Exploitation of Women

An Overview

Exploitation Of Women
An Overview

S Ojha

MD Publications Pvt Ltd
New Delhi
www.mdppl.com

Published by :

MD Publications Pvt Ltd
"MD House", 11, Darya Ganj,
New Delhi - 110 002
Phone : +91-11- 45355555
E-mail : contact@mdppl.com
Website: www.mdppl.com

ISBN : 978-81-7533-317-8

Published and Printed by Mr. Pranav Gupta on behalf of **MD Publications Pvt Ltd** at Repro India Limited.

Preface

The self-evident truth is that all men and women are brought into this world from the wombs of women in pain and travail. It is equally self-evident that the basis for the oppressive, sexual division of labor and the subjugation of women in the family under capitalism is women's reproductive function. The subjugation of women flows from dependency throughout pregnancy and while nursing - and that dependency, in turn, is actually the dependency of the human infant (which is the dependency of the human species, of human society upon women).

Despite its defiance, the male-dominated regime is retreating step by step. Yet at the same time, a reactionary, violent and suppressive force called fundamentalism is emerging. Misogynous in character, fundamentalism or religious fanaticism is threatening all the achievements of the civilized world, particularly those of women. Under the banner of Islam, the fundamentalists are denying the equality of women and men.

Upon investigation, working-class women are clearly the most oppressed, super-exploited sector of the entire proletariat. The greatest burdens are carried by racial and national minority women.

The root of women's subjugation and exploitation is not the human family as such, but the nuclear family as it is organized and exploited under advanced capitalism. The circulation of women through the waged labor force, women's principal identification of themselves as wives and mothers and thus only "temporary workers" (which produces negative or very weak class consciousness), and institutionalized discrimination against women all serve to facilitate the superexploitation of women under capitalism. This superexploitation is expressed by: 1) the denial by capital of compensation for labor consumed in production and reproduction of labor power; 2) the systematic undervaluation of waged female labor; 3) forcing women disproportionately into the worst and most degrading jobs; and 4) forcing women into part-time or full-time work in addition to full responsibility for domestic labor (thus married working women hold down two full-time jobs, but are paid wages for only one).

No group is in greater danger than the large number of women refugees and internally displaced persons. They are often single-handedly responsible for the survival of their children, even when their own survival is at stake. Every day provides challenges that increase the risk of physical danger: finding cooking fuel, carrying water (often for miles), obtaining sufficient food at distribution sites, and accessing primary health care for themselves and their families.

I am very grateful to Mr. Pranav Gupta, Director of MD Publications Pvt Ltd, New Delhi, for his kind cooperation and support for this book.

S Ojha

Contents

1

Violence Against Women

Violence against women is a technical term used to collectively refer to violent acts that are primarily or exclusively committed against women. Similar to a hate crime, this type of violence targets a specific group with the victim's gender as a primary motive. The United Nations General Assembly defines "violence against women" as "any act of gender-based violence that results in, or is likely to result in, physical, sexual or mental harm or suffering to women, including threats of such acts, coercion or arbitrary deprivation of liberty, whether occurring in public or in private life."

The 1993 Declaration on the Elimination of Violence Against Women noted that this violence could be perpetrated by assailants of gender, family members and even the "State" itself. Worldwide governments and organizations actively work to combat violence against women through a variety of programs. A UN resolution designated November 25th as International Day for the Elimination of Violence against Women.

Some historians believe that the history of violence against women is tied to the history of women being viewed as property and a gender role assigned to be subservient to men and also other women. In the 1870s courts in the United States stopped recognizing the common-law principle that a husband had the right to "physically chastise an errant wife". In the UK the traditional right of a husband to inflict moderate corporal punishment on his wife in order to keep her "within the bounds of duty" was removed in 1891.

The World Health Organization reports that violence against women puts an undue burden on health care services with women who have suffered violence being more likely to need health services and at higher cost, compared to women who have not suffered violence. Several studies have shown a link between poor treatment of women and international violence. These studies show that one of the best predictors of inter- and intranational violence is the maltreatment of women in the society.

TYPES OF VIOLENCE

DOMESTIC VIOLENCE

Women are more likely to be victimized by someone that they are intimate with, commonly called "Intimate Partner Violence" or (IPV). The impact of domestic violence in the sphere of total violence against women can be understood through the example that 40-70% of murders of women are committed by their husband or boyfriend. Studies have shown that violence is not always perpetrated as a form of physical violence but can also be psychological and verbal. In unmarried relationships this is commonly called dating violence, whereas in the context of marriage it is called domestic violence.

Instances of IPV tend not to be reported to police and thus many experts believe that the true magnitude of the problem is hard to estimate. Though this form of violence is often portrayed as an issue within the context of heterosexual relationships, it also occurs in lesbian relationships, daughter-mother relationships, roommate relationships and other domestic relationships involving two women. Violence against women in lesbian relationships is about as common as violence against women in heterosexual relationships. Violence against women by women also exists outside the sphere of relationship violence, probably even less research has been done on this subject.

Domestic violence (also known as domestic abuse, spousal abuse, or intimate partner violence) occurs when a family member, partner or ex-partner attempts to physically or psychologically dominate another. Domestic violence often refers to violence between spouses, or spousal abuse but can also include cohabitants and non-married intimate partners. Domestic violence occurs in all cultures; people of all races, ethnicities, religions, sexes and classes can be perpetrators of domestic violence. Domestic violence is perpetrated by both men and women. Domestic violence has many forms, including physical violence, sexual abuse, emotional abuse, intimidation, economic deprivation, and threats of violence.

Violence can be criminal and includes physical assault (hitting, pushing, shoving, etc.), sexual abuse (unwanted or forced sexual activity), and stalking. Although emotional, psychological and financial abuses are not criminal behaviors in some legal systems, they are forms of abuse and can lead to criminal violence. There are a number of dimensions including:

Mode- Physical, psychological, sexual and/or social

Frequency- on/off, occasional and chronic

Severity- in terms of both psychological or physical harm and the need for treatment

Transitory or permanent injury- mild, moderate, severe and up to homicide.

An important component of domestic violence, often ignored is the realm of passive abuse, leading to violence. Passive abuse is covert, subtle and veiled. This includes victimization, ambiguity, and neglect, spiritual and intellectual abuse. Recent attention to domestic violence began in the women's movement, particularly feminism and women's rights, in the 1970s, as concern about wives being beaten by their husbands gained attention. Awareness and documentation of domestic violence differs from country to country. Estimates are that only about a third of cases of domestic violence are actually reported in the United States and the United Kingdom.

According to the Centers for Disease Control, domestic violence is a serious, preventable public health problem affecting more than 32 million Americans, or more than 10% of the U.S. population. Popular emphasis has tended to be on women as the victims of domestic violence.

However, with the rise of the men's movement, and particularly masculism and men's rights, there is now advocacy for men victimized by women. In a special report on violence related injuries by the US Department of justice (in August 1997) hospital emergency room visits pertaining to domestic violence indicated that physically abused men represent just under one-sixth of the total patients admitted to hospital reporting domestic violence as the cause of their injuries. The report highlights that significantly more men than women did not disclose the identity of their attacker.

The term "intimate partner violence" (IPV) is often used synonymously. Family violence is a broader definition, often used to include child abuse, elder abuse, and other violent acts between family members. Wife abuse, wife beating, and battering are terms sometimes used, though with acknowledgment that many are not actually married to the abuser, but rather co-habiting or other arrangements. In more recent years, 'battering' or 'battered wife' has become less acceptable terminology, since abuse can take other forms than physical abuse and males are often victims of violence as well. Other forms of abuse may be constantly occurring, while physical abuse happens occasionally. These other forms of abuse have potential to lead to mental illness, self-harm, and even attempts at suicide.

The U.S. Office on Violence Against Women (OVW) defines domestic violence as a "pattern of abusive behavior in any relationship that is used by one partner to gain or maintain power and control over another intimate partner". The definition adds that domestic violence "can happen to anyone regardless of race, age, sexual orientation, religion, or gender", and that it can take many forms, including physical abuse, sexual abuse, emotional, economic, and psychological abuse.

The Children and Family Court Advisory and Support Service in the United Kingdom in its "Domestic Violence Policy" uses domestic violence to refer to a range of violent and abusive behaviours, defining it as:

Patterns of behaviour characterised by the misuse of power and control by one person over another who are or have been in an intimate relationship. It can occur in mixed gender relationships and same gender relationships and has profound consequences for the lives of children, individuals, families and communities. It may be physical, sexual, emotional and/or psychological. The latter may include intimidation, harassment, and damage to property, threats and financial abuse.

In Spain, the introduction of Ley Orgánica 1/2004, de 28 de diciembre, de Medidas de Protección Integral contra la Violencia de Género (Organic Law 1/2004 of December 28, of Measures of Integral Protection against Gendered Violence) defined several key terms. It defines la violencia de género (gendered violence) as una violencia que se dirige sobre las mujeres por el hecho mismo de serlo, por ser consideradas, por sus agresores, carentes de los derechos mínimos de libertad, respeto y capacidad de decisión (a violence that is directed at women for the very fact of being women and therefore being considered by their attackers as lacking the basic rights of freedom, respect, and decision making capability).

The new law establishes courts titled Juzgados de Violencia sobre la Mujer (Courts of Violence against Women) and suspends the presumption of innocence for men accused of domestic violence. Courts are empowered to hold closed door hearings before trial and evict men from their homes; suspend parental rights, child custody, or visitation rights; and bar men from possessing weapons.

FORMS OF ABUSE

Domestic violence can take the form of physical violence, including direct physical violence ranging from unwanted physical contact to rape and murder. Indirect physical violence may include destruction of objects, striking or throwing objects near the victim, or harm to pets. In addition to physical violence, spousal abuse often includes mental or emotional abuse, including verbal threats of physical violence to the victim, the self, or others including children, ranging from explicit, detailed and impending to implicit and vague as to both content and time frame, and verbal violence, including threats, insults, put-downs, and attacks.

Nonverbal threats may include gestures, facial expressions, and body postures. Psychological abuse may also involve economic and/or social control, such as controlling the victim's money and other economic resources, preventing the victim from seeing friends and relatives, actively sabotaging the victim's social relationships, and isolating the victim from social contacts.

PHYSICAL VIOLENCE

Physical violence is the intentional use of physical force with the potential for causing injury, harm, disability, or death, for example, hitting, shoving, biting, restraint, kicking, or use of a weapon.

SEXUAL VIOLENCE

Sexual violence is divided into three categories:

i. Use of physical force to compel a person to engage in a sexual act against his or her will, whether or not the act is completed;
ii. Attempted or completed sex act involving a person who is unable to understand the nature or condition of the act, unable to decline participation, or unable to communicate unwillingness to engage in the sexual act, e.g., because of underage immaturity, illness, disability, or the influence of alcohol or other drugs, or because of intimidation or pressure; and
iii. Abusive sexual contact

EMOTIONAL ABUSE

Emotional abuse (also called psychological abuse or mental abuse) can include humiliating the victim privately or publicly, controlling what the victim can and cannot do, withholding information from the victim, deliberately doing something to make the victim feel diminished or embarrassed, isolating the victim from friends and family, implicitly blackmailing the victim by harming others when the victim expresses independence or happiness, or denying the victim access to money or other basic resources and necessities.

Women who are being emotionally abused often feel as if they do not own themselves; rather, they may feel that their significant other has nearly total control over them. Women undergoing emotional abuse often suffer from depression, which puts them at increased risk for suicide, eating disorders, and drug and alcohol abuse. The emotional abuse of men is characterised by low self esteem.

Typical patterns of abuse involve humiliation and the undermining of perceived competence, especially in front of other people. This problem can be extended due to a widely held belief in society (including among males themselves) that men who are emotionally abused are in some way less masculine, causing men to feel embarrassed about seeking help.

ECONOMIC ABUSE

Economic abuse is when the abuser has complete control over the victim's money and other economic resources. Usually, this involves putting the victim on a strict "allowance," withholding money at will and forcing the victim to beg for the money until the abuser gives them some money. It is common for the victim to receive less money as the abuse continues. This also includes (but is not limited to) preventing the victim from finishing education or obtaining employment, or intentionally squandering or misusing communal resources.

STALKING

In addition, stalking is often included among the types of Intimate Partner Violence. Stalking generally refers to repeated behaviour that causes victims to feel a high level of fear.

VICTIMIZATION

STATISTICS

Domestic violence occurs across the world, in various cultures, and affects people across society, irrespective of economic status. In the United States, according to the Bureau of Justice Statistics women are about six times as likely as men to experience intimate partner violence. Percent of women surveyed (national surveys) who were ever physically assaulted by an intimate partner: Barbados (30%), Canada (29%), Egypt (34%), New Zealand (35%), Switzerland (21%), and United States (22%). Some surveys in specific places report figures as high as 50-70% of women surveyed who were ever physically assaulted by an intimate partner.

Others, including surveys in the Philippines and Paraguay, report figures as low as 10%. South Africa is said to have the highest statistics of gender-based violence in the world and this includes rape and domestic violence. 80% of women surveyed in rural Egypt said that beatings were common and often justified, particularly if the woman refused to have sex with her husband. In India, around 70% of women are victims of domestic violence. The Human Rights Watch found that up to 90% of women in Pakistan were subject to verbal, sexual, emotional or physical abuse, within their own homes.

Up to two-thirds of women in certain communities in Nigeria's Lagos State say they are victims to domestic violence. Statistics published in 2004; show that the rate of domestic violence victimisation for Indigenous women in Australia may be 40 times the rate for non-Indigenous women. The rate of intimate partner violence in the U.S. has declined since 1993. Results will vary, depending on specific wording of survey questions, how the survey is conducted, the definition of abuse or domestic violence used, the willingness or unwillingness of victims to admit that they have been abused and other factors.

Martin S. Fiebert examined 219 studies on intimate partner violence and concluded that "women are as physically aggressive, or more aggressive, than men in their relationships with their spouses or male partners". However, studies have shown that the nature and consequences of spousal violence are much more serious for women than for men; the severity of the abuse inflicted on women is worse.

A Canadian study showed that 7% of women and 6% of men end up abused by their current or former partners, but female victims of spousal violence were more than twice as likely to be injured as male victims. Women were also three times more likely to fear for their life, and twice as likely to be the targets of more than 10 violent episodes. Overall, female victims were twice as likely as male victims to be stalked by a previous spouse. Domestic violence against women in lesbian relationships is about as common as domestic violence against women in heterosexual relationships.

In the United States males experienced higher victimization rates than females for all types of violent crime except rape and other sexual assault; but 20 percent of all violent crimes experienced by women in the U.S. are cases of intimate partner violence, compared to 3 percent of violent crime experienced by men. According to the U.S. Bureau of Justice Statistics, "in 1994 for every 5 violent victimizations of a female by an intimate, there was 1 of a male. Intimates committed over 900,000 victimizations of females and about 167,000 victimizations of males."

There is currently limited research on the abuse of lesbian women by their lesbian partners; however an investigation by the Canadian Government saw some 19% of a survey of lesbian women respond to being victims of their partners.

During Pregnancy

Domestic violence during pregnancy can be missed by medical professionals because it often presents in non-specific ways. A number of countries have been statistically analyzed to calculate the prevalence of this phenomenon:

i. UK prevalence: 2.5-3.4%

ii. USA prevalence: 3.2-33.7%

iii. Ireland prevalence: 12.5%

iv. Rates are higher in teenagers

v. Severity and frequency increase postpartum (10% antenatally vs. 19% post-natally); 21% at 3 months post partum

There are a number of presentations that can be related to domestic violence during pregnancy: delay in seeking care for injuries; late booking, non-attenders at appointments, self-discharge; frequent attendance, vague problems; aggressive or over-solicitous partner; burns, pain, tenderness, injuries; vaginal tears, bleeding, STDs; and miscarriage.

Domestic violence can also affect the fetus, the subsequent baby, and existing children:

i. Pre-birth: prematurity, premature rupture of membranes, IUD

ii. Psychosocial: interference in relationship, witnessing of violence, eating and sleeping disorders, emotional neediness, withdrawn, over-compliant, clingy, aggressive, problems at school, suicidal ideation

iii. Legal: child protection issues, overlap with child abuse

iv. Long-term chronic ill-health

According to a July 2000 Centers for Disease Control (CDC) report, data from the Bureau of Justice, National Crime Victimization Survey consistently show that women are at significantly greater risk of intimate partner violence than are men. Data from the National Family Violence Survey, and from numerous peer-reviewed studies dating to as early as 1980 and a 2000 meta analysis contradict these data and consistently show that men and women suffer domestic abuse in at least equal rates.

The 2000 CDC report, based on phone interviews with 8000 men and 8000 women, reported that 7.5% of men claim to have been raped or assaulted by an intimate at some time in their life time (compared to 25% of women), and 0.9 percent of men claim to have been raped or assaulted in the previous 12 months (compared to 1.5% of women). In May, 2007, researchers with the Centers for Disease Control reported on rates of self-reported violence among intimate partners using data from a 2001 study. In the study, almost one-quarter of participants reported some violence in their relationships.

Half of these involved one-sided ("non-reciprocal") attacks and half involved both assaults and counter assaults ("reciprocal violence"). Women reported committing one-sided attacks more than twice as often as men (70% versus 29%). In all cases of intimate partner violence, women were more likely to be injured than men, but 25% of men in relationships with two-sided violence reported injury compared to 20% of women reporting injury in relationships with one-sided violence. Women were more likely to be injured in non-reciprocal violence.

While much attention has been focused on domestic violence against women, men's rights activists argue that domestic violence against men is a social problem that is also worthy of attention. Each year, 834,000 men are raped or physically assaulted by intimate partners an average 3.5 times/year for a total of 2.9 million assaults/year (4.9 million for women). Men in intimate relationships with other men are more likely to be raped or assaulted than men in heterosexual relationships.

According to the 2000 CDC/Justice study, "Approximately 23 percent of the men who had lived with a man as a couple reported being raped, physically assaulted, and/or stalked by a male cohabitant, while 7.4 percent of the men who had married or lived with a woman as a couple reported such violence by a wife or female cohabitant. These findings, combined with those presented in the previous bullet, provide further evidence that intimate partner violence is perpetrated primarily by men, whether against male or female intimates." A 2007-2008 online non-random, self-report survey is being conducted by researchers at Clark University and Bridgewater State College, which seeks to document the experiences and health of men who have sustained partner violence in the past year.

VIOLENCE AGAINST CHILDREN

When it comes to domestic violence towards children involving physical abuse, research in the UK by the NSPCC indicated that "most violence occurred at home" (78 per cent). 40 - 60% of men and women who abuse other adults also abuse their children. Girls whose fathers batter their mothers are 6.5 times more likely to be sexually abused by their fathers than are girls from non-violent homes.

VIOLENCE AGAINST TEENS

Teen dating violence is a pattern of controlling behavior by one teenager over another teenager who is in a dating relationship. While there are many similarities to "traditional" domestic violence there are also some differences. Teens are much more likely than adults to become isolated from their peers as the result of controlling behavior by their boyfriend/ girlfriend. Also, for many teens the abusive relationship may be their first dating experience and have never had a "normal" dating experience with which to compare it.

The World Conference on Human Rights, held in Vienna in 1993, and the Declaration on the Elimination of Violence against Women in the same year, concluded that civil society and governments have acknowledged that violence against women is a public health and human rights concern. Work in this area has resulted in the establishment of international standards, but the task of documenting the magnitude of violence against women and producing reliable, comparative data to guide policy and monitor implementation has been exceedingly difficult.

The World Health Organisation Multi-country Study on Women's Health and Domestic Violence against Women 2005is a response to this difficulty. Published in 2005 it is a groundbreaking study which analysed data from 10 countries and sheds new light on the prevalence of violence against women. It seeks to look at violence against women a public health policy perspective. The findings will be used to inform a more effective response from government, including the health, justice and social service sectors, as a step towards fulfilling the state's obligation to eliminate violence against women under international human rights laws.

TYPES

The form and characteristics of domestic violence and abuse may vary in other ways. Michael P. Johnson (1995, 2006b) argues for three major types of intimate partner violence. The typology is supported by subsequent research and evaluation by Johnson and his colleagues, as well as independent researchers.

Distinctions need to be made regarding types of violence, motives of perpetrators, and the social and cultural context. Violence by a man against his wife or intimate partner is often done as a way for men to control "their woman". Other types of intimate partner violence also occur, including violence between gay and lesbian couples, and by women against their male partners. Distinctions are not based on single incidents, but rather on patterns across numerous incidents and motives of the perpetrator. Types of violence identified by Johnson:

Common couple violence (CCV) is not connected to general control behavior, but arises in a single argument where one or both partners physically lash out at the other. Intimate terrorism is one element in a general pattern of control by one partner over the other. Intimate terrorism is more common than common couple violence, more likely to escalate over time, not as likely to be mutual, and more likely to involve serious injury.

Intimate terrorism (IT) may also involve emotional and psychological abuse.

Violent resistance (VR), sometimes thought of as "self-defense", is violence perpetrated usually by women against their abusive partners.

Mutual violent control (MVC) is rare type of intimate partner violence occurs when both partners act in a violent manner, battling for control.

Another type is situational couple violence, which arises out of conflicts that escalate to arguments and then to violence. It is not connected to a general pattern of control. Although it occurs less frequently in relationships and is less serious than intimate terrorism, in some cases it can be frequent and/or quite serious, even life-threatening. This is probably the most common type of intimate partner violence and dominates general surveys, student samples, and even marriage counseling samples.

Types of male batterers identified by Holtzworth-Munroe and Stuart (1994) include "family-only", which primarily fall into the CCV type, who are generally less violent and less likely to perpetrate psychological and sexual abuse. IT batterers include two types: "Generally-violent-antisocial" and "dysphoric-borderline".

The first type includes men with general psychopathic and violent tendencies. The second type is men who are emotionally dependent on the relationship. Support for this typology has been found in subsequent evaluations. Others, such as the US Centers for Disease Control, divide domestic violence into two types: reciprocal violence, in which both partners are violent, and non-reciprocal violence, in which one partner is violent.

THEORIES

There are many different theories as to the causes of domestic violence. These include psychological theories that consider personality traits and mental characteristics of the offender, as well as social theories which consider external factors in the offender's environment, such as family structure, stress, social learning. As with many phenomena regarding human experience, no single approach appears to cover all cases.

PSYCHOLOGICAL

Psychological theories focus on personality traits and mental characteristics of the offender. Personality traits include sudden bursts of anger, poor impulse control, and poor self esteem. Various theories suggest that psychopathology and other personality disorders are factors, and that abuse experienced as a child leads some people to be more violent as adults. Studies have found high incidence of psychopathy among abusers.

Dutton has suggested a psychological profile of men who abuse their wives, arguing that they have borderline personalities (between psychotics and neurotics), which are developed early in life. Gelles suggests that psychological theories are limited, and points out that other researcher have found that only 10% (or less) fit this psychological profile. He argues that social factors are important, while personality traits, mental illness, or psychopathy are lesser factors.

It should be noted that Borderline Personality Disorder as used in this context is outdated. Whilst it was originally believed that a person's psychological state was between neurotic and psychotic it is now recognised that BPD is the most severe and intransigent of the personality disorders.

SOCIAL THEORIES

Looks at external factors in the offender's environment, such as family structure, stress, social learning, and includes rational choice theories.

RESOURCE THEORY

Resource theory was suggested by William Goode (1971). Women who are most dependent on the spouse for economic well being having children to take care of, should they leave the marriage, increases the financial burden and makes it all the more difficult for them to leave. Dependency means that they have fewer options and few resources to help them cope with or change their spouse's behavior. Couples that share power equally experience lower incidence of conflict, and when conflict does arise, are less likely to resort to violence.

If one spouse desires control and power in the relationship, the spouse may resort to abuse. This may include coercion and threats, intimidation, emotional abuse, economic abuse, isolation, making light of the situation and blaming the spouse, using children (threatening to take them away), and behaving as "master of the castle".

SOCIAL STRESS

Stress may be increased when a person is living in a family situation, with increased pressures. Social stresses, due to inadequate finances or other such problems in a family may further increase tensions. Violence is not always caused by stress, but may be one way that some (but not all) people respond to stress.

Families and couples in poverty may be more likely to experience domestic violence, due to increased stress and conflicts about finances and other aspects. Some speculate that poverty may hinder a man's ability to live up to his idea of "successful manhood", thus he fears losing honor and respect. Theory suggests that when he is unable to economically support his wife, and maintain control, he may turn to misogyny, substance abuse, and crime as ways to express masculinity.

SOCIAL LEARNING THEORY

Social learning theory suggests that people learn from observing and modeling after others' behavior. With positive reinforcement, the behavior continues. If one observes violent behavior, one is more likely to imitate it. If there are no negative consequences (e.g. victim accepts the violence, with submission), then the behavior will likely continue. Often, violence is transmitted from generation to generation in a cyclical manner.

POWER AND CONTROL

In some relationships, violence arises out of a perceived need for power and control, a form of bullying and social learning of abuse. Abusers' efforts to dominate their partners have been attributed to low self-esteem or feelings of inadequacy, unresolved childhood conflicts, the stress of poverty, hostility and resentment toward women (misogyny), hostility and resentment toward men (misandry), personality disorders, genetic tendencies and sociocultural influences, among other possible causative factors. Most authorities seem to agree that abusive personalities result from a combination of several factors, to varying degrees.

A causalist view of domestic violence is that it is a strategy to gain or maintain power and control over the victim. This view is in alignment with Bancroft's "cost-benefit" theory that abuse rewards the perpetrator in ways other than, or in addition to, simply exercising power over his or her target(s). He cites evidence in support of his argument that, in most cases, abusers are quite capable of exercising control over them, but choose not to do so for various reasons.

An alternative view is that abuse arises from powerlessness and externalizing/projecting this and attempting to exercise control of the victim. It is an attempt to 'gain or maintain power and control over the victim' but even in achieving this it cannot resolve the powerlessness driving it. Such behaviours have addictive aspects leading to a cycle of abuse or violence. Mutual cycles develop when each party attempts to resolve their own powerlessness in attempting to assert control.

Questions of power and control are integral to the widely utilized Duluth Domestic Abuse Intervention Project. They developed "Power and Control Wheel" to illustrate this: it has power and control at the center, surrounded by spokes (techniques used), the titles of which include:

i. Coercion and threats

ii. Intimidation

iii. Emotional abuse

iv. Isolation

v. Minimizing, denying and blaming

vi. Using children

vii. Economic abuse

viii. Male privilege

The model attempts to address abuse by one-sidedly challenging the misuse of power by the 'perpetrator'. Critics of this model suggest that the one-sided focus is problematic as resolution can only be achieved when all participants acknowledge their responsibilities, and identify and respect mutual purpose.

The power wheel model is not intended to assign personal responsibility, enhance respect for mutual purpose or assist victims and perpetrators in resolving their differences. It is an informational tool designed to help individuals understand the dynamics of power operating in abusive situations and identify various methods of abuse.

ALCOHOL-RELATED AND NON-ALCOHOL RELATED VIOLENCE

Other factors associated with domestic violence include heavy alcohol consumption, mental illness, classism, various political and legal characteristics such as authoritarianism and dehumanisation.

PRESCRIPTION DRUGS

It is also important to this topic to understand the paradoxical effects of some sedative drugs. Serious complications can occur in conjunction with the use of sedatives creating the opposite effect as to that intended. Malcolm Lader at the Institute of Psychiatry in London estimates the incidence of these adverse reactions at about 5%, even in short-term use of the drugs. The paradoxical reactions may consist of depression, with or without suicidal tendencies, phobias, aggressiveness, violent behavior and symptoms sometimes misdiagnosed as psychosis. The contribution of these reactions is one possible component.

SEX AND GENDER

Modes of abuse are stereotyped by some to be gendered, females tending to use more psychological and men more physical forms. The visibility of these differs markedly. However, experts who work with victims of domestic violence have noted that physical abuse is almost invariably preceded by psychological abuse. Police and hospital admission records indicate that a higher percentage of females than males seek treatment and report such crimes.

CYCLE OF VIOLENCE

Frequently, domestic violence is used to describe specific violent and overtly abusive incidents, and legal definitions will tend to take this perspective. However, when violent and abusive behaviours happen within a relationship, the effects of those behaviours continue after these overt incidents are over. Advocates and counsellors will refer to domestic violence as a pattern of behaviours, including those listed above.

Lenore Walker presented the model of a Cycle of violence which consists of three basic phases:

1. Honeymoon Phase - Characterized by affection, apology, and apparent end of violence. During this stage the batterer feels overwhelming feelings of remorse and sadness. Some batterers walk away from the situation, while others shower their victims with love and affection.
2. Tension Building Phase- Characterized by poor communication, tension, fear of causing outbursts. During this stage the victims try to calm the batterer down, to avoid any major violent confrontations.
3. Acting-out Phase - Characterized by outbursts of violent, abusive incidents. During this stage the batterer attempts to dominate his/her partner (victim), with the use of domestic violence.

Although it is easy to see the outbursts of the Acting-out Phase as abuse, even the more pleasant behaviours of the Honeymoon Phase serve to perpetuate the abuse. Many domestic violence advocates believe that the cycle of violence theory is limited and does not reflect the realities of many men and women experiencing domestic violence.

GENDER DIFFERENCES

The role of gender is a controversial topic related to the discussion of domestic violence. Erin Pizzey, the founder of an early women's shelter in Chiswick, London, has expressed her dismay at how she believes the issue has become a gender-political football, and expressed an unpopular view in her book Prone to Violence that some women in the refuge system had a predisposition to seek abusive relationships.

She also expressed the view that domestic violence can occur against any vulnerable intimates, regardless of their gender. A Freudian concept, repetition compulsion, has also come up in modern psychology as a possible cause of a woman who was abused in childhood seeking an abusive man (or vice versa), theoretically as a misguided way to "master" their traumatic experience.

GENDER ASPECTS OF ABUSE

There continues to be discussion about whether men are more abusive than women, whether men's abuse of women is worse than women's abuse of men, and whether abused men should be provided the same resources and shelters that years of advocacy, money-raising, and funding has gained for women victims sekä Carney (2007). Martin S. Fiebert of the Department of Psychology at California State University, Long Beach, provides an annotated bibliography of a couple of hundred scholarly works, selected by him because he believes they support the claim that women are as physically aggressive, or more aggressive, than men.

In a Los Angeles Times article about male victims of domestic violence, Fiebert suggests that "...consensus in the field is that women are as likely as men to strike their partner but that - as expected - women are more likely to be injured than men. However, he noted, men are seriously injured in 38% of the cases in which "extreme aggression" is used." No statistic was given to shed light on how often "extreme aggression" occurs with women as the aggressor. The article goes on to say, "We've all learned to be wary of statistics, and Fiebert says studies abound on the subject. He notes, however, that those suggesting men are also frequent abuse victims should not be used to minimize the threat that women face from abusive boyfriends or spouses."

In a Meta-analysis, John Archer, Ph.D., from the Department of Psychology, University of Central Lancashire, UK, writes:

> The present analyses indicate that men are among those who are likely to be on the receiving end of acts of physical aggression. The extent to which this involves mutual combat or the male equivalent to "battered women" is at present unresolved. Both situations are causes for concern. Straus (1997) has warned of the dangers involved - especially for women - when physical aggression becomes a routine response to relationship conflict. "Battered men" - those subjected to systematic and prolonged violence - are likely to suffer physical and psychological consequences, together with specific problems associated with a lack of recognition of their plight. Seeking to address these problems need not detract from continuing to address the problem of "battered women."

Donald G. Dutton and Tonia L. Nicholls, from the Department of Psychology at the University of British Columbia also undertook a meta-analysis of data in 2005. They concluded:

> Clearly, shelter houses full of battered women demonstrate the need for their continued existence. Moreover, outside of North American and Northern Europe, gender inequality is still the norm (Archer, in press). However, within those countries that have been most progressive about women's equality, female violence has increased as male violence has decreased (Archer, in press). There is not one solution for every domestically violent situation; some require incarceration of a terrorist perpetrator, others can be dealt with through court-mandated treatment, still others may benefit from couples therapy. However, feminist inspired intervention standards that preclude therapists in many states from doing effective therapy with male batterers are one outcome of this paradigm. The failure to recognize female threat to husbands, female partners, or children is another (Straus et al., 1980 found 10% higher rates of child abuse reported by mothers than by fathers).
>
> The one size fits all policy driven by a simplistic notion that intimate violence is a recapitulation of class war does not most effectively deal with this serious problem or represent

the variety of spousal violence patterns revealed by research. At some point, one has to ask whether feminists are more interested in diminishing violence within a population or promoting a political ideology. If they are interested in diminishing violence, it should be diminished for all members of a population and by the most effective and utilitarian means possible. This would mean an intervention/treatment approach based on other successful approaches from criminology and psychology.

Theories that women are as violent as men have been dubbed "Gender Symmetry" theories. In the most serious violence the men do dominate for example in 1999 in the US, 1,218 women and 424 men were killed by an intimate partner, regardless of which partner started the violence and of the gender of the partner. On the other hand, Michael Kimmel of the State University of New York at Stony Brook found that men are more violent inside and outside of the home than women. Problems in conducting studies that seek to describe violence in terms of gender is the amount of silence, fear and shame that results from abuse within families and relationships.

Another is that abusive patterns can tend to seem normal to those who have lived in them for a length of time. Similarly, subtle forms of abuse can be quite transparent even as they set the stage for further abuse seeming normal. Finally, inconsistent definition of what domestic violence is makes definite conclusions difficult to reach when compiling the available studies. Both men and women have been arrested and convicted of assaulting their partners in both heterosexual and homosexual relationships. The bulk of these arrests have been men being arrested for assaulting women. However, in the case of reciprocal violence, frequently only the male perpetrator is arrested. Determining how many instances of domestic violence actually involve male victims is difficult.

Male domestic violence victims may be reluctant to get help for a number of reasons. Another study has demonstrated a high degree of acceptance by women of aggression against men. Murders of female intimate partners by men have dropped, but not nearly as dramatically. Men kill their female intimate partners at about four times the rate that women kill their male intimate partners. Research by Jacquelyn Campbell, PhD RN FAAN has found that at least two thirds of women killed by their intimate partners were battered by those men prior to the murder. She also found that when males are killed by female intimates, the women in those relationships had been abused by their male partner about 75% of the time.

Some researchers have found a relationship between the availability of domestic violence services, improved laws and enforcement regarding domestic violence and increased access to divorce, and higher earnings for women with declines in intimate partner homicide. However, both men and women are far less likely to be abused when married to each other. The bulk of injuries from domestic violence involve co-habitation or the distresses of relationship break-ups. Gender roles and expectations can and do play a role in abusive situations, and exploring these roles and expectations can be helpful in addressing abusive situations, as do factors like race, class, religion, sexuality and philosophy. None of these factors cause one to abuse or another to be abused.

Concerns About Social Programs dealing with Violence

In 1997, the Canadian Advertising Foundation ruled that a National Ad campaign that featuring Nicole Brown Simpson's sister Denise with the slogan entitled, "Stop violence against Women" was in fact portraying only men as aggressors, and that it was not providing a balanced message and was in fact contributing to gender stereotyping.

Domestic Violence in Same-sex Relationships

Domestic violence also occurs in same-sex relationships. In an effort to be more inclusive, many organizations have made an effort to use gender-neutral terms when referring to perpetratorship and victimhood. Historically domestic violence has been seen as a family issue and little interest has been directed at violence in same-sex relationships. It has not been until recently, as the gay rights movement has brought the issues of gay and lesbian people into public attention, when research has been started to conduct on same-sex relationships. Several studies have indicated that partner abuse among same-sex couples (both female and male) is relatively similar in both prevalence and dynamics to that among opposite-sex couples.

Gays and lesbians, however, face special obstacles in dealing with the issues that some researchers have labeled "the double closet". A recent Canadian study by Mark W. Lehman suggests similarities include frequency (approximately one in every four couples); manifestations (emotional, physical, financial, etc.); co-existent situations (unemployment, substance abuse, low self-esteem); victims' reactions (fear, feelings of helplessness, hyper vigilance); and reasons for staying (love, can work it out, things will change, denial). At the same time, significant differences, unique issues and deceptive myths are typically present.

Lehman points to added discrimination and fear gays and lesbians can face; dismissal by police and some social services; a lack of support from peers who would rather keep quiet about the problem in order not to attract negative attention toward the gay community; the impacts of HIV status or AIDS in keeping partners together, due to health care insurance/ access, or guilt; outing used as a weapon; and encountering supportive services that are targeted and/or structured for the needs of heterosexual women and which may not meet the needs of gay men or lesbians.

DIAGNOSIS PLANNING

The American Psychiatric Association planning and research committees for the forthcoming DSM-V (2012) have canvassed a series of new Relational disorders which include Marital Conflict Disorder Without Violence or Marital Abuse Disorder (Marital Conflict Disorder With Violence). Couples with marital disorders sometimes come to clinical attention because the couple recognizes long-standing dissatisfaction with their marriage and come to the clinician on their own initiative or are referred by an astute health care professional.

Secondly, there is serious violence in the marriage which is -"usually the husband battering the wife". In these cases the emergency room or a legal authority often is the first to notify the clinician. Most importantly, marital violence "is a major risk factor for serious injury and even death and women in violent marriages are at much greater risk of being seriously injured or killed (National Advisory Council on Violence Against Women 2000)."

The authors of this study add that "There is current considerable controversy over whether male-to-female marital violence is best regarded as a reflection of male psychopathology and control or whether there is an empirical base and clinical utility for conceptualizing these patterns as relational." Recommendations for clinicians making a diagnosis of Marital Relational Disorder should include the assessment of actual or "potential" male violence as regularly as they assess the potential for suicide in depressed patients.

Further, "clinicians should not relax their vigilance after a battered wife leaves her husband, because some data suggest that the period immediately following a marital separation is the period of greatest risk for the women. Many men will stalk and batter their wives in an effort to get them to return or punish them for leaving. Initial assessments of the potential for violence in a marriage can be supplemented by standardized interviews and questionnaires, which have been reliable and valid aids in exploring marital violence more systematically."

The authors conclude with what they call "very recent information" on the course of violent marriages which suggests that "over time a husband's battering may abate somewhat, but perhaps because he has successfully intimidated his wife. The risk of violence remains strong in a marriage in which it has been a feature in the past. Thus, treatment is essential here; the clinician cannot just wait and watch." The most urgent clinical priority is the protection of the wife because she is the one most frequently at risk, and clinicians must be aware that supporting assertiveness by a battered wife may lead to more beatings or even death.

RESPONSE TO DOMESTIC VIOLENCE

The response to domestic violence is typically a combined effort between law enforcement agencies, the courts, social service agencies and corrections/probation agencies. The role of each has evolved as domestic violence has been brought more into public view. Domestic violence historically has been viewed as a private family matter that need not involve government or criminal justice intervention. Police officers were often reluctant to intervene by making an arrest, and often chose instead to simply counsel the couple and/or ask one of the parties to leave the residence for a period of time. The courts were reluctant to impose any significant sanctions on those convicted of domestic violence, largely because it was viewed as a misdemeanor offense.

Activism, initiated by victim advocacy groups and feminist groups, has led to a better understanding of the scope and effect of domestic violence on victims and families, and has brought about changes in the criminal justice system's response. Several projects have aided in filling the voids in the justice system as it pertains to the protection of victims. One such initiative, The Hope Card Project, makes an attempt to remedy several problems through the issuance of an ID card to victims of abuse. The card is used to identify both parties in a domestic violence protection order and provides additional resources to the victim through a voucher program for services.

"There is no photograph on a protection order, so a photograph is a bonus, not a necessity. There are several methods used to obtain the photograph. Some jurisdictions have a photograph taken of the offender during the first hearing while both parties are present. Another method is for officers to take a photograph in the field or retrieve a booking photograph from their local jail. In a lot of cases the victim brings a photograph and it is scanned. Lastly, the new online site has some state motor vehicle department photograph databases connected for that purpose. This is the ideal method."

MEDICAL RESPONSE

Medical professionals, who have contact with abuse victims through medical visits, have a role to play in helping domestic violence victims. Many cases of spousal abuse are handled solely by medical professionals and do not involve the police. Sometimes cases of spousal abuse are brought into the emergency room, while many other cases are handled by family physician or other primary care provider. Doctors and other medical professionals are in position to empower victims, give advice, and refer them to appropriate services. The health care professional in the United Kingdom, the United States, and elsewhere has not always met this role, been uneven in quality of care, and in many cases has been unhelpful due to misunderstandings they have about domestic violence.

Myths that have prevailed in the past and influenced how a doctor approaches a case, where domestic violence may be involved, include the belief that domestic violence is rare, that women are responsible for the violence, and it is inevitable. Washaw (1993) suggests that many doctors prefer not to get involved in people's "private" lives. Clifton, Jacobs, and Tulloch (1996) found that training for general practitioners in the United States about domestic violence was very limited or they had no training. Abbott and Williamson found that knowledge and understanding of domestic violence was very limited among health care professionals in a Midlands, United Kingdom County, and that they don't see themselves as being able to play a major role in helping women in regards to domestic violence.

Furthermore, in the biomedical model of health care, injuries are often just treated and diagnosed, without regard for the causes. As well, there is substantial reluctance for victims to come forward and broach the issue with their physicians. On average, women experience 35 incidents of domestic violence before seeking treatment. In the U.S., the Institute of Medicine recognized the shortcomings of the health care system in its

2002 report entitled Confronting Chronic Neglect and attributed some of the problems cited to a lack of adequate training among health professionals. Health professionals have an ethical responsibility to recognize and address exposure to abuse in their patients, in the health care setting.

For example, the American Medical Association's code of medical ethics states that "Due to the prevalence and medical consequences of family violence, physicians should routinely inquire about physical, sexual, and psychological abuse as part of the medical history. Physicians must also consider abuse in the differential diagnosis for a number of medical complaints, particularly when treating women."

LONGER TERM HEALTH EFFECTS

New research illustrates that there are strong associations between exposure to domestic violence and abuse in all their forms and higher rates of many chronic conditions. The strongest evidence comes from the Adverse Childhood Experiences (ACE's) series of studies which show correlations between exposure to abuse or neglect and higher rates in adulthood of chronic conditions, high risk health behaviors and shortened life span.

Evidence of the association between physical health and violence against women has been accumulating since the early 1990s. More recently work by such researchers as Corso have begun to quantify the economic impact of exposure to violence and abuse. A recent publication Hidden Costs in Health Care: The Economic Impact of Violence and Abuse makes the case that such exposure represents a serious and costly public health issue that should be addressed by the health care system.

Medication

A number of medications have been used for control of aggression. Good evidence exists on the efficacy of clozapine. Evidence also exists for SSRIs (selective serotonin re-uptake ihibitors), like "Prozac", hormonal antiandrogenic agents, beta-blockers, quetiapine and ariipiprazole. Lithium and anticonvulsants are widely used but their efficacy is not strongly supported.

Law enforcement

In the 1970s, it was widely believed that domestic disturbance calls were the most dangerous type for responding officers, who arrive to a highly emotionally charged situation. This belief was based on FBI statistics which turned out to be flawed, in that they grouped all types of disturbances together with domestic disturbances, such as brawls at a bar. Subsequent statistics and analysis have shown this belief to be false.

Statistics on incidents of domestic violence, published in the late 1970s, helped raise public awareness of the problem and increase activism. A study published in 1976 by the Police Foundation found that the police had intervened at least once in the previous two years in 85 percent of spouse homicides. In the late 1970s and early 1980s, feminists and battered women's advocacy groups were calling on police to take domestic violence more seriously and change intervention strategies. In some instances, these groups took legal action against police departments, including in Oakland, California and New York City, to get them to make arrests in domestic violence cases. They claimed that police assigned low priority to domestic disturbance calls.

The Minneapolis Domestic Violence Experiment was a study done in 1981-1982, led by Lawrence W. Sherman, to evaluate the effectiveness of various police responses to domestic violence calls in Minneapolis, Minnesota, including sending the abuser away for eight hours, giving advice and mediation for disputes, and making an arrest. Arrest was found to be the most effective police response. The study found that arrest reduced the rate by half of re-offending against the same victim within the following six months. The results of the study received a great deal of attention from the news media, including The New York Times and prime-time news coverage on television.

Many U.S. police departments responded to the study, adopting a mandatory arrest policy for spousal violence cases with probable cause. By 2005, 23 states and the District of Columbia had enacted mandatory arrest for domestic assault, without warrant, given that the officer has probable cause and regardless of whether or not the officer witnessed the crime. The Minneapolis study also influenced policy in other countries, including New Zealand, which adopted a pro-arrest policy for domestic violence cases. However, the study was subject of much criticism, with concerns about its methodology, as well as its conclusions.

The Minneapolis study was replicated in several other cities, beginning in 1986, with some of these studies has producing different results. In the replication studies, arrest seemed to help in the short run in some cases, but those arrested experienced double the rate of violence over the course of one year. Criminologists do not fully understand the reasons why deterrent effects do not last over time. But they suggest that abusers may initially fear punishment, though many cases do not make it all the way through the criminal justice process. If the victim is uncooperative during investigation, the prosecutor may choose not to pursue the case. If the case is pursued through the criminal justice system, sometimes the resulting sentence is minor. Subsequently, any fear that the abuser has of punishment may have diminished.

DOMESTIC RESPONSE OF LAW ENFORCEMENT TODAY

Each agency and jurisdiction within the United States has its own Standard Operating Procedures (SOP) when it comes to responding and handling domestic calls. Generally, it has been accepted that if the understood victim has visible (and recent) marks of abuse, the suspect is arrested and charged with the appropriate crime. However, that is a guideline and not a rule. Like any other call, domestic abuse lies in a gray area. Law enforcement officers have several things to consider when making a warrantless arrest:

Are there signs of physical abuse?

Were there witnesses?

Is it recent?

Was the victim assaulted by the alleged suspect?

Who is the primary aggressor?

Could the victim be lying?

Could the suspect be lying?

Along with protecting the victim, law enforcement officers have to ensure that the alleged abusers' rights are not violated. Many times in cases of mutual combatants, it is departmental policy that both parties be arrested and the court system can establish truth at a later date. In some areas of the nation, this mutual combatant philosophy is being replaced by the primary abuser philosophy in which case if both parties have physical injuries, the law enforcement officer determines who the primary aggressor is and only arrests that one. This philosophy started gaining momentum when different government/ private agencies started researching the effects. It was found that when both parties are arrested, it had an adverse affect on the victim. The victims were less likely to call or trust law enforcement during the next incident of domestic abuse.

INTERVENTION

In 1981, the Duluth Domestic Abuse Intervention Project became the first multi-disciplinary program designed to address the issue of domestic violence. This experiment, conducted in Duluth, MN, frequently referred to as the "Duluth Project." It coordinated agencies dealing with domestic situations, drawing together diverse elements of the system, from police officers on the street, to shelters for battered women and probation officers supervising offenders.

This program has become a model for other jurisdictions seeking to deal more effectively with domestic violence. Corrections/probation agencies in many areas are supervising domestic violence offenders more closely, and are also paying closer attention to the victim's needs and safety issues. There has been controversy as the Duluth framework depends on a strict "patriarchal violence" model and presumes that all violence in the home and elsewhere has a male perpetrator and female victim. Also evidence of success of the model is limited, with scholarly analysis and critique.

Many victims leave their abusers, only to return. Research has shown that a major factor in helping a victim to establish lasting independence from the abusive partner is her or his ability to get legal assistance. Economists at the Brennan Center for Justice analyzed Bureau of Justice Statistics data to determine what accounted for the nationwide reduction in reported abuse. Their findings revealed that one significant factor was the availability of legal services to assist abuse victims. Another major study by economists at Colgate University and the University of Arkansas flatly stated that the only public service that reduces domestic violence in the long term is legal aid. Legal assistance can provide essential safety planning, buttress a family's economic position through child or spousal support, allay fears planted by the batterer about loss of custody, and help victims to secure needed government benefits.

DIAGNOSIS PLANNING

The American Psychiatric Association planning and research committees for the forthcoming DSM-V (2012) have canvassed a series of new Relational disorders which include Marital Conflict Disorder without Violence or Marital Abuse Disorder (Marital Conflict Disorder with Violence). Couples with marital disorders sometimes come to clinical attention because the couple recognizes long-standing dissatisfaction with their marriage and come to the clinician on their own initiative or are referred by an astute health care professional. Secondly, there is serious violence in the marriage which is - "usually the husband battering the wife".

In these cases the emergency room or a legal authority often is the first to notify the clinician. Most importantly, marital violence "is a major risk factor for serious injury and even death and women in violent marriages are at much greater risk of being seriously injured or killed (National Advisory Council on Violence Against Women 2000)." The authors of this study add that "There is current considerable controversy over whether male-to-female marital violence is best regarded as a reflection of male psychopathology and control or whether there is an empirical base and clinical utility for conceptualizing these patterns as relational."

Recommendations for clinicians making a diagnosis of Marital Relational Disorder should include the assessment of actual or "potential" male violence as regularly as they assess the potential for suicide in depressed patients. Further, "clinicians should not relax their vigilance after a battered wife leaves her husband, because some data suggest that the period immediately following a marital separation is the period of greatest risk for the women. Many men will stalk and batter their wives in an effort to get them to return or punish them for leaving. Initial assessments of the potential for violence in a marriage can be supplemented by standardized interviews and questionnaires, which have been reliable and valid aids in exploring marital violence more systematically."

The authors conclude with what they call "very recent information" on the course of violent marriages which suggests that "over time a husband's battering may abate somewhat, but perhaps because he has successfully intimidated his wife. The risk of violence remains strong in a marriage in which it has been a feature in the past. Thus, treatment is essential here; the clinician cannot just wait and watch." The most urgent clinical priority is the protection of the wife because she is the one most frequently at risk, and clinicians must be aware that supporting assertiveness by a battered wife may lead to more beatings or even death.

STATE VIOLENCE

Labor camps

Many women underwent extrajudicial punishment in labor camps of Nazi Germany and the Soviet Union. Their suffering was described in memories of former Gulag women prisoners Yevgenia Ginzburg, Eufrosinia Kersnovskaya and others.

War and Militarism

Militarism produces special environments that allow for increased violence against women. For example, during World War II, the Japanese military established brothels for soldiers exploiting women for the purpose of creating access and entitlement for men. Another example of violence against women incited by militarism during war took place in the Kovno Ghetto. Jewish male prisoners had access to (and used) Jewish women forced into camp brothels by the Nazis, who also used them. The 1998 United Nations International Criminal Tribunal for Rwanda recognized rape as a war crime.

Violence in Empowerment Systems

Shelter workers are often reduced them to contributing to violence against women by exploiting their vulnerability in exchange for a paying job.

ACTIVISM

Many activists believe that working towards the elimination of domestic violence means working to eliminate a societal hierarchy enforced through sexism. Women of Color Against Violence cited racism within the anti-violence movement and suggest that violence against women will not end until the anti-violence movement re-directs its goal from "ending violence against women" to "ending violence against women of color." The same conclusion can be drawn for other systems of oppression.

Criticism

In 1997, the Canadian Advertising Foundation ruled that a National Ad campaign that featuring Nicole Brown Simpson's sister Denise with the slogan entitled, "Stop violence against Women" was in fact portraying only men as aggressors, and that it was not providing a balanced message and was in fact contributing to gender stereotyping. The

United Nations defines violence against women as any act of gender-based violence that results in, or is likely to result in, physical, sexual or mental harm or suffering to women, including threats of such acts, coercion or arbitrary deprivation of liberty, whether occurring in public or in private life.

There are many forms of violence against women, including sexual, physical, or emotional abuse by an intimate partner; physical or sexual abuse by family members or others; sexual harassment and abuse by authority figures (such as teachers, police officers or employers); trafficking for forced labour or sex; and such traditional practices as forced or child marriages, dowry-related violence; and honour killings, when women are murdered in the name of family honour. Systematic sexual abuse in conflict situations is another form of violence against women.

Scope of the problem:

In a 10-country study on women's health and domestic violence conducted by WHO,

Between 15% and 71% of women reported physical or sexual violence by a husband or partner.

Many women said that their first sexual experience was not consensual. (24% in rural Peru, 28% in Tanzania, 30% in rural Bangladesh, and 40% in South Africa).

Between 4% and 12% of women reported being physically abused during pregnancy. More about the study

About 5,000 women are murdered by family members in the name of honour each year worldwide.

Trafficking of women and girls for forced labour and sex is widespread and often affects the most vulnerable.

Forced marriages and child marriages violate the human rights of women and girls, but they are widely practiced in many countries in Asia, the Middle East and sub-Saharan Africa.

Worldwide, up to one in five women and one in 10 men report experiencing sexual abuse as children. Children who experience sexual abuse are much more likely to encounter other forms of abuse later in life.

Health effects

Health consequences can result directly from violent acts or from the long-term effects of violence.

Injuries: Physical and sexual abuse by a partner is closely associated with injuries. Violence by an intimate partner is the leading cause of non-fatal injuries to women in the USA.

Death: Deaths from violence against women includes honour killings (by families for cultural reasons); suicide; female infanticide (murder of infant girls); and maternal death from unsafe abortion.

Sexual and reproductive health: Violence against women is associated with sexually transmitted infections such as HIV/ AIDS, unintended pregnancies, gynaecological problems, induced abortions, and adverse pregnancy outcomes, including miscarriage, low birth weight and fetal death.

Risky behaviours: Sexual abuse as a child is associated with higher rates of sexual risk-taking (such as first sex at an early age, multiple partners and unprotected sex), substance use, and additional victimization. Each of these behaviours increases risks of health problems.

Mental health: Violence and abuse increase risk of depression, post-traumatic stress disorder, sleep difficulties, eating disorders and emotional distress.

Physical health: Abuse can result in many health problems, including headaches, back pain, abdominal pain, fibromyalgia, gastrointestinal disorders, limited mobility, and poor overall health status.

Social and economic costs

The social and economic costs of violence against women are enormous and have ripple effects throughout society. Women may suffer isolation, inability to work, loss of wages, lack of participation in regular activities, and limited ability to care for themselves and their children.

Though risk factors vary, some characteristics seem to increase the likelihood of violence. The potential risk factors can be grouped into the following subsets.

Individual: Personal attributes associated with higher risk of violence include: a young age, lower socio-economic status, limited education, a history of abuse and substance use, and, for partner violence, the choice of partner. Partner traits that put women at risk include alcohol or drug use, low educational level, negative attitudes about women, and witnessing domestic violence against women or being abused as a child.

Family and relationship: Within families, risk of violence increases with marital conflicts, male dominance, economic stress and poor family functioning.

Community: Within communities, the risk is higher where there is gender inequality, and a lack of community cohesion or resources.

Societal: On a broader level, higher risk is found in societies with traditional gender norms or a lack of autonomy for women, and where there are restrictive laws on divorce and ownership and inheritance of property, or when there is social breakdown due to conflicts or disasters.

Prevention and response

More evaluation is needed to assess the effectiveness of violence prevention measures. Interventions with promising results include increasing education and opportunities for women and girls, improving their self-esteem and negotiating skills, and reducing gender inequities in communities.

Other efforts with positive success include: work with teenagers to reduce dating violence; supportive programmes for children who have witnessed intimate partner violence; mass public education campaigns; and work with men and boys to change attitudes about gender inequities and the acceptability of violence. Advocacy for victims, better awareness of violence and its consequences among health workers, and wider knowledge of available resources for abused women (including legal assistance, housing and child care), can lessen the consequences of violence.

WHO response

WHO and partners collaborate to decrease violence against women through initiatives that help to identify, quantify and respond to the problem, including:

i. Building evidence on the scope and types of violence in different settings as a key step in understanding the magnitude and nature of the problem at a global level.

ii. Developing guidance for Member States and health professionals to prevent violence and strengthen health sector responses to it.

iii. Disseminating information to countries and supporting national efforts to advance women's rights and prevent violence.

iv. Collaborating with international agencies and organizations to deter violence against women globally.

2

Violence Against Tribal Women

Alcoholism has been a major problem in the tribal areas of Orissa State in India. The tribal population in Orissa is 25 percent and the majority leaves in remote areas in difficult terrains. Women have been the worst affected because of excessive alcohol consumption by their men folks. Violence against women has been one of the negative consequences of excessive drinking by men. Consumption of liquor leaves very little income to purchase essential commodities for daily use. It is estimated that 20 percent of the income is spent on consuming country liquor.

This is highly prevalent among the younger men. Additionally the degradation of natural resources and limited income earning opportunities has led to the tribal populations living in very dismal conditions. The country liquor industry flourished due to the heavy demand by the tribal population. On the other hand it also generated revenue of 40 crores of Rupees annually. Indebtedness to non-tribal money-lenders is a common problem in these areas. Many tribals have lost their land due to excessive borrowings.

There is a need to reduce or completely stop this practice by banning sale of country liquor in the tribal areas. Further, recognition of village organizations to influence decision-making at the micro-level especially women focussed would prove to be constructive in bringing about changes in the present conditions.

TRIBAL WOMEN'S INITIATIVE

In March 1993 on the eve of the International Women's Day, the first Tribal Women's Convention was held in Biswanathpur in Kalahandi (Tribal) district of Orissa. Women workers of 24 non-governmental organisations from 11 districts of the state, along with 415 tribal women representatives took part in the convention. The major objective of this convention was to pressurise the Government in taking actions to improve the socio-economic conditions of the tribal people in a sustainable manner.

The problems that they seriously wanted the government to address include: degradation of the ecology on which their livelihoods were based; wage discrimination against women and; initiating a movement to ban the sale of country liquor. Further a ten point cluster of demands was submitted by the representatives to the Chief Minister of the State. The ban on the sale of country liquor was the most serious and needed attention. On the other hand it was difficult to implement due to the high revenue that it generated.

THE APPROACH

The non-acceptance by the National political party to stop the sale of country liquor led to women strengthening their movement against this practice. Pressure groups at various levels were established. Tribal women with help of the NGO women workers conducted workshops, rallies, street plays and other forms of meetings to sensitize the people on the evils and hazards of country liquor. Such methods of sensitization had far reaching effects. Certain incidents of harassment by drunken men stirred the movement further and added to the pressure on the government to take serious steps.

Eventually these efforts made an impact on the ruling political party and the Chief Minister of Orissa state announced the ban on sale and manufacture of country liquor on 18 April 1994.

The Impact:

- The banning of country liquor received wide social acceptance all over the state from all stratas of the society.

- Tribal women supported the ban and vowed to co-operate further in order to sustain this effort like raising awareness about the evils of liquor consumption in different areas and meetings.
- Tribal women have been able to influence decision making at the grass root level as they feel empowered due to the success of their movement. Some women have been able to achieve special positions in terms of decision making especially to fight against forces of exploitation and injustice.
- Law enforcing agencies of the state regarding the illicit sale and manufacture of country liquor are forging strong ties with grass roots organisations to implement stringent measures against this practice.
- The success of this movement has spread not only to other parts of the state but also other states of India.
- Media reporting on this feature played an important role in not only spreading the message but also creating awareness about the evils of country liquor consumption.

OTHER PARTS OF THE GLOBE

The essential Navajo value is that while men and women are distinct, they relate as complementary equals. That kind of relationship creates, or should create, an environment that views violence toward women as deviant behavior. Under Navajo common law, violence toward women, or mistreatment of them in any way, is illegal. A man who battered his wife was considered irrational and thus could no longer lead a war party, a hunt, or participate in either. He could not be trusted to behave properly.... He was thought of as contrary to Lakota law and lost many privileges of life and many roles in Lakota society and the societies within the society.

What we do know is that in most Native American societies men's and women's roles were delineated in such a way that violence against women among their own groups did not seem to be a common and regular practice. We were always taught that women were sacred and that everything in the home belonged to the women. Our extended families used to live together and no one would have ever thought of abusing women and children. It wasn't until families started to move into town or to move away from each other that we started to hear stories about someone beating up his wife. The physical abuse of American Indian women is a subject now emerging from the Netherlands of ignorance which has surrounded the lives of contemporary indigenous people in the United States.

That American Indian tribes have been recognized as the first sovereign within the boundaries of the United States is not a fact consciously acknowledged by many citizens governed by the other two sovereigns: the state and the federal governments. Many presume that American Indians are just another ethnic minority within this republic. Additionally, non-Indians often assume that the popular media's depictions of contemporary Indian life are accurate. The purpose of this chapter is to discuss openly the issue of the physical abuse of American Indian women in a manner that reflects the authors' knowledge of how American Indian people live. This chapter confronts presumptions or pre-existing notions about the indigenous people of the United States that pervade popular culture.

American Indian societies generally hold a common world view that seeks to achieve balance or harmony in all relationships. The cultural principles of American Indians, reflected in this world view, do not espouse or approve of the abuse of women. While this statement encompasses the approximately 550 tribes recognized by the federal government, the authors' knowledge of the traditional values and beliefs of contemporary tribal people sustains the broad application. Although there are differences among the tribes, respect for the physical integrity of women is not an area where cultural values among tribes differ significantly.

Individuals in any society have always attempted to use physical force to control others and American Indians are not exempt from what continues to be an unfortunate human behavior. The fact that individual members of tribes, predominantly male, engage in the physical abuse of women does not mean that such behavior satisfies a culturally approved norm. Like non-Indian jurisdictions in the United States that use various means to redress abusive situations, there are certain differences in the way tribes, as nations, protect their female members. Rather than a single Indian model, there are many; each tribe's practices derive from a blend of its cultural, historical, and contemporary experiences.

Initially, this chapter will examine the sovereign nature of the tribal nations within the parameters of both international law and United States jurisprudence. This chapter will also address the way in which some international instruments relate to the rights and protection of indigenous people, including specific provisions for protecting women. Furthermore, this chapter will provide an overview of the American Indians' shared world view, revealing values in sharp contrast to those of the majority of American society. The lives of indigenous peoples are anchored upon communal values, rather than individualism, as the primary guide to behavior. Finally, this chapter will demonstrate how some tribes seek to protect their female members through codes, customary law, and intervention programs which provide services to victims, abusers, and their families.

The powers of Indian tribes are, in general, 'inherent powers of a limited sovereignty which has never been extinguished.' Before the coming of the Europeans, the tribes were self-governing sovereign political communities. Like all sovereign bodies, they then had the inherent power to prescribe laws for their members and to punish infractions of those laws.

American Indian tribes existed as sovereign nations before the European invasion of the North American continent. This sovereign status persisted through the subsequent wars and resolutions of conflicts among the European powers. Each European power dealt in practical ways with the tribal nations to maintain a competitive advantage with other nations. France and England, for instance, recognized the tribes as sovereign nations if this recognition would give them an advantage over a competitor in trade or military alliances.

Similarly, the newly formed United States treated the tribes as sovereign nation-states. The history of the encounters among all of the sovereigns reflects pragmatic concerns, with theoretical frameworks as a delayed or collateral development. As noted, both European colonial powers, and the United States Constitution originally recognized American Indian Tribes as nations. Supreme Court decisions have continued to uphold this political status. The autonomy of Native American tribes to act as discrete governments persists even though congressional acts and federal court decisions have limited the power of the Indian sovereigns.

The American Indians' status as tribal nations immediately distinguishes them from other ethnic populations within the United States. The tribal status as a sovereign is both pre-constitutional and extra constitutional. In jurisprudential terms, this means that the equal protection and due process doctrines do not necessarily resolve issues in Indian law. Although a unique nation-to-nation status exists between tribes and the federal government, shifting federal policies since the formation of the United States have limited, defined, and complicated tribal autonomy.

Legal complexity arises from the conflict inherent between tribal sovereignty and the concurrent doctrine of the federal government as trustee for the tribal dependent. Unlike other U.S. citizens, American Indians as individuals have overlapping citizenship rights within three sovereigns - tribal, state, and federal. The nature and extent of tribal autonomy is a recurring legal question that complicates interactions among these three sovereigns. The tribal sovereign's status is key to understanding how American Indian governments act to protect women.

Tribes use inherent authority and cultural means which are distinct from the authority and means used by state and federal governments. Like non-Indian jurisdictions, tribes protect women through governmental structures. Some tribal governments are similar to non-Indian governmental entities, where executive, legislative, and judicial branches are identifiable. These descriptors, however, do not necessarily define how these branches operate in tribal governments. In some Pueblo communities, for instance, domestic disputes are resolved through traditional proceedings conducted by the Governor of the Pueblo, who is not categorically a judicial officer.

The protection of women by tribal governments stems from cultural values. Tribal societies retain and integrate cultural values into the contemporary responsibility of tribal governments. The goal of maintaining harmony among members of the community perpetuates traditional dispute resolution methods that employ elders, peacemakers, and designated persons (such as the Pueblo Governor) to serve as mediators and decision makers. Traditional tribal methods of dispute resolution do not fit within the adversarial model, but rather aim to restore harmonious relationships among spouses, domestic partners, family, clan, and community members. To be valid judgments about how women fare in these tribal communities must be based upon the legal and cultural frameworks that apply to the indigenous people of the Americas.

Recent attempts by the international community to address the status of the indigenous peoples of the world include an examination of Native American tribes. In the countries invaded by European powers, the natives resisted the invaders' common initial practice of exterminating indigenous populations as human beings, nations, or as cultures. Historically, under international law, native populations became protected from annihilation and were allowed to assimilate into the dominant political society. In the post-colonial period, nation-states resisted recognizing distinct ethnic and cultural groups within a country's boundaries.

Whether in the former U.S.S.R. with its multitude of ethnic populations, numerous Latin American countries with Indians, or Sweden, Norway, and Finland with the Samis, the dominant nations argued that no distinctions existed among their citizens and that all possessed only one national identity. Later instruments, such as Convention 169, the Convention Concerning Indigenous and Tribal Peoples in Independent Countries of the International Labour Converence ('ILO'), generated new ways of perceiving and respecting the rights of indigenous people in the collective and as individuals. International law is now wrestling with the persisting question of how to treat the distinct indigenous populations found everywhere in the world.

The emerging norms, most recently stated in the products of the U.N. Working Group on Indigenous Populations, expand the view of the indigenous peoples. Consequently, the nature of their rights is changing. Current dialogue involves the nation-states, the indigenous peoples (usually represented by nongovernmental organizations), and the international structure or forum such as the United Nations (U.N.), that mediates this dialogue. Significant differences exist among proponents about key concepts and definitions regarding the legal status of indigenous populations and land. One of the central disputes is the indigenous populations' demand to qualify as autonomous nation-states and their resistance to a less autonomous status as 'a people' or 'a minority.'

American Indians continue to possess the key characteristics of the sovereign state: a distinctive permanent population; a defined territory, with identifiable borders; a government exercising authority over territory and population; and the capacity to enter into relationships with other nation-states. In this regard, the American Indian nations can generate models on how indigenous peoples can protect their communal interests, including the well-being of their female members.

The protection of women as members of indigenous communities has not been specifically addressed by international legal doctrines. Rather, women have been considered in a generic sense. All women who are noncombatants are among those persons protected by the Geneva Accords. Civilized nation-states have a responsibility to honor and enforce this treaty, which protects women from deprivation of basic needs and from physical abuse during wartime. Only recently has physical abuse against women in non-combat situations become part of the international law dialogue.

Additionally, specific instruments bar unequal treatment of women by nation-states. While some instruments proscribe the abuse of women through denial of political and social rights, these provisions are directed only at the dominant nation-states. National power cannot be used to burden or disable women who are members of an indigenous population. International organizations utilize these international legal doctrines to determine whether a country discriminates against its female population. In two cases adjudicated by the U.N. Committee on Human Rights the panel concluded that laws in Mauritius and Canada violated women's rights under the International Covenant on Civil and Political Rights (the 'Covenant').

While Lovelace v. Canada demonstrates how international law has protected indigenous women, a factually similar U.S. case, Santa Clara Pueblo v. Martinez, illustrates how the sovereignty doctrine distinctively affects the treatment of American Indian women. Both cases involved female tribal members who married non-members. The women's relationships with their tribes substantively changed as a result of their marriages to non-members. Sandra Lovelace, for example, lost her membership rights and benefits. In both cases, however, male members who also married outside the tribe were not subject to the same disqualifications.

These similar factual situations, however, did not produce the same legal conclusions. In Lovelace, the U.N. Committee found gender discrimination in the Canadian law based on the provisions in the Covenant. Thereafter, the Canadian national government stated that it would enact a statutory revision. Martinez yielded a result opposite to Lovelace because of the different law used in a federal forum. The Supreme Court determined that the Santa Clara Pueblo, as a sovereign, was immune from suit and that protecting the sovereignty of the tribe precluded the federal government from interfering with the tribe's right to control qualifications for membership.

Martinez is based upon U.S. law and the federal policy affirming tribal sovereignty as a legal doctrine. The Covenant provisions used in Lovelace probably could not apply in

Martinez to obtain a decision favoring the female plaintiff and her children; the U.S. tribes have not signed the Covenant and are thus not bound by its provisions. Additionally, the Covenant favors indigenous people in their autonomy. It states that, 'all peoples have the right of self-determination. By virtue of that right they freely determine their political status and freely pursue their economic, social and cultural development.' It is not yet known where indigenous women as a specific class may obtain enforceable rights in the emerging picture in international law.

Indigenous women can seek the protection of their rights under international provisions that protect all women against rights abuses by nation-states. It is, however, doubtful whether these current instruments protect indigenous women within their tribal governments. Where the Covenant applies, as in Lovelace, indigenous women are not distinct from all women with identifiable rights and potential remedies. The provisions prohibit gender discrimination, abuse of women's personal security, and loss of any rights or equality because the women are married.

Convention 169 of the ILO also prohibits gender-based discrimination. Yet, the ILO directs its force against nation-states with indigenous peoples within their boundaries, not against indigenous peoples and their governments. The ILO also provides that 'the social, cultural, religious and spiritual values and practices of these peoples shall be recognized and protected.' The ILO does not, however, indicate if or how the individual rights of women are to be balanced against the interests of their indigenous community.

In 1992, the Working Group on Indigenous Population released the Draft Declaration on the Rights of Indigenous People 'Draft Declaration' While the Draft Declaration addressed 'peoples' and their rights, it failed to delineate rights for individuals. The 1993 revisions to the Draft Declaration injected individual's rights into the provisions, yet the document retained its collective focus. Therefore, tribal power and laws employed in Martinez may be valid under some provisions of the Draft Declaration. While the Working Group grounded the Draft Declaration's provisions in a communal perspective of rights, there is a potential for conflict with law and instruments based on individualistic principles of gender equality. If gender equality becomes a fundamental international norm, American Indian tribes could face challenges to their customary legal practices.

The Convention on the Elimination of All Forms of Discrimination Against Women ('Women's Convention') created another potential conflict between international legal doctrine and federal law. The Women's Convention constructed its declaration on strict equality principles, but failed to specifically address indigenous people and tribal women. This Convention could prohibit a ruling similar to Martinez because the Convention's declaration provides that women shall have 'equal rights with men with respect to the nationality of their children.' Similarly, the Women's Convention declared that a woman who marries an alien cannot lose her nationality, be forced to acquire her husband's nationality, or be rendered stateless. Since the Women's Convention does not specifically address indigenous peoples, it is conjectural to state definitively that this equality doctrine conflicts with U.S. law.

American Indian nations with recognized sovereignty are a contrast to other peoples who lack this source of jurisprudential power. Despite these contrasts, the tribes can provide some models of governance and the use of custom for contemporary indigenous peoples. Tribal governments are implementing models through their laws, courts, and intervention programs to protect their female members. Martinez and the ongoing work in tribal communities to protect women are congruous. Both types of actions, defining membership and protecting members, are an exercise of the tribal sovereign's power. Moreover, the use of the tribal sovereign's powers is bound to the cultural context of the American Indian world.

Both Martinez and the protective efforts of domestic violence laws are the product of important tribal values. To understand the Martinez decision and the tribal laws, one must consider the world view which guides the indigenous people of the U.S. For each tribe of men Usen created He also made a home. In the land for any particular tribe He placed whatever would be best for the welfare of that tribe. When Usen created the Apaches He also gave them their homes in the West. He gave them such grain, fruits, and game as they needed to eat.... He gave them a pleasant climate and all they needed for clothing and shelter was at hand. Thus it was in the beginning: the Apaches and their homes each created for the other by Usen himself. When they are taken from these homes they sicken and die.

And God blessed them, and God said unto them, Be fruitful, and multiply, and replenish the earth, and subdue it; and have dominion over the fish of the sea, and over the fowl of the air, and over every living thing that moveth upon the earth.

A commonality of values and perceptions exists among the many indigenous peoples in the U.S., which contrasts starkly with the values and views historically asserted by the majority culture in the United States. While this statement may generalize too broadly about both viewpoints, the American Indians' shared viewpoint about both their reality and the contrast is evident. A comparison of the two groups' viewpoints on community, the individual, and conflict resolution reveals the difference between the communal perspective of native peoples and the individual rights focus of Euro-Americans.

The political philosophy of John Locke, influential in the formation of the United States government, presents communities as the basic political entity protecting individual rights. The drafters of the Constitution did not seek the participation of the Indian nations in the 'mutuality of concession' that created the U.S. Constitution, the social contract that guides the majority culture in the United States. The preclusion of the indigenous nations from the Constitutional Convention is not the sole explanation for the difference between indigenous and Euro-American cultures. Both cultures value the maintenance of community through law or customary rules of conduct, but this facial resemblance between the two societies cannot mask the differences.

In establishing the function of law derived from distinct values, indigenous people and the dominant U.S. culture do differ. Native American tribes subscribe to communal values as the guiding principle for the laws that govern an individual's conduct. This preference does not mean that individual interests are ignored. Native American laws strive to protect individuals, at the same time preserving the cultural beliefs and practices of the collective framework. Thus, tribal societies are built on community or relational foundations. The relational foundation does not mean that individual rights are inconsistent with tribal interests. The key questions are: 1) which rights and values ought to exist; and 2) how can designated rights be held by an abstract individual, independent of social context, relationships with others or historical setting?

For tribal people, the real-life relational framework is the key to how individuals should treat each other. The Navajo Nation Peacemaker Court materials represent one example of this framework. The materials state as the operating principles for those before that traditional body: ' K'ei is kinship which arranges correct conduct of the individuals within a family unit.... Doonee is the clan group where rules of correct conduct, with fellow clan groups of the same tribe, are foremost.... Bahoddaatah is the innate nature and responsibility of an individual's existence.'

These concepts anchor the standards of respect and responsibility which the Peacemaker court employs to review members' conduct when conflicts must be resolved. Conflict among individuals is a universal feature of human society. The survival of an organized community depends on the resolution of the inevitable conflicts between the interests of individual members and the interests of the community as a whole. The resolution of conflicts and the maintenance of a universal harmony is a primary concern for indigenous nations and their members, but the cultural guide utilized is distinct from that of predominantly Western societies. Individual interests are considered as part of a larger perspective.

The individual and the community are part of the kinship that exists among all life forms and the environmental elements. Harmony is the desired result of the relationship with all life forms, including humans, animals, and plants. For tribal people, conflict arises when the individual is out of balance or in disharmony with other community members and elements in the universe. Restoration of the individual's physical and mental well-being requires the involvement of others in understanding the problem and its resolution.

Traditional forms of problem resolution include non-adversarial forums where respected elders, family, and clan members contribute to the outcome. When the resolution occurs, the individual and the community can resume a life that promotes harmonious relationships. Accommodation and compromise, not win-or-lose strategies, contribute to the desired traditional outcome. This type of accommodation and compromise of individual interests may not be understood or appreciated by persons outside the tribe. Internal decision-making and the resolution of intra-tribal conflicts have traditionally not included outsiders, including non-member Indians.

A non-Indian's lack of appreciation for tribal autonomy and its importance in Native American communities is reflected in the chapters written about Martinez. Martinez disturbed many non-Indians, especially feminists, because the Court's holding denied full tribal membership to children of a female tribal member who married outside of the tribe. Some commentators made an equal protection argument, which would have the effect of treating a tribe-specific rule as common to all Native American tribal nations.

Responses such as this overlook the unique status of American Indian tribes as sovereigns outside the usual realm of American constitutional law. As a result, commentators ignore the repeated affirmations that issues in Indian law require a non-constitutional analysis. These non-Indian and feminist views overlook the premise that only the essential quality of a particular tribe's sovereignty can explain outcomes similar to and different from Martinez. The tribe's power to self-define by establishing the qualifications for membership is key to sovereignty and to understanding Martinez.

It is not clear, for instance, how critics of Martinez respond to the Navajo Nation's custom that empowers a matrilineal and matrilocal society, so as to define important legal rights by the mother's clan. In the Onondaga Nation, tribal males, whose rights and status are subject to the Onondaga Faithkeepers' authority, can neither vote for these leaders nor have non-member spouses reside on tribal land. The Faithkeepers are selected and appointed by, and are accountable to, the Clan Mother. A broad brush approach demanding equality for women and men in all tribal situations would trample upon both the power of the tribal sovereigns and the values used to construct their governments.

Indian feminists have rejected the Western feminist approach to gender equality by retaining the cultural framework and a commitment to the tribal nations' autonomy. Rayna Green, a Cherokee, states:

For Indian feminists, every women's issue is framed in the larger context of Native American people. The concerns which characterize debate in Indian country, tribal sovereignty and self-determination, for example, put Native American tribes on a collision path with regulations like Title 9 and with Equal Opportunity and Affirmative Action. Tribes insist that treaty-based sovereignty supersedes any other federal mandate. While many Native American women have personal difficulty with the application of tribal sovereignty to affirmative action in tribal hiring, for example, most agree that sovereignty is best debated without special exception.

This statement, acknowledging that contemporary Indian women experience personal difficulties, is not that of an atypical Indian feminist. Rayna Green notes, however, that conservation and innovation continue to exist in tribal societies because Indian women insist on taking their traditional places as healers, legal specialists and tribal government leaders. The return to tradition, retraditionalization, coupled with the evolution of gender roles in American Indian society continue the complementary and mutual roles enjoyed by women and men.

Complementary roles arise from the deepest traditional beliefs tribal people hold about how they were created and should function in the universe. One Indian feminist, Paula Gunn Allen, echoes a pervasive understanding 'that primary power - the power to make and to relate - belongs to the preponderantly feminine powers of the universe.' The strictly drawn gender lines of the majority culture fail to explain much in indigenous belief systems where the creative force is exclusively feminine. Although this spirit or creative force can change forms (including manifesting itself as a male if necessary), the maintenance of a complementary social structure remains essential if a tribe is to deal effectively with internal and external matters.

In the complementary relational system of the tribe, membership in the tribe and who can undertake roles are key concerns. The tribal nation's ability to define membership, its qualifications, benefits and responsibilities is explicitly connected to the customary values of a tribe. The tribes face enormous challenges in melding traditional values with the demands of operating a contemporary government responsive to members' needs. Tribes manage this task by relying on a historically successful approach: they conserve and innovate.

Through a combination of conservation and innovation in their customs and practices, the indigenous peoples of the Americas survived the injection of European populations, life forms, and ideas into their lives. Consequently, it is foolhardy to think that American Indians can be unchangingly defined by a historically set point. Such a view treats American Indians as living artifacts and ignores their ability to develop by reinterpreting custom. The reinterpretation of traditional beliefs and behavior has led numerous tribes to select women as the tribal nation's chief official. In sharp contrast, the United States has yet to entrust the Presidency to a woman. It is not surprising that tribes have acted to share leadership roles with women.

Tribes in the nineteenth century ensured women their own property rights. This was long before the state or federal governments allowed women to own property or treated women as legal or political actors. The contents of tribal domestic abuse codes appear to be grounded in the traditional willingness of tribes to respect women in complementary roles which promote tribal well-being. The protection of the physical security of female tribal members is considered critical for two reasons: it maintains continuity with customary values, and it meets the duties of a government to promote the well-being of all members.

Despite problems associated with poverty, unemployment, alcoholism, and inadequate education, contemporary tribes strive to return to their traditional values and beliefs. A failure to do so can only lead to increased problems, as abused individuals treat others in an abusive manner. For instance, abuse of female tribal members frequently results in abuse to children, and eventually spreads throughout the tribal community. Resolution, remediation, and prevention must reach beyond the individual female victims and incorporate offenders into the process. Additionally, any steps taken should preserve cultural values which honor families and clans in relational networks.

Effective tribal law and intervention results in the protection of individuals and the restoration of offenders to community participation. Both outcomes are needed to strengthen a community. In essence, tribes should strive to protect their female members through a system which preserves the cultural values of the tribe. Without culturally appropriate means to lessen the social disruption, tribal societies risk losing their identity as distinct cultures and sovereigns. A commitment to traditional relational values, such as those which stress family and clan honor, should help to alleviate problems associated with the physical and psychological abuse of female tribal members. A review of some protective models from American Indian tribes demonstrates that tribes are engaged in an earnest effort to preserve their tribal uniqueness through codes, court orders, and interventions which stress the protection of women.

In perseveration society, beliefs... were handed down by all the people to the coming generations. In order for a tiyospaye to live in unity and cooperation, it was necessary for all to live according to the same beliefs/laws/values. This resulted in unity. When people living together do not share the same beliefs/laws/values, there will be confusion. Individuals will not have a foundation from which to guide their self-conduct. Individuals will live according to different values, and the society made up of those individuals will exist in confusion as to what is considered proper behavior.

This portion of the chapter will focus on contemporary tribal activities, tribal laws, the common law of tribal courts, and tribal intervention programs in operation. This approach is distinguishable from anthropological studies, in which information is gathered by interviewing members of a society about their perceptions or reliance on Human Relations Area Files (reports compiled by anthropologists detailing their observations and interpretations of the societies studied). We have reservations about how salient some of these studies are to contemporary tribal people in the United States. Practices reported in some studies do not comport with what we have observed in contemporary tribal societies.

Consequently, this chapter offers a review which is an emerging picture of how tribes protect their female members. This review presents a discussion of the legal treatment of domestic violence by fourteen United States tribes. It is not intended to be a description of the state of the law among all 537 tribes. Rather, this chapter is a general survey of existing tribal law on domestic violence. The selected tribal laws were not chosen to represent the way that all tribes should approach domestic violence.

Instead, they serve as a starting point from which to analyze the issues that arise when tribal communities confront issues of domestic violence. The laws demonstrate the effort of tribes to ensure the physical security of women within their respective jurisdictions. Of the tribes examined, almost all have specific laws which address domestic violence. Many of these tribal codes have common provisions.

The most frequently recurring provisions are those defining domestic violence and identifying the persons protected under the law. While our focus is on the protection of women, these laws are framed in much broader terms. In this review, we look closely and consider these codes not only in terms of the protections they afford women, but also in terms of the protections afforded to all members of tribal society. Additionally we also consider how the laws reflect and impact tribal society. A discussion of the above identified provisions will follow. Unique provisions will also be discussed in so far as they reveal the cultural perspectives that distinguish tribal societies.

We begin with an overview of the persons protected by tribal law and the behavior proscribed by these codes. All of the tribal codes reviewed identify the persons protected and set forth what constitutes domestic violence, domestic abuse, or spousal abuse. The tribal provisions vary in that some tribes ascribe protection to a broad group of persons, while others protect a narrow group of persons. Generally, women who are spouses and family and household members are protected persons. Tribes, however, vary in their provisions by further qualifying the definition of 'spouse' and 'family and household member' or by further expanding the protected class. A minority of tribes restrict the definition by age and marital status.

Most tribes broaden the definition to include relationships without reference to marital status or age. The Navajo Nation clearly identifies the protected class and uses the identification to expand the class beyond that of several state family violence protection provisions in the United States. Others protect a broad class through the use of a general term such as 'persons' when describing the individuals protected.

The Navajo Nation, the Jicarilla Apache tribe, and the Standing Rock Sioux have provisions which specifically identify a broad class of protected individuals. The Navajo Nation Domestic Abuse Protection Act specifically and unequivocally provides for the protection of a wide class of persons. Under this law, the protected class includes persons who have been directly affected by domestic abuse.

The Act specifically includes any current or former member of the abuser's household or immediate residence area; anyone currently or previously involved in an intimate relationship with the abuser; any person who interacts with the abuser in an employment, academic, recreational, religious, social or other setting; any offspring of the abuser; any relative or clan member of the abuser; any elderly person; or any vulnerable person, including the emotionally and physically disabled. The Rules for Domestic Violence Proceedings for the Courts of the Navajo Nation require that the definition of domestic violence, which makes reference to the protected parties, be supplemented by Navajo common law principles, such as the principle that recognizes that special reciprocal relations exist in Navajo society among spouses and family members.

A succession of violent acts resulting in the death of Navajo women at the hands of their husbands and boyfriends brought domestic violence to the center of Navajo public attention. Witnesses presented testimony to subcommittees of the Navajo Nation Council at public hearings held in conjunction with the Navajo Nation Judicial Branch. 'Jane Begay,' the name used by one witness who did not wish to reveal her true identity, was one woman who offered testimony. A portion of her testimony, as related by one observer, is as follows:

He would wait until she was asleep, then violently pull her from bed to confront her about her infidelity or the illegitimacy of the older child. It got to the point where she was afraid to sleep. She once stayed up four days in a row. She would do the chores, but forget what she was doing. The last night, when she was completely exhausted, she ran from the house without her shoes. She went up into the mountains, and covered herself with pine needles so she couldn't be found.... The audience was still as she told her story.

She told it quietly, with soft emotion and tears and people were ready to join in them. She softly told the story of being trapped by a brutal cowboy, naively tied to him by a belief she was 'married' to him. She was driven from her grandparent's home by rape and molestation, severely treated by her parents, treated as a captive by the denying father of her children, and given more abuse by her own family when she returned to it. She painted the picture of a brutal, male world, where abuse, accusations of sexual misconduct, and attempted rape were commonplace.

Women on the Council, on the Navajo Nation bench, and within the government and the community were instrumental in the lengthy process involved in the passage of the Act. This involvement ranged from insisting that the issue be addressed to drafting the law and working on its passage. The voice that 'Jane Begay' found that day was heard. Perhaps she spoke because the reality of domestic violence was too important to be left to the boredom and detachment of statistics and official reports. What she related required tremendous courage?

She exposed herself and her relatives to those who knew her, and her story dealt with taboo subjects: mistreatment by men and sexuality. Her family's response revealed the breakdown of her 'special reciprocal relations' in Navajo society that should have shielded her. Her story was filled with relatives she shared households with: grandparents, aunts, parents, and cousins. The Nation, in the resolution approving the Domestic Abuse Act, speaks of the Navajo tradition of protecting household members from violence. Jane's story illustrates the breadth of the household.

The Jicarilla Apache Tribal Code broadly defines domestic violence as 'an act of abuse by a perpetrator on a family member or household member of the perpetrator.' Included within the definition of a 'member' of the perpetrator's family or household are current and former spouses, people related by blood, people related by an existing or prior marriage, people currently or formerly residing with the perpetrator, or a person with whom the perpetrator has a child in common, regardless of whether the parents of the child have been married or have lived together at any time. Under the purpose section of the code, elders, adults, and children are identified as intended beneficiaries of the code.

The domestic abuse chapter of the Standing Rock Code also protects a broad class of individuals under the definition of 'family' or 'household members.' While the Standing Rock Code protects the same parties as the Jicarilla Code, the Standing Rock Code also includes persons who are in a dating relationship and, for purposes of the issuance of a domestic violence protection order, any other person with a sufficient relationship as determined by the court. The purpose section of the code states that it is the intent of the Council that 'criminal laws be enforced without regard to whether the persons involved are family members, are or were married, cohabitating, or involved in a relationship.'

The above tribal codes clearly extend the protected class beyond the conventional boundaries of the nuclear family. The persons protected by these tribal codes reflect the extensive degree of interaction in the Indian community between and among extended family members and within societal units unique to tribal society, such as clans. Other tribes, such as the Salt River Pima-Maricopa and the Oglala Sioux, protect a broad class through use of the term 'persons.' Although the Oglala Sioux Domestic Abuse Code does not define the protected class as clearly as other codes, the arrest provisions of the code reveal who is to be protected.

It is mandatory to arrest someone pursuant to the code for: assaulting another 'person' he/she lives with or used to live with; contacting a 'victim' in violation of an order of protection; threatening with a dangerous weapon; and placing the 'victim' in immediate fear of bodily harm following a call to the police. The terms used to refer to the protected class are 'persons' and 'victims.' The only restriction on the term 'persons' is that the persons currently reside or formerly resided together. The term 'persons' apparently encompasses both immediate and extended family members, within or without a legally recognized marriage relationship, as well as others without blood relationship.

Likewise, the Salt River Pima-Maricopa Tribe's Department of Public Safety Policy (DPS) protects 'persons' with whom the alleged assailant currently resides or formerly resided. Therefore, the Oglala Code and Salt River Policy exceed most other tribal provisions in 'persons protected,' by using the general term 'persons,' to include persons without regard to age, marital status, or blood relationship. The Salt River Pima-Maricopa DPS Policy also illustrates how some tribes protect victims of domestic abuse through the use of existing criminal code provisions.

While the term 'persons' in the Oglala Code and Salt River Pima Policy encompasses a potentially limitless class, the requirement that 'persons' currently reside or formerly resided together arguably restricts protection to those individuals who typically live together, such as family members and couples. Despite this, all persons in a domestic living arrangement are essentially protected, no matter what relationship exists between the parties. There are other tribal provisions which are narrower in comparison to the above mentioned provisions.

Generally, these codes protect household members and relatives from acts of violence. While these provisions are more limited, it is important to note that the majority of these codes protect the broader relational network which exists in Indian communities. Take for example, the protections afforded under the law of the Pascua-Yaqui. The Pascua-Yaqui law specifically protects children under fifteen who are the victims of domestic violence and for all other offenses requires that the relationship between the victim and the defendant is one of marriage or former marriage, or of persons of the opposite sex residing or having resided in the same household, or [that] the victim and the defendant or the defendant's spouse are related to each other by consanguinity or affinity to the second degree.

Thus, the protected class would include married and divorced persons, a partner or unrelated individual of the opposite sex currently or previously residing in the same household, children and stepchildren of the defendant, and other relatives of the defendant or the defendant's spouse, who are related by blood, ancestry or marriage to the second degree. Another example can be found in the Cherokee Nation Code. The Cherokee Nation's 'protected class' includes those who are most in need of protection by society: the aged, the young, and the physically challenged. Additionally, the tribe's code covers 'parents.'

Parents often are targets of abuse from older teenage children, alcohol- or chemically-dependent adult children, or mentally unstable adult children. In tribal communities, it is not unusual to have extended family members live in one household. Often, adult children remain in their parents' household or parents will move in with their adult children. Households consisting of three generations are not unusual in Native American society. A substantial number of tribal domestic violence codes, however, limit their protections to adults only. Some tribal codes are more restrictive than others. These tribes include the Rosebud, Crow, Fort Belknap, Zuni, and the Menominee.

Rosebud and Crow domestic violence codes contain similar provisions regarding 'protected parties.' Both codes cover family or household members. Under Rosebud law, a 'family' or 'household member' is 'a relative, spouse, former spouse, adult or elderly person related by marriage or an adult or elderly person who resides or formerly resided in the residence. 'The purpose section of the domestic abuse code indicates that the protected class includes people regardless of whether they 'are family members, were or are married, cohabiting or involved in a relationship.' While the terms 'relative' and 'spouse' ensure the protection of minors such as teenage spouses and children, the inclusion of 'adult,' in reference to persons presently or formerly residing together, excludes minors who cohabitate or reside in the household but are not related.

Under Crow Law, 'family member' or 'household member' is defined as a spouse, adult person related by marriage, or adult person who resides or formerly resided in the same residence. Due to the use of the word 'adult' and the definition of 'spouse' which excludes the victim spouse, this code apparently provides no protection to minors unless they are emancipated by marriage. Its narrow protection, however, is expanded in situations where the victim has been placed in immediate fear of bodily harm.

The code allows a law enforcement officer to arrest a perpetrator when responding to a domestic violence call involving 'persons (of any age) residing together or who have resided together in the past.' The protected class is small and centered around relationships created by marriage or residency. Adult status is required unless the relationship involving a minor is created by a legal marriage. The requirement of marriage or co-residency combined with adult status limits the class. Blood relations are included only if the residency and adult requirements are met. The Fort Belknap Code defines 'abuse' without reference to the protected class.

However, the protected class can be found in the provisions for arrest. Persons can be arrested for past or future domestic abuse of a 'spouse' or 'family member,' but as with both the Crow and Oglala Codes, it is only the abusing spouse who is included in the definition of 'spouse.' The Fort Belknap Code defines 'family members' as 'a spouse, former spouse, adult person related by blood or marriage [or] any person residing in the home who is dependent upon the head of the household,' including elders and children. The Fort Belknap provision is more expansive than the Crow provision, as it includes adult blood relatives and dependents of any age that reside in the home.

The protected class is also limited under both Menominee law and Zuni law, to include a spouse or former spouse, adults residing together, adults who formerly resided together, and adults who have had a child together. The Zuni Code also protects 'persons' who have a child or had a relationship with the offender. This provision does not require the 'person' to be an adult. Otherwise, the Zuni and Menominee codes only protect those within a legal marriage or adult relationships involving cohabitation or children.

Restricting protection to adults is significant. Generally, restrictions to adults occur when describing relationships between couples. These restrictions may occur because domestic violence is typically thought of as occurring only between married couples and because marriage is generally thought of as occurring between adults. Restricting a protected category to adults excludes minors from the class.

This result has varying degrees of impact. Under codes which are not entirely restricted to adults, certain minors are protected nevertheless because they fall within other categories that do not require adult status. On the other hand, minors who cohabitate or who have had a child out of wedlock are excluded in some of the aforementioned codes yet abusive behavior may begin in the dating relationship of minors. Additionally, the high rate of teen pregnancy may result in couples living together prior to attaining adult status. Thus, restricting the protected class to adults is likely to exclude minors in need of the same protections as adults. Abuse which occurs between minor siblings and against parents by minors may also be excluded in codes which apply to adults only.

The extended family plays a significant role in tribal life. Evidence of this role may be noted in the statutory presence which the extended family has in most tribal laws regarding domestic abuse. Many of the tribes clarify their intent to include members of the immediate and extended family by expressly listing children, the elderly, persons related by blood, and persons related by marriage within the protected class. Additionally, some tribes even protect persons who fall outside the extended family. These protections demonstrate the great emphasis certain tribes place on addressing group disharmony and maintaining proper relationships within tribal communities.

To the extent tribes are interested in protecting the same relationships as do states, this influence is understandable. To the extent, however, that tribes seek to develop laws to protect relationships inherent in the particular tribe, to reflect the composition of tribal households, and to describe the households and relationships commonly occurring on the reservation in the protected class, state law may be either too narrow or too reflective of mainstream society.

The unique relationships among tribal people may add parties uncommon to state law, or require different descriptors. The importance of protecting and maintaining the relationships within the extended family is also reflected in tribal court opinions and orders. In Moran v. Rosebud Housing Authority, for example, the Rosebud Sioux Court of Appeals narrowed a broad injunctive order issued to protect a victim of abuse from violent behavior. The tribal court took this action to allow the defendant and her children to visit the defendant's grandmother. This decision was in accord with the important concept of tiyospaye, the Lakota word meaning 'the relatives living together.'

Among Navajos, where clan and kinship relations are central and create strong duties and responsibilities, members may say of a wrongdoer, ' e acts as if he has no relatives.' This statement is intended to describe a person who fails to act responsibly toward members of his own clan. Other tribes share in this belief and practice of respecting extended family relationships. These beliefs are reflected in enacted codes or through the recognition of these beliefs and through tribal common law.

It is the intent of the Jicarilla Apache Tribal Council that the official response to cases of domestic violence shall be that violent behavior is not to be tolerated or excused, whether or not the abuser is intoxicated. The elders, adults, and children of our Tribe, and of the entire community residing on the Jicarilla Apache Reservation, are to be cherished and treated with respect. The behavior proscribed by the tribal codes varies from a broad range of behavior to certain criminal offenses against persons generally associated with domestic violence.

The Oglala Sioux Domestic Abuse Code defines abuse as 'physical harm, bodily injury, assault or the infliction of fear of imminent physical harm, bodily injury or assault.' The Crow provisions differ slightly from the Oglala Sioux code. In addition to the acts included in the Oglala code, abuse under Crow law includes bodily 'harm' or imminent bodily 'harm' to any family or household member. Under the Salt River

Policy, an officer can arrest a person for simple assault or battery, aggravated assault and battery, and a violation of an order of protection restraining the person or excluding the person from the residence.

The Rosebud Sioux and the Menominee codes are similar in that they proscribe abusive acts committed with specific intent. The Rosebud Sioux define domestic abuse as a crime and prohibit purposely or knowingly causing bodily injury or apprehension of bodily injury to a family member or household member. Bodily injury includes physical pain, illness, or an impairment of one's physical condition. Causing apprehension includes any physical act intended to cause another person to reasonably fear imminent serious bodily injury or death. Under the Menominee Code domestic violence is defined as intentional infliction of physical pain, physical injury or illness, intentional impairment of physical condition, or a physical act that may cause the other person to reasonably fear imminent engagement in any of the above.

The Zuni Pueblo, Jicarilla Apache, and Navajo tribes broaden the behavior which is categorized as domestic violence. This is accomplished by including other types of offenses proscribed under the tribes' general criminal code. Under Zuni law, domestic violence includes any act or incident which constitutes a crime under the Zuni Tribal Code resulting in physical harm, bodily injury, or assault, or a threat which places a person in reasonable fear of imminent physical harm or bodily injury. The Jicarilla Apache Domestic Violence Code states that abuse includes, but is not limited to, assault and battery as defined in the Jicarilla Apache Tribal code. Navajo law incorporates criminal offenses more liberally by proscribing 'domestic violence,' including any conduct that constitutes an offense under Navajo law.

The Navajo domestic violence law includes the following acts upon a victim: assault, battery, threatening, and coercion, and confinement, damage to property, emotional abuse, and harassment. In addition, any other conduct that constitutes a tort under Navajo law qualifies as domestic violence. Navajo law also clearly provides that domestic abuse does not include a victim's reasonable act of self-defense. Under the Rules for Domestic Violence Proceedings, when parties fall out of harmony, they must proceed in a cautious way in their relations with each other (hozhogo), and any definition of domestic violence must be interpreted in such a way as to identify any instances of disharmony.

The Navajo, the Jicarilla Apache, and Cherokee Nation codes also specifically include sexual offenses in their definition of abuse. The Cherokee Nation further defines domestic abuse as causing or attempting to cause serious physical harm or threatening another with imminent serious physical harm. This definition includes, but is not limited to, assault, battery, and aggravated assault and battery against family or household members.

The Pascua-Yaqui Tribal Code forbids behavior by specifying acts beyond assault, physical injury, and intimidation. The code defines domestic violence as any act which is a dangerous crime against children. These acts range from murder to drug offenses. Domestic violence also includes custodial interference, unlawful imprisonment, kidnapping, criminal trespass, and disorderly conduct.

TRIBAL REMEDIES AND SANCTIONS

There was no evidence of penal systems. Only the worst lawbreakers were labelled, but remained an integral part of the community because of their important roles in defining the boundaries of appropriate and inappropriate behavior. Their actions were viewed as the result of natural human error which required corrective intervention by elders. Customary penalties were used for the purpose of helping the offender make amends and to restore self-respect and dignity. The goal was to cure and cleanse the offender of the bad thoughts causing the negative behavior.

This was accomplished by having the offender apologize and be forgiven by the victim, their relatives, and village officials who were present at a gathering. (The terms gathering and family gatherings are translated words used to describe the traditional court process for conflict and dispute resolution. In this process the first level of intervention begins with the family patriarch or other related elder designated by the family). The objective of this process was not to punish the offender; rather, the focal point of customary justice and sanctions was atonement by the offender to the entire social group.

This viewpoint towards crime has continued with some variations. Criminal and civil acts have been redefined in written law and order codes adopted by most Pueblos and approved by the Secretary of Interior. Formal structures such as tribal courts and law enforcement exist in most Pueblos. Research conducted in two Pueblo communities indicate that tribal [traditional] methods for handling offenders are still being used to deal with contemporary problems.

The majority of the tribal codes reviewed provide greater or equal protection to victims of domestic violence when compared to the states in which these tribes are located. This is accomplished by proscribing a wide range of acts and behavior, and by protecting the physical integrity of an expansive class. The effectiveness of these provisions obviously is contingent upon the enforcement and actual reporting of incidents, as well as the final action taken against perpetrators.

Some tribes blend methods of traditional dispute resolution into the formal judicial process. This practice is evident in the specific provisions of the Navajo Nation's Domestic Abuse Protection Act and Supreme Court Rules for Domestic Violence. The judges of the Navajo Nation courts established the Peacemaking system in 1982. Peacemakers work with people to help them take care of their problems on their own. Peacemakers are community leaders who employ the traditional Navajo method of 'talking things out' to resolve problems. The Peacemakers use traditional methods of mediation and arbitration, but it should be noted that Navajo mediation and arbitration is different from the American 'mediation' and 'arbitration' models.

Many counselors to victims of domestic violence feel that mediation is inappropriate between the victim and the abuser. The Peacemakers are tied to each of the seven district courts of the Navajo Nation. Other tribes, such as the Pueblos, accomplish this blend through the general recognition of traditional methods of dispute resolution. One example is the Pueblo of Laguna. The tribe incorporates the traditional method of dispute resolution into its formal judicial system. The Pueblo recognizes the traditional authority of village officials to assist village members in resolving disputes without resorting to the court.

The person seeking relief, however, possesses the choice of utilizing the traditional method of dispute resolution or of going to court. In addition, the Pueblo has a special method of dispute resolution for married couples, involving sponsors of couples who marry in the traditional manner. The sponsors assist married couples in resolving their disputes by reminding them of their marriage vows, counseling them, and bringing the extended family into the dispute resolution process. This method is available to those couples who choose to use it. This practice is common to other New Mexico Pueblos. Sponsors, however, have now assumed more of a ceremonial role in the traditional marriage ceremony.

As a result, couples are less inclined to utilize this traditional method. The Pueblo of Laguna, like several other Pueblos and tribes, does not have a specific code on domestic violence. Primarily the domestic abuse codes reviewed are divided into three basic categories. The Zuni, Pascua-Yaqui, Standing Rock, Oglala, and Jicarilla tribes have enacted provisions which combine criminal and civil sanctions and remedies.

Other tribes, such as the Navajo Nation and the Cherokee Nations, have enacted codes which provide civil remedies and sanctions only. While these codes refer to the criminal sanctions available, the actual prosecution for acts of domestic violence is treated separately under a tribe's criminal law. The domestic violence codes of the Rosebud Sioux, Crow, Fort Belknap, and the Menominee Nation qualify as another category. Under this category, the tribal codes are strictly criminal in nature. Civil remedies and sanctions only are available under the civil law of the tribe.

The purpose of this Chapter is to recognize domestic abuse as a serious crime against our society and to assure the victim of domestic abuse the maximum protection from abuse which the law and those who enforce the law can provide. Many tribal domestic abuse provisions include criminal sanctions and provide for arrest of those persons committing certain acts of domestic abuse. Both mandatory and discretionary arrest provisions are common. Those tribes with mandatory arrest provisions for the commission of certain acts of domestic abuse or violation of orders of protection include: Oglala, Jicarilla, Crow, Fort Belknap, Salt River Pima-Maricopa, Pascua-Yaqui, Zuni, Standing Rock, Rosebud, and Menominee. Even the Navajo Nation, which has a civil domestic abuse code, provides for the mandatory arrest of persons who violate domestic abuse protection orders.

Under some of these tribal codes, a mandatory cooling-off period of 12 to 72 hours or a holding period follows the mandatory arrest. In tribal communities, mandatory arrest serves the same purpose as in other non-Indian communities: protection of the victim's safety. The plain language in many provisions makes it clear that the arrest is intended to serve as a cooling-off period. It also serves as a period during which the abuser can regain his sobriety given the high correlation between alcohol and criminal arrests on tribal lands. Nearly all tribal codes that allow for mandatory arrest also permit a police officer to file a complaint or an arrest report with the prosecutor for further action. The victim is generally not required or file or to agree to the filing of a complaint.

Mandatory arrest is not without its unique problems in tribal communities. Incarceration has never been a traditional method of punishment in Indian societies. In this respect, mandatory arrest and incarceration are serious measures as well as reminders of the loss or breakdown of traditional constraints on tribal societal behavior. In 1883, incarceration was introduced into tribal societies by the federal government with the advent of Courts of Indian Offenses and Indian police. While incarceration has been present in some tribes for at least one hundred years, inadequate jail facilities pose problems. Many tribes do not have jail facilities, and must utilize other tribal or state facilities, at high costs. The utilization of non-tribal jail facilities can also require distant trips for law enforcement and family members.

In addition, some tribal community activists challenge mandatory arrest provisions as violative of the rights of alleged abusers, including the presumption of innocence until guilt is proven. As in the non-Indian world, there is concern that the mandatory arrest provision will be abused by women who employ it against their spouse without sufficient grounds. Despite these countervailing factors, a significant number of tribes include mandatory arrest provisions in their laws addressing domestic violence in their communities.

Once a defendant is found guilty, the tribal code provisions generally provide for incarceration, fines, probation, or counseling. The Jicarilla and Oglala codes, for example, provide that a court may require chemical dependency evaluations if alcohol or drugs are a factor in a particular case. The Menominee, Jicarilla, and Oglala require that the defendant participate in a domestic violence program. The Jicarilla and the Oglala also require the counselor, domestic violence program, or other service provider to make reports to the court; sanctions against the perpetrator are provided for failure to comply with a court order requiring counseling, treatment, or participation in a program.

In terms of sentencing, Pascua-Yaqui law specifically allows probation for a first offense and dismissal of the charge if probation is successfully completed. The Pascua-Yaqui court also may require a defendant to pay restitution and undergo counseling. The Oglala Sioux allow for the suspension of a jail sentence for a first offense. Most tribes that will provide criminal sanctions, however, set minimum jail sentences ranging from 10 days to 30 days to a maximum sentence of 6 months for a first offense. For a second offense, tribes require minimum jail sentences ranging from 10 to 90 days with a maximum of 6 months.

For a third or subsequent offense, the Fort Belknap Indian Reservation requires a 6-month minimum sentence, while the Rosebud Sioux Code mandates a minimum of 30 days. Many tribes require a $500 maximum fine, and in addition to imprisonment, provide counseling for substance abuse, anger control, and domestic relations. Also, both the Fort Belknap Indian Community and the Rosebud Sioux Tribe provide counseling by a medicine man recognized in the community by those persons who practice traditional Indian religion.

The importance of allowing counseling by traditional or professionally trained counselors from within the Indian community cannot be overstated. The counselors approach issues from a cultural and traditional perspective with an understanding of the impact that contact with Western culture has had on the roles of tribal men and women. Utilizing these counselors affirms native people in their own culture and provides a basis for confronting the problem from a tribal perspective. Putting domestic violence in the proper cultural perspective is critical in Indian communities.

Accomplishing this goal requires a general knowledge of historical events regarding Indian people as well as specific knowledge of a tribe's history. It also necessitates a familiarity with a specific tribe's traditional concepts of male/female relations and counseling skills. Tradition and culture can play a role in modifying behavior to the extent that either traditional or trained counselors in the community can provide information to reinforce both victims and abusers with an understanding of traditional values and traditional male/female relations. Using tradition to approach contemporary issues in Indian society is what many call 'retraditionalization.'

It is also important that the needs of both abusers and victims be addressed because of the relational structure of Indian tribes. In tribal societies, men, women, and children are related not only to one another, but to the larger community. In this respect, tribes differ from small town and city populations. This approach is of tremendous value, whether tribes utilize peacemakers, medicine people, sponsors, or other persons to provide a traditional approach to contemporary problems.

Tribal codes also provide civil remedies and sanctions to curb domestic violence. The majority of tribal codes allow for the issuance of protective orders on an emergency basis, regardless of whether the codes permit only civil remedies or both criminal and civil remedies. The Jicarilla Code allows a court to issue a temporary order of protection as a condition of release of the defendant when the defendant is before the court after mandatory arrest. This court can issue the temporary orders at its own discretion, without an application to the court for a civil protection order. Under the Jicarilla Code, an order of protection can provide for the temporary exclusion of the defendant from the residence and for restricted contact with the victim.

The Menominee Ordinance contains an interesting provision regarding orders of protection. It provides that a jailed party can be released if the accused agrees to apply for and comply with a judge's order prohibiting any interference with the other party. Significantly, the Oglala Code maintains that when there is an allegation of an imminent and present danger, a standing order of protection will exist pending a full hearing. The order may restrain acts of domestic abuse, exclude the abusing party from a shared residence, and prohibit contact with the victim. The Jicarilla and Standing Rock Sioux Codes also permit the issuance of a temporary restraining order under similar conditions.

Most other tribes allow for the issuance of a temporary restraining order without further hearing if, upon the court's review of the pleadings and evidence, there is reasonable cause to believe that an act of domestic violence may be or has been committed. Most temporary protection orders grant limited relief to the victims of domestic violence. This relief includes: restraining the abusing party from acts of domestic abuse; excluding the abusing party from a shared residence; restraining contact with the victim; restricting proximity to the victim; awarding temporary custody; and establishing temporary visitation of minor children. Upon award of a final restraining order, some tribes provide for counseling, give temporary use and possession of property to the victim, require an accounting for all transfers made after the order is entered, mandate payment of rent and child support, and allow any other relief necessary.

Four tribes have provisions in their codes requiring mandatory reporting of possible domestic violence. All four require reporting by medical personnel, such as physicians, nurses, and community health workers. Moreover, the Oglala and Crow Codes require physician assistants, hospital interns, residents, field health nurses, and dentists to file a report when they suspect domestic abuse. Additionally, the Standing Rock and Jicarilla Codes require mental health workers to report domestic abuse.

Outside of the medical profession, the Jicarilla Code mandates that school teachers, social workers, and probation officers report domestic abuse. The Standing Rock Code requires social workers, counselors, and personnel of domestic violence programs and shelters to report suspected situations of domestic abuse. The Oglala and Crow Codes additionally require social workers, parent aides, adult service workers, law enforcement officers, court workers, alcohol program workers, and domestic violence personnel to report domestic abuse. Under Oglala, Jicarilla, and Crow Law, the failure to report domestic abuse is a criminal offense.

We want none of your laws or customs that we have not willingly adopted for ourselves. We have adopted many. You have adopted some of ours - votes for women for instance - we are as well behaved as you and you would think so if you knew us better.

There is often a difference between what the law provides and what is actually implemented. This is as true in Indian communities as it is in non- Indian communities. Therefore, the existence of a domestic abuse code does not necessarily mean that all aspects of the code function as the written law mandates. This is often the result of uneven enforcement and the lack of resources within a tribal community, and/or the effectiveness of those resources. This review of the domestic abuse codes of tribal communities is only a part of the picture. Another part of the picture comes from a look at the actual impact being made in these communities. It is important to reflect on what the codes themselves reveal, before we address intervention work at the community level.

In certain respects, the codes reflect the tribal influence as it is represented by the many references to the extended family, the allowances for restitution, and counseling by medicine people. In other ways, the codes directly incorporate tribal thought, such as in the policy, finding, and purpose sections of the Navajo code. Mostly, the tribal codes evidence the incorporation and influence of western jurisprudence.

Perhaps this is inevitable in light of the Indian Civil Rights Act (ICRA), and the tendency of tribes to look at both state and other tribal codes for guidance when developing their particular code. When tribes develop laws to deal with areas of such critical social concern as domestic abuse, careful deliberation is required when outside laws and procedures are considered. Equal consideration should be given to indigenous concepts of law and to traditional methods of dispute resolution when developing tribal law. ICRA standards notwithstanding, tribes can infuse their law with principles and methods which reflect their values, precepts, and approaches to dispute resolution in far greater ways than present codes currently reflect.

The stage when a court implements orders and intervention occurs is the most critical point in the entire dispute resolution process. To successfully address domestic abuse in Indian communities, the needs of both the abused and the abuser require attention. Both parties need insight into their behavior and must take action to foster change based on this insight. Typically, 'needs' are met as a result of intervention. Intervention may occur as the result of a court order or through informal methods, such as through a person's self-referral to a counselor or through traditional dispute resolution.

A list of grantees of federal assistance for victims of federal crimes in Indian country reveals that thirty-seven tribes received funds in 1994 to provide assistance for victims of domestic violence. These recipients include the Native Indian Crisis Association (NICA) Domestic Abuse Shelter run by the Blackfeet of Montana. The primary purpose of this program is to provide shelter for abused victims and their children. Victims residing at the shelter are provided transportation, legal advocacy, counseling, and assistance in locating permanent safe housing. The tribe provided an alternate home for the project while the house, which opened in May of 1990, was undergoing renovation. Previously, the nearest available shelter had been located 130 miles away. A counselor staffs the program and provides group and individual counseling on education and job skills. There is also a victim advocate/house parent who provides support, advocacy, and assistance to victims.

Another example is Tender Hearts Against Family Violence, Inc., a program which began in 1988 with Victims of Crime Assistance funding. Located in Fort Yates, North Dakota, the program is seeking to set up a satellite office in McLauglin, South Dakota, for those victims who reside on the South Dakota side of the Standing Rock Reservation. The Reservation straddles the boundaries of the two states. The Tender Hearts program is a crisis-intervention program and works in conjunction with other tribal, state, and IHS resources.

The program has support groups for men and women with most of the participants attending as a result of a court-order. The program assisted in the effort to enact the Standing Rock Domestic Abuse Code. For the years 1991 and 1992, Tender Hearts found that 95% of domestic abuse victims were women. A total of 211 cases of domestic violence were prosecuted through Standing Rock Tribal Court from October 1990 to September 1991. The Sacred Shawl Society is an example of an intervention program which provides a cultural context in which to deal with domestic violence.

This approach is, at once, comforting and challenging to Indian people. Sacred Shawl is located in Pine Ridge Village on the Oglala Sioux reservation, with a reservation-wide network of counselors and safe-houses. The Society provides services such as family and victim counseling, legal assistance, emergency shelter, transportation, and limited financial assistance. Sacred Shawl receives no federal or tribal funds, but it receives grant assistance and benefits from grassroots fund raising. The Society's work revealed that the general public, the court system, the abuser, the children, and the victims were living in ignorance of Lakota values regarding domestic violence.

As a result, the Society began to provide education regarding Lakota thought and philosophy on domestic violence. In her chapter on the work of the Society, Debra White Plume describes the pre-reservation Lakota philosophy regarding spousal abuse, the role of adult men and women in pre-reservation society, and the Lakota values and social law regarding wife battering using Lakota words. Plume explains the concept of tiyospaye - relatives living together in unity and cooperation, which is based on people living together according to the same beliefs, laws, and values. She describes how the Lakota society has been affected by the dissolution of traditional ways.

Traditionally, wife battering was neither accepted nor tolerated. Spousal abuse, however, emerged as the result of the disintegration of Lakota ways of life and with the introduction of alcohol into the society. The Sacred Shawl Society's approach to domestic violence first involves articulating the traditional concepts of Indian society relative to the relationship between men and women. Further, the present relationship between men and women in tribal society is examined against the backdrop of these traditional concepts.

An important aspect appears to be an examination of the treatment of domestic violence in the society before outside influences affected the concepts. Contemporary tribal societies face problems because of the disruption of the roles of men and women, the displacement of traditional values, and the introduction of countervailing and contrary values. This culture-oriented approach plays a role in any action taken by tribal communities to address domestic values. In tribal communities, both the abused and the abuser can gain from this knowledge.

The use of community members in intervention and counseling programs can result in the development of counseling methods which draw on the strengths of the culture. Developing a domestic abuse approach premised on the Indian value of harmony within a community ensures that the needs of the direct and indirect victims of violence, as well as the perpetrator, will be considered. Indian societies are based on different values and beliefs than other societies. Borrowing an individualistic approach focusing on the victim from outside tribal society only adds to the conflict.

INDIANS OUTSIDE THE TRIBAL SYSTEM

When I first came into a shelter in the city, I felt confused. I tried to explain my feelings but nobody understood.... I couldn't just go and do what they asked of me.... I didn't have a phone. I had no neighbors. Abuse on the reserve can be much hidden. We have focused on tribal laws and systems, but we must also consider the large urban Indian population. Generally, a large part of the urban Indian population maintains ties with the reservation, by moving between the reservation and urban areas. The urban centers, however, are increasingly becoming permanent homes to a large number of Indian people.

For this reason, it is important to consider the needs of the urban population. For those who maintain close ties to the reservation, tribal resources remain available. Urban Indians are no less Indian than Indian people who reside on the reservation. Thus, state judges and service providers must be aware of the need for approaches to domestic violence which consider the cultural needs of Indian people. The need for approaches to domestic violence which take culture into consideration is just as great among urban Indian families as it is at the tribal level.

Indian women and other women of color confront the same cultural insensitivity and racism at urban domestic violence shelters as they do elsewhere. These shelters can be unaware of the cultural resources which should be used to assist Indian victims of domestic violence. Consequently, shelters which provide services specifically directed at Indian women in urban centers are greatly needed. The Eagle's Nest, in St. Paul, Minnesota, is such a program. The program is the result of the work of the Women of Nations, an advocacy group for battered American Indian women.

The program provides shelter to native victims and uses traditional teachings, resources, and practices to overcome the damage that results from the abuse. These practices range from burning sage and cedar to calm the spirit to teaching traditional craftwork and survival skills. Participation in spiritual ways familiar to Native women is also available. In urban centers with large Indian populations, statistics reveal the presence of native people at shelters and within the court system. Just as tribes cannot successfully address tribal domestic violence by adopting the same approaches to domestic violence as the non-Indian society, neither can individual Indian people nor their families be expected to completely benefit from programs operated for majority clients.

The intertribal community is a resource which can be utilized to assist in dealing with domestic violence in the Indian urban community. Urban Indian centers, with the multi-tribal membership among service providers and recipients, are important in providing varied and culturally appropriate intervention services to Indian victims and offenders. Tribal input from local reservations, from which the urban Indian community populations come, can assist in efforts to assess the needs of the urban population.

State courts have jurisdiction when domestic violence occurs outside tribal boundaries. The state courts and human services allied in domestic law proceedings can work to cooperate with the urban Indian organizations and centers as well as with local tribes. This cooperation should also include state subsidies for services, like those subsidies provided to other entities. Financially limited urban Indian organizations and centers cannot be expected to relieve the state of its responsibilities for intervention and its costs. Agreements between states and tribes are essential so that the urban and reservation Indians can obtain culturally appropriate and effective assistance to remove domestic violence from their lives.

You see, we have power. Men have to dream to get power from the spirits and they think of everything they can - songs and speeches and marching around, hoping that the spirits will notice them and give them some power. But we have power... Children. Can any warrior make a child, no matter how brave and wonderful he is?

In the instance of the Cherokees, we are fortunate to have many strong women. I have attained a leadership position because I am willing to take risks, but at the same time, I am trying to teach other women, both Cherokees and others, to take risks also.... Friends describe me as someone who likes to dance along the edge of the roof. I try to encourage young women to be willing to take risks, to stand up for the things they believe in, and to step up and accept the challenge of serving in leadership roles.

If I am to be remembered, I want it to be because I am fortunate enough to have become my tribe's first female chief. But I also want to be remembered for emphasizing the fact that we have indigenous solutions to our problems. Cherokee values, especially those of helping one another and of our interconnections with the land, can be used to address contemporary issues.

Our review of some tribal methods of protecting women from domestic violence affirms two continuing foundations in the life of indigenous people in the United States. The first of these foundations is the persisting role of the tribe as a sovereign, the first sovereign within the national boundaries of the United States. Tribes retain their sovereignty in the context of international law, especially in the law of nations relating to indigenous people. International norms and emerging instruments, however, address tribal people in the collective, as distinct groups within a larger nation-state. The status and rights of indigenous women in relation to their tribal communities have only recently been directly addressed in international law. Consequently, it is the sovereignty of tribes within the United States borders that most directly affects the way indigenous women are protected in their tribal communities.

The power of the sovereign remains integral in drafting tribal law, rendering judicial orders, and establishing intervention programs to protect women. This is in contrast to other ethnic populations in the United States who use non- governmental organizations to promote their interests. The tribe's status as a separate governmental entity allows tribes to address their concerns regarding the well being of women, families, and tribal members through enactment of tribal law. The tribe's separate status affects the relationship between tribes and the state and federal governments and it is the tribe which provides the first line of protection to women within their jurisdiction.

Second, this review addresses the societal resources which tribal governments use in resolving family, clan, and tribal disputes, as well as the use of cultural beliefs and practices in addressing domestic violence. The resulting tribal codes, court orders, and intervention programs can be distinct in multiple ways. The traditional models of tribal law and practice contrast with the Euro-American approaches within the United States borders, but some are distinct among the over 500 tribes. The use of Peacemakers by the Navajo and the Seneca is one generalized response to any relational dispute.

The use of traditional marriage sponsors in Laguna Pueblo, who take on a responsibility to the couple at betrothal expecting to assist the couple if marital problems arise, is another. Each tribe's experiences, in combination with other factors, produce a model of law and practice tailored to a tribe's needs. In the aggregate, the tribes produce many models. Yet underlying the tribal variation is the common world view that is of key importance to American Indians. The indigenous peoples of the Americas have a shared belief that achieving harmony and balance are the goals of their societies.

Both men and women in a tribal society are guided by communal rather than individualistic values; the pursuit of harmony and balance extends to the roles and responsibilities of each. Consequently, any analysis of the way that tribes respond to the needs of female victims of violence must include a concern for, and response to, the abuser, the children, and other members of the extended family, clan, and tribe. A strict gender equality model of law and practice ignores the traditional and evolving ways in which tribal societies structure complementary roles for their members.

The constitutional equal-protection-based criticism of Martinez reveals how narrow perspectives miss much about contemporary tribal life. Besides ignoring the legal doctrine of tribal sovereignty, the gender equality viewpoint fails to recognize both the indigenous peoples' view of male/female relationships as complementary and the abilities of indigenous people to conserve and innovate in order to promote tribal interests and continuity. The approach of retraditionalization through intervention programs, which restore men and women to complementary relationships, relies on applying long-held tribal values in a contemporary context.

The tribal ability to use these customary values is demonstrated when tribal nations select women as their governmental leaders and in tribal efforts to protect women from violence. While the tribal codes reveal some similarities to state codes, several reveal an expansive view of the protected class of individuals and relationships. The non-restrictive view of protected persons reflects the belief and policy that violence reaches beyond individual victims within the immediate family and damages the extended family and others in the tribal community. The behaviors that trigger the protective measures include not only the threatened and resulting injury to victims, but also to property.

Additionally, protected relationships can justify a legal response from law enforcement agents and the courts. Especially noteworthy is the protection provided by the Navajo tribe in the workplace and educational environment. If violence occurs or is threatened, the victim and others can invoke protective measures. The tribal courts mandate a mix of temporary and permanent remedies that are both similar and dissimilar to those utilized in non-Indian jurisdictions. Mandatory jailing for short-term cooling off, sentencing, and mandatory completion of counseling and remediation programs bear some similarity to state laws.

Some tribal intervention programs operate on culturally-based goals distinct from non-Indian programs; more is involved than stopping the abuse cycle. The goal of intervention programs like the Sacred Shawl Society is to restore victim and abuser to a functional and productive status within the personal and tribal network. The problems of alcoholism, drugs, poverty, inadequate housing, and high unemployment among Indians are formidable, but the culturally-based programs do not allow these elements to excuse the abusive behavior.

These contemporary aggravations make difficult the critical task facing tribal people and their government of using every resource, old and new, to promote the safety and well-being of all members. The tribal codes, court orders, and programs in this study demonstrate the initial effort involved to deliver the justice promised in words. Like all other governments, the tribes will be judged by their performance; the test is whether women believe that tribal action affirmatively protects them. The indigenous nations in this study provide encouraging models for protecting women inseparable from the nations' distinct tribal sovereignty. These tribes also demonstrate that the indigenous cultures within the United States are vital contemporary societies, rather than mere historical artifacts.

3

Family Violence Against Married Women

As Goode (1971) argued, force is a resource that men may use when they lack other (economic) resources to induce desired behavior. Other scholars have argued that women who depend on a partnership because they have children or few economic alternatives may be more tolerant of abuse and less willing to leave abusive relationships. Still others have argued that discrepancies in the resources of partners, which challenge men's status expectations, may lead men to use force to reinstate their dominance. Finally, others have proposed that cross-cultural models of domestic violence against women should account for local, family characteristics that may facilitate or impede such violence.

A composite score for assets typically owned by men captures household economic status. Number of living sons, number of living daughters, and prior work for cash measure a wife's socioeconomic dependence on marriage. The relative education of spouses and their relative contributions to the expenses of marriage capture economic dependence as well as status inconsistency of the wife vis-à-vis her husband. Measures of family organization include residence with marital relatives, proximity of women's natal or biological kin, and endogamous marriage or marriage to a blood relative. Multivariate methods are used to assess the effects of these variables, after controls, on women's attitudes about wife beating and divorce and experience of physical abuse in the prior year.

Domestic violence refers to "assaultive and coercive behaviors that adults use against their intimate partners", and recent surveys have shown that domestic violence against women is widespread. Twenty-five percent of women interviewed in The 1995 - 1996 National Violence Against Women Survey reported that they were raped and/or physically assaulted by a current or former spouse, cohabiting partner, or date in their lifetime.

The lifetime prevalence of physical domestic violence has ranged from 17% to 48% among groups of women in Africa and from 40% to 52% among ever-married women in Colombia, Peru, and León, Nicaragua. Levels of lifetime and even recent physical domestic violence against women have been similarly high in parts of Asia. Studies of domestic violence in the Middle East are rare, but one third of ever-married Egyptian women have reported being beaten since marriage, and 30% of married Arab women in Israel have reported recent physical or sexual abuse. (Comparing estimates of abuse across contexts warrants some caution because of variation in the measurement of abuse across settings and variability in estimates of abuse within each setting).

In theory and research to explain domestic violence against women, scholars have given considerable attention to the role of resources in households and intimate partnerships. Goode (1971) argued that force, like money or personal attributes, is a resource that individuals may use to induce desired behavior or to deter unwanted actions. Goode predicted that individuals may rely on force when they lack resources of other kinds, or when other resources have failed to achieve desired ends. In studies of domestic violence against women, scholars have tested Goode's hypothesis by estimating the effects of a husband's or household's socioeconomic status on physical abuse of the wife.

Research in parts of India has shown that the unadjusted odds of wife beating are higher in households owning fewer consumer durables, and in rural Bangladesh, landholdings have been negatively associated with wife beating by a husband or his family. In Bangkok, Thailand, a combined index of family income and husband's education and occupational prestige has been negatively associated with physically abusing wives, and a measure combining individual income, education, and occupational prestige has been negatively associated with partner assaults among adult heterosexual couples in the U.S.

Research in North America has shown that a family's or husband's income is consistently negatively associated with physically abusing a wife, but that the relationships of men's education and employment with such abuse are less consistent. Smith (1990) and others have argued that evidence of an income-abuse association is consistent also with stress theory, insofar as low income induces stress that leads to violence. The relationship of a husband's socioeconomic status and marital violence through induced stress has had empirical support in urban Thailand.

Critics of Goode (1971) have argued that a male partner's lack of income or other economic resources is insufficient to explain abuse against women and that women's socioeconomic dependence on the partnership may better explain this abuse. Scholars have argued that married women with children and little other financial support may see few alternatives to marriage, which leads them to be more tolerant of an abusive husband. Contrary to these expectations, having sons in parts of South Asia has been either unrelated to or negatively associated with domestic violence against women, and homemakers have been less likely than working women to be in violent marriages in Kentucky.

In-depth data from 40 families in the U.S., however, have shown that unemployed and poorly educated women are less likely to seek outside intervention after spousal beatings than employed women with more schooling. Moreover, a study of cohabiting adults in the U.S. has shown that women's psychological dependence, or their perception that wives would be hurt more than husbands by divorce, is positively associated with minor physical violence. The same study also showed that women's economic dependence, as measured by whether the wife was employed, had young children, and earned 25% or less of total income, is positively associated with severe physical violence.

In rural Bangladesh, participants in programs that facilitate group-based savings and provide credit to women have had a two-thirds lower risk of domestic violence compared to non-participants, but cases of aggravated violence also have been observed among participants. In another study of married women in rural Bangladesh, the risk of physical beating was not associated with individual membership in a savings program, but declined as the percentage of members in the community increased. Other critics of Goode (1971) have argued that models of domestic violence against women need to distinguish those relationships in which the distribution of resources between partners disrupts "culturally defined... status expectations".

According to status-inconsistency theorists, if the psychological and/or economic resources of a woman exceed either those of her male partner or some culturally acceptable level, atypical disadvantages in the partner's status will threaten his masculine identity and motivate him to use violence to reinstate his dominance. Among currently or previously married women in Kentucky, life-threatening violence has been more common among wives whose educational and occupational attainments exceeded those of the husband. In the U.S. more generally, men have been more likely to be physically violent toward female partners with higher incomes, but not with more education.

In Canada, the adjusted probability that a man will use coercive tactics to control his partner has been greatest when the female partner was working for pay and the man was not. Absolute differences between spouses in years of education and scores for occupational prestige, however, were not associated with a husband's physical abuse of his wife in Bangkok, Thailand after adjusting for the household's socioeconomic status and other factors.

Discrepancies in the above findings may have resulted from differences across studies in the samples, analytic methods, and measures used. Scholars have argued that the concept of violence is multidimensional, and each dimension may be variously associated with absolute and relative resources. Reporting on violence also may be linked to group differences in the acceptability of violence. Further, using absolute differences in partners' years of education or scores for occupational prestige to measure status inconsistency disallows nonlinear effects.

An alternative measure of status inconsistency might distinguish women who have more of a resource from those having the same amount or less of that resource than their partner. Discrepancies in findings also may have resulted from omitting contextually relevant causes of domestic violence against women. Where multigenerational co-residence and extended kinship are common, several features of family organization may precipitate or impede such violence. The custom of patrilocal residence, whereby a son remains in the father's house and a daughter moves out after marriage, may reduce a woman's power because the co-residing husband and parents-in-law share authority over her actions.

In rural Bangladesh, women living with senior marital relatives have had less family power, but a lower likelihood of physical abuse as well. Women living near their natal or biological kin also may be better able to negotiate conflicts in the marital home. Research in India has shown that women with closer ties to natal kin have more control over finances, decision-making power, and mobility, and the presence of the wife's family has been negatively associated with domestic violence against women in South India and Cambodia.

Finally, in societies where endogamous marriage occurs, endogamously married women may be protected from domestic violence for several reasons. Namely, the socioeconomic background of the spouse is more certain, spousal differences in age tend to be smaller, the socioeconomic resources of women's kin are more accessible, and parents tend to value daughters who are available to provide support. The empirical literature suggests other determinants of domestic violence against women for which analyses should control.

These determinants include a woman's religious affiliation, age group, location of residence, duration of marriage, and experience of a child's death. Among women and men in the U.S., being Catholic rather than nonreligious has been associated with less tolerance for wife beating, and in Egypt, attitudes about women's roles as well as the frequency of practices such as female genital cutting have varied between Muslims and Christians. Several national surveys of married women outside the West have shown that women's higher age and rural residence are associated with lower likelihoods of experiencing spousal abuse in the prior year but that duration of marriage has inconsistent effects on such abuse.

In León, Nicaragua a higher lifetime prevalence of physical or sexual abuse has been observed among the mothers of children who died before age five years. In sum, the causes of domestic violence against women are poorly understood in non-Western settings, and are especially understudied in the Middle East. Cross-cultural research also has not accounted simultaneously for the potential influence of the household's economic status, wife's socioeconomic dependence or status inconsistency in marriage, and family organization in social context.

A description of the setting is useful to contextualize these four hypotheses. In Egypt, familial solidarity is based on bonds connecting male members of the same paternal lineage, so older married men often are family heads, and brothers share authority in family decisions. Beliefs in gender complementarity in Egypt reinforce the poor representation of women in public life. For example, despite increasing access to education among girls, a higher percentage of girls than boys never attend school (14.4% vs. 7.8%), and less than half of ever-married women of reproductive age agree that education should prepare women for work. As a result, men still represent over two thirds of the formal work force and hold a majority of public offices.

Islamic laws pertaining to inheritance favor men, husbands, and sons over women, wives, and daughters. Ethnographic research in poor neighborhoods of Cairo has shown that concerns about women's dependence and status inconsistency in marriage are salient among women and men. In this research, some informants argued that marriages reflecting the socioeconomic asymmetries observed in society are preferable. Male informants agreed that marrying a woman of higher social standing would "test their dignity".

Other informants warned, however, that marrying "too far up" could be problematic for women. Four other characteristics of family organization in Egypt may influence the treatment of married women, as well as their attitudes about divorce and physical abuse of wives. First, although having children enhances the social identity of Egyptian women, laws governing divorce in Egypt ultimately grant child custody to the husband. Thus, a woman's dependence on marriage to retain custody of her children may discourage thoughts of divorce and increase her tolerance for abuse.

Second, endogamous marriages comprise roughly one third of marriages in Egypt. Such marriages may protect women for the reasons described above; endogamous marriage may benefit men, however, because related spouses "jointly owe their obligations" to the same male relatives. Third, over half of ever-married Egyptian women aged 15 - 49 years in 1995 lived with their husband's family at the start of marriage. Finally, despite the frequency of living with marital kin, married women often maintain ties with their natal family.

The above forms of gender inequality and kinship are especially pronounced in Upper or Southern Egypt. In the year 2000, 52% of ever-married women of reproductive age had no schooling, and 15% were working for cash. Also in 2000, 48% of marriages were endogamous, and ever-married women at the end of their reproductive years had 6.0 children, on average. Compared to their spouse in 1995, 66% of women were at least 5 years younger, 42% had less schooling, and 15% had more schooling.

Minya, the site of this study, is a poor, agrarian Upper Egyptian governorate that begins about 200 kilometers south of Cairo and extends about 80 kilometers along the Nile. About 20% of the population lives in urban areas, but the habitable land is at most 30 kilometers wide and lies mostly on the west bank of the river. Roughly 80% of residents are Muslim, and about 20% are Coptic Christian, which is the main Christian sect in Egypt that evolved from the teachings of Saint Mark in the first century A.D.

In 1995, 55% of adult women (aged 20 - 24 years) compared to 16% of adult men had no education, and 11% of ever-married women aged 15 - 54 years were working for cash. In the same year, 51% of married women aged 15 - 54 years were married to a blood relative. The risk of mortality among children aged less than five years was higher for girls than boys, in part because girls have received poorer care. Thus, Upper Egypt and Minya governorate in particular are settings where the educational system and labor market remain highly patriarchal, and where most women rely on their family's socioeconomic resources.

STUDY POPULATION AND DATA

This analysis is based on data from a representative sample of households in seven districts in Minya governorate (two districts were excluded for reasons of security). Data collection for this study was implemented with the Two Governorate Linkages Survey, a five-round longitudinal study of child morbidity and women's reproductive experience that was undertaken in Qaliubia and Minya governorates during 1995 - 1997. In Minya, multistage, cluster-sampling procedures were used to identify a target sample of 40 households in each of 2 clusters in 38 primary sampling units (villages or urban neighborhoods), and 3,125 households were included over the course of the study.

Trainees for the survey interviews were female residents of Minya who had completed at least secondary schooling. The training session lasted one week and included didactic explanations of the questionnaire and techniques of structured interviewing, daily tests and exercises, role plays, and mock interviews with women having the characteristics of eligible study participants. A subset of the best trainees was selected to complete the fieldwork. Two local supervisors oversaw daily operations of the fieldwork and conducted periodic re-interviews to check the consistency of reporting on selected questions.

For the duration of data collection, project investigators made weekly trips from Cairo to meet with resident supervisors and interviewers, to review questionnaires, and to conduct retraining sessions as needed. Of the questionnaires administered, a household listing permitted recording of age, gender, relationship to household head, education, and main occupation for each member; births and migrants at each round; and survival status, marital status, and work status of each member for the round of first residence and subsequent rounds. A household characteristics questionnaire included questions about the dwelling; access to electricity, water, and sanitary facilities; and ownership of consumer goods and durables.

A woman's questionnaire included questions on age, age at marriage, marital status, education, work, pregnancies and fertility, health knowledge and practices, and use of contraception and was administered to all ever-married women aged 15 - 54 years or any main caretaker of a child aged less than 5 years. A child's questionnaire focused on the health and nutritional status of resident children aged less than 5 years. A women's status module was adapted from one developed for a national survey in Egypt. This module included questions on gender preferences, perceptions of child illness, marital history, mobility, decision making, and work.

This module also included questions about any beating in adulthood (the age of physical maturity), any severe beating in adulthood (e.g., that required a doctor, whether or not one was sought), times beaten in the year before interview, help seeking after episodes of abuse, and safe places to go to avoid abuse. Before round five of the larger survey, separate consent was obtained to administer this module to all women in Minya who had received the woman's questionnaire described above. Women were informed prior to participation that some questions might be sensitive, that their participation was voluntary, that they may refuse to answer any question, and that they may end the interview at any time.

Interviewers were instructed to administer the module in private. The total eligible sample for the women's status module included 3,194 women aged 15 - 54 years. Two hundred forty-two (8%) never married or currently unmarried women were dropped from the analysis. Another 292 (9%) eligible women who did not complete the module, 75 (2%) eligible women with missing data on attitudes toward and experiences of beating in the prior year, and 63 (2%) eligible women with item non-response for covariates of interest were dropped from the analysis. This analysis thus was based on married women aged 15 - 54 years in Minya with complete data on relevant variables (N = 2,522).

DEPENDENT VARIABLES

The first outcome measures whether the respondent reported to have been beaten in the year before interview. This outcome indicates exposure to physical abuse that likely succeeded the timing of covariates in the analysis. Physical violence in the prior year also was frequent enough among women in Minya that multivariate analysis of this outcome was possible. The second and third outcomes measure women's tolerance for physical abuse of wives and their expectations about a woman's likelihood of seeking divorce.

The second outcome indicates whether the respondent reported that a husband is never, seldom/sometimes, or often justified in beating his wife. The third outcome measures the extent to which a respondent expected that a wife would seek a divorce in response to circumstances that locally signify an unsatisfactory marriage and/or a negligent husband. This measure is based on women's responses to questions about whether a wife would be unlikely, somewhat likely, or very likely to ask for a divorce if the couple is unable to have children, the couple is unable to have a son, the husband is disrespectful of the wife's parents or senior relatives, the husband fails to support the family, the husband beats his wife regularly, the husband flirts with other women, and the husband is sexually unfaithful.

A principal components analysis of these items was performed, and the first principal component accounted for 46% of the variance in the original items (not shown; available upon request). Scoring coefficients for the first principal component were used to derive a score reflecting each woman's overall expectation about the likelihood that a wife would seek divorce for the above reasons. Because the distribution of these scores was slightly right-skewed, women's scores were grouped into quartiles and a four-category, ordinal measure of women's overall expectations about a wife's likelihood of seeking divorce was constructed.

INDEPENDENT VARIABLES

An exogenous score for household wealth was developed from responses to questions about the assets and amenities of each respondent's household. Questions about assets ascertained whether the respondent's household (often the male member(s)) owned each of the following items: bicycle, motorcycle, private car, transport equipment, residential building, commercial building, farmland, and other land, poultry, livestock, and farm tools. Questions about amenities of the respondent's household ascertained the following information: availability of electricity, type of flooring, number of rooms, source of water, and type of toilet.

Using a method developed by Filmer and Pritchett (1999), each of the above items was recoded and included in a principal components analysis (not shown; available upon request). The first principal component accounted for 15% of the total variance in the original items. I used estimated scoring coefficients for this component to compute a score for household wealth for each respondent. Exogenous measures of a woman's economic and social dependence on her husband include whether the respondent ever worked for cash or kind, the respondent's number of living sons, and the respondent's number of living daughters.

An exogenous measure for women's relative economic dependence or status inconsistency in marriage includes whether the respondent had more years of schooling, the same amount of schooling, 1 – 5 fewer years of schooling, or 6 – 17 fewer years of schooling compared to her husband. The category denoting a woman's greater educational attainment than her husband captures status inconsistency, or atypical discrepancies in the educational attainment of spouses. Categories denoting a woman's lesser educational attainment than her husband capture women's fewer professional opportunities.

A second exogenous measure of status inconsistency captures relative financial contributions to the marriage and indicates whether the husband paid less of the marital expenses (the atypical situation in Egypt), or paid the same amount or more. Measures of family organization include whether the respondent lived with a parent-in-law, brother-in-law, or husband; whether her husband was a blood relative; and whether her natal family lived in the same neighborhood or village.

Demographic controls include the respondent's age (< 25, 25 – 34, e" 35 years); religion (Christian vs. Muslim); duration of marriage (0 – 4, 5 – 9, 10 – 14, e" 15 years); numbers of deceased sons and daughters (0, 1, e"2), and residence (urban vs. rural). Descriptive and Multivariate Analyses In the descriptive analysis, I computed relative frequency distributions of covariates that depict the major characteristics of married women of reproductive age in Minya. For these women, I estimated the reported prevalence of having ever been beaten during adulthood and of having ever been severely beaten during adulthood.

Also presented are estimates for the percentage of women who sought help for any beatings in adulthood and who reported having a safe place to go to avoid abuse. Finally, I estimated the prevalence of any beating in the year before interview, the relative distribution of women by number of reported beatings in the prior year, and the relative distribution of women by reports that a husband is never, seldom or sometimes, or often justified in beating his wife. In all multivariate analyses, robust standard errors were estimated for model coefficients to account for within-cluster correlation of responses resulting from the multistage, clustered sample design.

Finally, estimated coefficients from the model represented by equation (1) were used to compute predicted probabilities of physical abuse. The purpose of this step was to assess the extent to which family organization and socioeconomic dependence on marriage drive the risk of experiencing physical abuse among married women of all economic backgrounds in this setting. The basic idea was to estimate predicted probabilities of experiencing physical abuse in a 12- month period, by level of household wealth, for the two hypothetical groups of women having characteristics associated with the highest likelihood and the lowest likelihood of abuse.

This task was accomplished by (a) assigning the subgroup of women at each level of wealth those characteristics that were at least marginally associated with a higher (or lower) likelihood of abuse, (b) allowing non-significant covariates to assume their observed values for each woman in the subgroup, (c) estimating and exponentiating the linear prediction for each woman in the subgroup, and (d) computing average predicted probabilities for each wealth subgroup having more than one woman (The average number of women per wealth subgroup was 30, and the range across subgroups was 1 – 115.). Confidence intervals for these predictions were computed in the same manner to assess whether predicted probabilities of abuse differed significantly for the two hypothetical groups of women at each level of household wealth.

Compared to other women in the governorate, 37% were living in relatively poor households (score for household wealth < 0), and 46% were living in relatively wealthy homes (score > 0). Scores for household wealth were moderately correlated with the number of years of schooling among respondents' husbands. Forty-five percent of husbands had no schooling, and 28% of husbands had completed at least secondary school. Socioeconomic dependence of women on marriage was widespread. Only 15% of respondents had ever worked for cash or kind. Fifty-one percent of respondents had at least two living sons, and 47% had at least two living daughters.

Sixty-five percent of respondents had no formal schooling, and only 17% had at least some secondary schooling. Compared to their husband, 51% of respondents had the same amount of schooling (often both had none). Just over one fifth (21%) of respondents had 1 - 5 fewer years of schooling, and 19% of respondents had 6 - 17 fewer years of schooling. Most respondents (97%) reported that their husband had contributed more to the expenses of the marriage. Despite high levels of dependence among married women, status inconsistencies were apparent, as 10% of respondents had more schooling than their husband.

Regarding family organization and other demographic characteristics, over 95% of respondents reported that their marriage was arranged (and although not shown, 27% reported that they could not have refused the arranged marriage). Fifty-one percent of respondents were married to a blood relative, and 15%, 24%, and 92% of respondents lived with a parent-in-law, brother-in-law, and spouse, respectively. Three quarters of respondents had biological family living in the same village or neighborhood. Forty-one percent of respondents were aged 35 years or older, and 47% had been married to their current spouse for 15 or more years.

A large minority of respondents was Christian (23%, of whom almost all were Copts). About 18% of respondents were living in urban areas. Roughly one quarter of respondents reported that at least one son and at least one daughter had died.

Twenty-seven percent of respondents reported that they had ever been beaten during adulthood. Four percent reported that they had experienced a severe beating in adulthood. Thirty-eight percent of women who had ever experienced a beating in adulthood did not talk to someone after the beating to get help, and 44% reported that they did not have a safe place to go to avoid being beaten. Over 9% of respondents experienced a beating in the prior year, and 5% reported three or more beatings in the prior year. Only 27% of respondents reported that a husband is never justified in beating his wife, whereas 52% reported that a husband is seldom/sometimes justified, and 21% reported that a husband is often justified.

As expected, household wealth was strongly negatively associated with beatings in the prior year: An increase of one unit in the score for household wealth was associated with a 17% lower likelihood that women experienced a beating. Moreover, a one unit increase in the score for household wealth was associated with a 19% lower likelihood of reporting that a husband is more often justified in beating his wife.

Household wealth also was marginally positively associated with women's likelihood of reporting that a wife is more prone to seek a divorce. Regarding expectations about the effects of a woman's socioeconomic dependence on marriage, prior work for cash or kind was not associated with the likelihood of having been beaten, nor of reporting that a wife is more prone to seek a divorce. Women who had ever worked for cash or kind, however, were 42% less likely to report that a husband is more often justified in beating his wife.

Moreover, compared to women with the same amount of schooling as their husband, women with 6 – 17 fewer years of schooling were 49% more likely to have been beaten. Women with 6 – 17 fewer years of schooling also were marginally more likely to report that a husband is more often justified in beating his wife. Women with 1 – 5 fewer years of schooling were no more likely to have been beaten, and were 24% more likely to report that a wife is more prone to seek divorce.

Compared to women without sons, women with two or more sons were (a) 63% more likely to have been beaten, (b) marginally more likely to report that a husband is more often justified in beating his wife, and (c) marginally less likely to report that a wife is more prone to seek a divorce. Having daughters was not associated with either the likelihood of a beating or attitudes about seeking divorce or beating wives.

Regarding expectations about the effects of a woman's status inconsistency relative to her husband, women with more schooling than their husband were not more likely to have been beaten, and were marginally more likely to report that a woman is more prone to seek a divorce. (In estimated models not shown, having relatively more schooling was associated with a marginally lower likelihood of having been beaten, but these results are not presented because they were not robust across all estimated models.)

Surprisingly, women who had paid the same amount or more of the marital expenses were more likely to report that wife beating is justified. In general, measures for marital and natal family organization were associated in the expected ways with the physical abuse of married women in Minya. Although living with a parent-in-law was not associated with either recent beatings or women's attitudes about divorce or wife beating, women who were living with a brother-in-law were marginally more likely to have been beaten and to report that a husband is more often justified in beating his wife.

Living with one's husband also was associated with a marginally higher likelihood of having been beaten but was not associated with attitudes about divorce or wife beating. Women who had natal family living in the same neighborhood or village were 37% less likely to have been beaten than women without natal family living nearby. Although being married to a blood relative was not associated with the likelihood of having been beaten, endogamously married women were 26% more likely than non-endogamously married women to report that a husband is more often justified in beating his wife. Women in endogamous marriages also were 18% less likely to report that a wife is more prone to seek divorce.

Regarding the effects of demographic controls, women aged 35 years or older were 59% less likely than their younger counterparts to have been beaten in the prior year, but the attitudes of older and younger women about beating wives and seeking divorce were similar. None of the other demographic controls was associated with the likelihood of having been beaten, but several were associated with women's attitudes about beating wives and seeking divorce. Women married for 15 or more years were marginally more likely to report that a husband is more often justified in beating his wife.

Christian women and women living in urban areas were 23% and 58% less likely than their respective counterparts to report that a husband is more often justified in beating his wife. Because divorce generally is not accepted among Coptic Christians in Egypt, Christian women also were 87% less likely than Muslim women to report that a woman is more prone to seek a divorce. Predicted Probabilities of Physical Abuse Estimates are presented by level of household wealth for the two hypothetical groups of women having characteristics associated with the highest and lowest risks of physical abuse, according to significant and marginally significant coefficients in the model for abuse.

Characteristics associated with the highest risk of physical abuse include having at least two living sons, having 6 – 17 fewer years of schooling than one's husband, living with one's husband and any brothers-in-law, living without family in the same neighborhood or village, and being aged less than 25 years. Characteristics associated with the lowest risk of physical abuse include having no living sons, having more schooling than one's husband, living without one's husband and any brothers-in-law, having family in the same village or neighborhood, and being aged 35 years or older. Predicted probabilities of abuse at each level of household wealth are significantly different. The predicted probability of physical abuse exceeds.40 among high-risk women living in relatively poor households (scores in the range of -3.5 – -2.5).

High-risk women living in relatively wealthy households (scores in the range of 3.0 – 5.0), however, still have a.15 –.20 predicted probability of experiencing physical abuse. By contrast, women having characteristics associated with the lowest risk of physical abuse have a.05 or lower predicted probability of experiencing physical abuse, regardless of the household's level of wealth. These findings highlight that socioeconomic dependence on marriage and family organization strongly drive the risk of experiencing physical abuse among married women of all economic backgrounds in this setting.

This chapter advances our understanding of the influence of household wealth, a woman's socioeconomic dependence or status inconsistency in marriage, and local family organization on the physical abuse of married women in Minya, Egypt. Findings also may inform an understanding of the causes of physical abuse against married women in settings that maintain similar inequalities in the socioeconomic resources of women and men. Reports from married women of reproductive age in Minya indicate that 27% have experienced at least one beating in adulthood.

This estimate is consistent with that from the 1995 Demographic and Health Survey in Egypt, which indicated that one third of ever-married Egyptian women of reproductive age had been beaten since marriage. The estimate for Minya is lower than most available estimates of lifetime physical abuse from Sub-Saharan Africa and Latin America, but is higher than most available estimates from Europe and the U.S.

The frequency of severe beating in Minya also is notable, with 4% of married women reporting that they had been beaten in adulthood to the extent that a doctor was needed (whether or not one was sought). Regarding the determinants of physical abuse among married women in Minya, multivariate findings support and show that women in wealthier households were less likely to have been beaten in the prior year. This finding is consistent with Goode's (1971) adaptation of resource theory to the question of domestic violence against women. This finding also corroborates empirical evidence from Western and non-Western contexts showing that the household's or husband's socioeconomic status is negatively associated with various forms of domestic violence against women.

Because data on levels of stress were unavailable for the marital kin of women in this sample, however, it was not possible to evaluate whether stress mediated the relationship between the households or husband's economic status and physical abuse of married women in Minya. Findings also support, which concerns the net effects of women's socioeconomic dependence on their experiences of physical abuse and attitudes about wife abuse and divorce. First, having fewer years of schooling than one's husband, and thus fewer economic alternatives to marriage, was associated with a higher likelihood of having been beaten in the prior year and of reporting that a husband is more often justified in beating his wife.

Second, women with two or more living sons were more likely to have been beaten, marginally more likely to report that a husband is more often justified in beating his wife, and less likely to report that a wife is more prone to seek divorce for identified reasons. Differences in the effects of having sons in Minya versus having sons in India or Bangladesh may be attributable to differences in divorce laws across these settings. As already noted, mothers in Egypt depend on sons for financial support in old age, yet Egyptian law ultimately grants custodial rights to husbands in cases of divorce. Thus, motherhood enhances a woman's social identity, but also secures her dependence on marriage to maintain custody of her children.

In India and Bangladesh, all major religions have their own laws governing a person's rights in marriage, divorce, guardianship, and other personal matters. Thus, although divorce may have many negative consequences for Indian and Bangladeshi women, its implications for their custodial rights may vary more than in Minya. Regarding the effects of status inconsistency between a woman and her husband (hypothesis 3), the number of respondents who had more schooling (n = 242) or who paid as much or more of the marital expenses (n = 65) may have been insufficient to detect significant differences in the likelihood of recent physical abuse for these groups.

Yet, having more schooling than one's husband was associated with a marginally higher likelihood of reporting that a woman is more prone to seek a divorce. The latter finding suggests that women with relatively more schooling may see alternatives to marriage and thus may be less prone to abuse. This finding corroborates the view of informants in urban Cairo that women who marry lower- status men will "question their authority as head of the household".

Regarding the effects of family organization, findings show that women living farther from natal family and living with senior marital relatives were more likely to have been beaten in the prior year. Both findings corroborate the idea that isolation from supportive kin is an important independent determinant of a married woman's risk of experiencing physical abuse. At the same time, the finding that endogamous marriage was unrelated to physical abuse in Minya suggests that endogamous marriage is not protective for women, as expected.

Moreover, endogamously married women were more likely to report that a husband is more often justified in beating his wife and were less likely to report that a woman is more prone to seek a divorce. The association of endogamous marriage and these attitudes suggests that the obligations of related spouses to common male relatives may foster more tolerance for mistreatment and may impair a woman's perceived ability to seek divorce.

Overall, findings suggest that cross-cultural research on domestic violence against women should account for contextually relevant family characteristics, especially where extended forms of kinship are common. Predicted probabilities of physical abuse that were derived from multivariate analyses reveal important implications for theory about the forces driving married women's risk of physical abuse in settings such as Minya, Egypt.

Most notably, the likelihood of physical abuse may be substantially higher for women who are economically dependent on marriage and who lack access to social support than for women who are economically independent and who have access to such support, regardless of the level of household wealth. Thus, although greater household wealth may have a net negative effect on the likelihood that married women experience physical abuse, having access to social and economic resources outside of marriage may offer women the most consistent protection against such abuse.

The findings presented above inform several recommendations for policy. In general, changes in policy might focus on the sources of women's socioeconomic dependence on marriage. Establishing community-based sources of support would provide recourse for abused women who live far from natal family. Such services already are needed for the large percentage of abused women who neither seek help nor have safe places to go to avoid being beaten, and the need for such services may escalate if increasing percentages of married women live far from natal kin.

Given that the laws in Egypt still award custody of children to husbands in cases of divorce, reforms that leave decisions about child custody to the discretion of a judge also may alleviate women's reliance on abusive marriages to retain custody of their children. Further efforts also could be made to reduce disparities in women's and men's access to education so that equal opportunity, at least in this respect, is the normative backdrop against which women and men choose their mate in marriage.

Findings from this analysis, and certain limitations, also provide new ideas for research. First, because frequent beatings in the prior year were rare in Minya, multivariate analysis of recent, and regular abuse was not possible. New studies of domestic violence in Egypt could include a wider range of questions about the nature, severity, and timing of physical, sexual, and psychological abuse to ensure accurate estimates of the overall prevalence of domestic violence against women, and it's various types.

Second, only female respondents reported on the occurrence of beatings, and studies have shown that reports of physical abuse can be unreliable. Thus, if ethically feasible, new studies might include interviews with husbands and wives about the occurrence of domestic violence, and analyses can assess the effects of covariates on domestic violence against women that are confirmed by one or both partners.

Third, this study was undertaken before divorce laws in Egypt changed to make it easier for a woman to obtain a divorce without her husband's consent. Proponents of this law have argued that women need to be able to escape marriages in which they are abused but are unable to prove such abuse to a judge's satisfaction. Thus, new studies might evaluate the association of women's socioeconomic dependence with their attitudes about abuse and their experiences of abuse in this new legal environment.

Fourth, the collection of data for this analysis occurred during the final round of a larger longitudinal study in Minya, and so data on women's attitudes as reported at interview may be endogenous to physical abuse that occurred in the prior year. Problems of temporality in the measurement of attitudes that could mediate the relationship between underlying variables and episodes of domestic violence precluded formal path analysis using these data.

Other scholars have faced similar limitations on drawing causal inferences from analyses of cross-sectional data. Thus, new studies might follow a prospective design that involves the measurement of underlying and proximate attitudinal variables at reasonable times prior to the measurement of domestic violence. Fifth, some variables that may be associated with domestic violence against women were not available, including poverty-induced stress among men, men's ideals about their familial roles, and exposure of either partner to domestic violence in childhood, and chronic use of drugs or alcohol by either partner.

Although asking questions about the abuse of drugs or alcohol might be difficult in Egypt, new studies could include interviews with husbands about their reactions to economic hardship and their ideals about men's family roles. New studies also could include interviews with husbands and wives about their experiences of maltreatment or observations of domestic violence in childhood. Finally, this analysis focused on recent physical abuse among married women only. The prevalence of domestic violence and its determinants, however, could differ among widowed and especially divorced women.

Fortunately, only 2% of the original sample of women was divorced at the time of the survey, and the lifetime prevalence of physical abuse was similar among divorced and married women (28% vs. 29%, respectively). To study domestic violence among all women, new studies could include marital histories and questions about the timing of major acts of violence. Implementing the above recommendations for research would help to assess the robustness of the findings here – that socioeconomic dependence and social isolation are important causes of domestic violence against women from all economic strata.

CASE STUDY

ALBANIA: VIOLENCE AGAINST WOMEN IN THE FAMILY 'IT'S NOT HER SHAME'

"Every day... if I had bruises around one eye, he hit the other one, every day for three years so that you would not be able to recognize me, my face wasn't a human face"

"I am carrying the past around inside me. No one can see my heart, how it is inside."

An estimated one in three women in Albania have been hit, beaten or subjected to other physical violence within their families. Some have been raped, some have been killed. Husbands, former husbands and partners are responsible for most of these acts of violence against women – abuses which are often condoned by the wider community. Violence against women is widely tolerated on grounds of tradition, even at the highest levels of the government, police and judiciary.

Violence against women is an abuse of the human rights of women and girls. It violates their rights to mental and physical integrity, to liberty and security of the person, to freedom of expression, the right to choice in marriage and the basic requirement of non-discrimination. Violence may amount to torture and in extreme cases, may violate the right to life. There is no specific legislation against domestic violence in Albania. A general acceptance of violence in the family is imbedded in Albanian society, and thus many women do not understand the concept of domestic violence as a criminal offence. An activist from an Albanian non-governmental organization (NGO) said: "They have seen their mothers beaten, and they think it is normal to be beaten, or to be shouted at by the husband or brother or mother-in-law, and that it is their husband's right to beat them."

But there is movement for change in Albanian society. In January 2006 a coalition of Albanian NGOs presented a petition to parliament signed by 20,000 Albanians calling for a change in the law to help prevent violence within the family.

THE EXTENT OF THE VIOLENCE

"They say in Albania, one in three women are beaten by their husbands, in Shkroda we say it's two and a half out of three." A doctor in the town of Shkodra.

"Violence happens everywhere: at the police station, at home, at school - there is a cycle of violence in the whole society," an NGO activist told Amnesty International. "Most women do not usually report such violence to the police: they don't understand that it is a criminal act, and many of them are violent to their own children - they see it as a tool for education".

Much violence within the family involves guns. The large number of small arms and light weapons in circulation in Albania - an estimated 200,000 - contributes to high levels of gun crime, including in domestic violence. Research by forensic practitioners has documented an increase in intimate partner violence over the past five years. Doctors from the Department of Forensic Medicine in Tirana found that between 2001 and 2003 cases involving violence in the family made up 71 per cent of all assault cases referred to them. Sixty-eight per cent of the victims were women.

However, the most comprehensive survey, the Albania Reproductive Health Survey 2002 conducted by the Ministry of Health, found Albanian women reporting much lower levels of violence. Eight per cent of Albanian women reported physical violence as compared to, for example, 29 per cent of women in Romania. Significantly, 31.2 per cent of previously married women reported violence, as opposed to 7.5 per cent of women who were still married or in a relationship. The survey found that 52.5 per cent of women who had suffered violence had never talked to anyone about it.

The persistent under-reporting of intimate partner violence indicates not merely a reluctance to report domestic violence to the authorities, but women's lack of awareness that it is something that they can or should report.

A CULTURE OF VIOLENCE

Albania's history of internal repression during the communist era followed by years of political instability has left a legacy of violence which recent governments have sought to address. Notions of honour (nderi) and shame (turpi) prevent women from telling anyone about domestic violence for fear that it would bring shame on the honour of their family.

"I stayed married to him for 18 years because of the family, and because of the shame; it was the idea of the shame that kept me there all of that time."

Notions of gender and gender relations in Albania are informed by cultural beliefs which draw on customary law, known as the Kanun. These are used to justify the control of women's behaviour, including by ill-treatment. In extreme cases women and girls believed to have transgressed notions of family honour have been murdered.

In September 2004 Gjin Martincanaj was sentenced to seven years and four months' imprisonment for shooting dead his 21-year-old daughter Grosha Martincanaj, after she went missing for three days and refused to explain where she had been. Her sister reportedly told the press, "Our father did right to kill her; he did his duty as the parent of a girl who shamed her family".

Since the early 1990s there has been resurgence in the use of customary practices, including blood feuds and revenge killings, especially in the north of the country. The use of the Kanun appears not only to be reviving, but also to be spreading beyond its traditional provisions, which exempted women from blood feuds.

PATTERNS OF ABUSE

A number of women who have suffered violence agreed to be interviewed by Amnesty International, despite their fear of bringing "dishonour" to their families. Their courage deserves recognition and the support of their government and the international community.

"The beating started from the first day after we married. He was jealous all the time; we were looking at photographs of when I was single - there was a photograph of me with my first cousin - and he hit me because he was jealous. I was completely shocked - my father had never hit my mother. But I thought it would not happen again."

"After we got married he got worse, more and more jealous. He was so jealous and got angry when people said hello to me in the street, and when we got home he would beat me. He would not even let me talk to my family: when I stopped to talk to my mother in the street, he just carried on walking, and when we got home he would take a wooden stick and beat me."

"I never understood why he was angry. When I was awake, I thought perhaps I had made a noise, or left a spoon in the wrong place, but even when I was asleep he would come in and grab me out of bed by the leg, and threaten to kill me. He would ask me why I was still alive, and tell me that I should kill myself".

"He would hit me, he would slap me, and then when he used the telephone cable I was very scared because he was drunk and out of control; and I became really frightened."

"He came home and threatened to kill me with a pistol in front of the children, and the children protected me and came and stood in front of me and they said, "You have to kill us first".

"He kicked me, punched me, and knocked me unconscious, he used verbal abuse, he used all kinds of violence, and - I don't know how to say it - he wanted to have sex with me."

Many of the women interviewed by Amnesty International had tried several times to leave their husband before they finally left him. Their reasons for returning to a violent marriage included economic hardship, a lack of housing, the need for their children to have a father, family pressure – or just the hope that the man they loved would stop beating them.

Reports from women's organizations suggest that an unknown number of women choose suicide as their only means of escaping domestic violence. Other women, after years of violence, have eventually resorted to violence themselves: more than 20 women are currently serving sentences for killing their husbands.

Some women never hear from their husbands or partners again. But for others, the violence does not stop even after divorce. A study of decisions taken by five district courts between 1990 and 1998 showed that in 35 per cent of criminal proceedings related to violence against women, the perpetrator was the woman's former husband.

WOMEN'S RIGHTS IN ALBANIA

All states have a duty under international human rights law to prevent, prohibit and punish violence against women, regardless of the perpetrator; the state also has a duty to provide redress, including compensation.

Albania is bound by the Convention on the Elimination of Discrimination against Women. According to the Albanian Constitution, all international conventions ratified by Albania are part of domestic legislation and take precedence over national laws. The Constitution also provides for equality before the law and prohibits discrimination. In theory therefore, Albanian women enjoy the same rights as men. In practice, they face widespread discrimination in almost all aspects of political, economic, social and cultural life. The

Albanian Criminal Code fails to separately define or criminalize domestic violence, and no distinction is made between violent crimes (including rape) perpetrated by strangers and those by family members.

IMPUNITY

"It's a problem of Albanian reality; women do not get access to justice"- An officer from the Serious Crimes Police, Tirana.

POLICE INDIFFERENCE

"There are reports in this region that women say they have called the police and that we don't come – maybe they don't give the right address." Qani Balija, Deputy Director, Vlora Police.

When women try to seek help, they rarely gain protection or justice because of the authorities' reluctance to take action. In the absence of a law criminalizing domestic violence, the police generally fail to recognize violence in the family as a criminal matter and fail to investigate allegations of domestic violence. One woman described how the police failed to respond to her repeated calls for help after her husband beat her. "I called every hour, every hour and a half. The police officer said, 'Don't call us, don't you feel embarrassed?'… and then he insulted me. I never again called the police."

The problems go beyond police attitudes. There are also procedural problems, including a failure to log calls relating to domestic violence and to disaggregate statistics. Even if the police respond to a call, they claim that they may not always have the powers to intervene. A Serious Crimes Police officer said: "Under the Criminal Code, for example – for [domestic] violence, we do not have a control mandate [search warrant to enter a property], so the women have to go to the judge. Sometimes we have entered without the control mandate – but we cannot just go on the word of the woman to prove a crime."

CRIMINAL PROSECUTIONS

"Few women are prepared to bring such prosecutions. They are psychologically tired of dealing with the court, and with their problems, and they just don't want to deal with it any more. They have to do all the work to get a divorce or prosecution: the burden lies entirely on the woman in such cases." Besa Saraçi, Women's Advocacy Centre.

Prosecutors fail to pursue complaints of domestic violence except in cases of death or serious injury, or threats with firearms or other weapons. They sometimes even impede women's attempts to pursue cases. According to a Shkodra NGO, a woman came to them, her face freshly bruised after her husband had beaten her. She had been examined by a local forensic doctor, but as the authorized photographer had not been present, she had her photograph taken by a street photographer. The prosecutor had refused to accept the photograph as evidence (even though it was accompanied by a forensic medical certificate), and criminal proceedings were not started.

Amnesty International reviewed 34 court decisions in cases relating to domestic violence which were prosecuted between March 2002 and November 2005. Most used accelerated trial procedures, where the case is judged exclusively on the basis of evidence collected during the judicial investigation and contained in the court dossier. Amnesty International found that evidence of previous incidents of domestic violence was rarely examined and provisions allowing violence in the family to be treated as an "aggravating circumstance" were almost never invoked.

Hazir Isaj, a police officer, was convicted by the Shkodra District Court on 14 April 2003 of the manslaughter of his wife Drita Isaj, after an argument in which she allegedly threatened him with a kitchen knife. He then pulled out his gun, and told her that unless she left, he would kill her. Drita then grabbed the gun and pulled it to her chest saying, "Go on then kill me!". Hazir reportedly told her that he could not kill the mother of his children, but in the struggle the gun went off fatally wounding Drita. He pleaded guilty and was sentenced to two years and three months' imprisonment, reduced to 18 months.

On 17 January 2006, Zef Shkjepana was sentenced by Shkodra District Court to three months' imprisonment for threatening to kill his wife, Alma Shkjepana, and to 17 months' imprisonment for possession of unlicensed arms and ammunition. Alma Shkjepana had told police that her husband had beaten her, repeatedly, and had threatened to shoot her dead. The final sentence was 10 months' imprisonment.

Amnesty International also reviewed seven cases in which eight women were convicted for killing or attempting to kill their husband (or in one case, their father). Delegates interviewed five of these women at Women's Prison 325 in Tirana. None had been able to afford to hire a lawyer and they were therefore represented by court-appointed lawyers.

CIVIL DIVORCE PROCEEDINGS

Instead of lodging criminal complaints against their abusive partners, women tend to escape violent marriages through divorce. Although domestic violence is a major factor in many divorce cases, women generally choose not to raise this in proceedings. Their reasons include the shame that a public disclosure would bring on their family and the difficulty in proving their case. In 511 divorce cases brought before the Tirana First Instance Court in 2000, domestic violence was cited as a cause in only 39 cases, and figures for 2001 to 2004 are comparable.

In Shkodra, staff at the Hapat e Leht¸ counselling and advice centre said that judges refuse to recognize domestic violence as a factor in divorce cases, and that; consequently, domestic violence appears not to exist. Women seeking to leave violent men are rarely able to support or house themselves and their children. No state provision is available; in cases of divorce financial settlements are rarely enforced by the courts.

CHALLENGING VIOLENCE

"There are no structures, no institutions, you have to do it on your own, there's no protection. I could not have done it without the shelter and the telephone line. Thank god for the shelter that gave me help and the hope to start my life again".

Women's organizations in Albania have worked since 1996 to challenge violence against women. They have run awareness-raising programmes, trained state officials and documented domestic violence. They have also established telephone help-lines, counselling centres, and shelters and given free legal assistance and employment advice.

NGOs are pressing forward on the legislative front too, with the drafting and presentattion to parliament of the draft law on the prevention of violence within the family. NGOs see the draft law as a catalyst for change, but recognize the problems that may accompany its introduction. One NGO, Useful to Albanian Women, stated, "Domestic violence can only be reduced through parallel processes in the economy, and in women's self-confidence, empowerment and self-esteem."

The Family Code which entered into force on 21 December 2003 replaced all previous legislation relating to the family and marriage and provided new legal protection for women. In particular, Article 62 allows courts to issue an order removing a violent spouse from the family home. However, this article has scarcely ever been invoked, since the necessary supporting legislation is lacking. One aim of the new draft law is to allow such measures to be implemented.

The draft law envisages an integrated response by government agencies, including police, medical practitioners and social workers, to cases of family violence. It also sets out a civil process for protection orders, implementing Article 62 of the Family Code.

Amnesty International welcomes the substance of the draft law, in particular: the creation of a body to coordinate responses to protect and provide redress to victims of domestic violence; the establishment of anti-violence units at police stations, and the training of police officers; and instructions to police authorities to record their findings in the event of a reported incident, and to start investigations. Amnesty International's concerns about the draft law relate to the definition of family violence. In particular it is not clear whether the law applies to co-habitees.

4

Women and Family Violence

To every gathering of Muslim women, Maria added a smile. She came to Islam early, marrying a Muslim man and accepting the religion at 13 years old. She embraced it wholeheartedly, learning from the sisters as she went along. By age nineteen, she became the mother of a much-beloved baby boy. She and her son attended Jumu'ah prayers every Friday. When the women decided to gather in one another's homes two Saturdays a month, Maria made an effort to come to each meeting. By this time, her son was nearly two years old, and Maria was separated from her husband and living with her non-Muslim mother. Often, the talk turned to the difficulties of marriage. Maria listened, sympathized, and smiled. One day, the sisters decided to organize a retreat to discuss family issues.

At the retreat, Maria and the 15 or so other women talked, laughed, and shared a potluck brunch. They began to discuss the topic of marriage. Maria had a question. She wanted to know how a woman knows when her divorce is final. As the women focused on Maria's question, she told them her horror story of suffering, abuse, being divorced, taken back, divorced again, lied to, and finally stalked by her husband. He told her the divorce was final one day, and the next day that it was not final, and that it was her Islamic duty to obey him in everything.

She remained Muslim, but did not know enough of her new religion to assert her rights. Her tires had been slashed, her home watched, her peace threatened, and she was afraid. The sisters were shocked. They should not have been. According to a survey of the 63 Muslim community workers, leaders, and individuals done in 1993 by the North American Council for Muslim Women, domestic violence (including everything from hitting to incest) against Muslim women and children occurred in ten percent of the population of Muslims. If verbal and psychological abuse were added to this, the figure would rise considerably.

By comparison, seven percent of American women in general were physically abused, and 37% were verbally or emotionally abused in 1993, according to the Family Violence Prevention Fund. A comprehensive study in 1993 by the Commonwealth Fund found that in one year alone nearly four million American women suffered abuse at the hands of their husbands or male friends, and that a woman is abused every nine seconds. The Family Violence Prevention Fund also reports that 34% of men and women have directly witnessed an act of domestic violence. This number is higher than the combined numbers of adults who have witnessed robberies or muggings.

Maria continued to attend the sisters' meetings as the sisters began to focus on the problem of domestic violence in their community. She was not the only victim. The sisters protested to their Imam when they discovered that a community leader involved with their children had used violence against his wife. It became obvious to them that some community education was in order. Meanwhile, Maria's ex-husband had begun to frequent another Muslim community in the area but continued to alternately harass her and to entice her to continue her relationship with him. He began to use their son as a way to gain access to her, and he continued to disturb her sense of security and to assess his control over her.

AUTHORITARIAN FAMILY STRUCTURES

An authoritarian family structure predisposes many Muslims in America to be abused in some way and possibly to become the victims of violence. Generally, husband's dominance's in the family structure, the more likely wife and child abuse become. In the most abusive homes, the father believes and socializes his wife and children to believe that whatever he wants the family to do is the same as what Allah wants them to do. He, in effect, makes himself into something of a god. Of the eight to ten million Muslims in America, more than half are African-American, a small but growing number are European American, and the rest are immigrants (first, second, or third generation) from Middle Eastern, Southwest Asian, and other countries.

African American Muslim families suffer from the influence of the overwhelming incidences of abuse and violence in the general society and from the historical experience of slavery, which encouraged fractured families. While African-Americans who have been Muslim for many years are as self-directed as any community, new Muslim families who are searching for stability and morality often look to the immigrant communities for leadership and mentoring. Unfortunately, the most negative behavioral common denominator between the African-American and the immigrant Muslim communities is a socialization process which presents the parents, particularly the father, as having the last word on everything, and teaches children to be unquestioningly obedient as part of their devotion to faith.

The overwhelming majority of immigrant Muslims comes from repressive countries where political power is held by officials who secure or maintain their leadership through unethical, un-Islamic, and sometimes brutal means. These tyrannical governments tend to produce extended families and societies where only the man at the top can pronounce what is right or wrong, what is acceptable or unacceptable, and who is good or bad. Muslim American immigrants fleeing oppressive governments may not yet have realized that their own family dynamics are a microcosm of the tyranny and despotism they so actively oppose, and mistakenly think a tyrannical family structure is an Islamic one.

The atmosphere in too many of these families is repressive, non-communicative, top-down, and male-dominated, where the leadership title that is worn is primary and which never allows or plans for asking why or how the family functions. Surprisingly, in the homes of most Muslims, focusing on the rules and desires of the parents almost always takes precedence over any focus on Allah. Most Muslim parents do not give their children any Qur'anic proof behind their opinions, do not allow themselves to be questioned, and no not invite discussion or reflection on ideas even though Allah continuously instructs Muslims to think and to reflect. Parents rarely see the connection between parents (instead of Allah) as the focus of the family structure, and shirk associating partners with Allah.

In order to end domestic violence, we must understand what it is that we are dealing with. The Family Violence Prevention Fund described abuse as "a pattern of purposeful behaviors, directed at achieving compliance from or control over, the victim." When these escalate to violence, creating "domestic violence," the definition becomes, "a pattern of assaultive and coercive behaviors, including physical, sexual, and psychological attacks, as well as economic coercion that adults or adolescents use against their intimate partner."

According to the US Department of Justice report in 1991, men against women commit 95% of assaults on spouses or ex-spouses. (Abused females may also abuse their children, and are sometimes the primary abusers.) Most of the control mechanisms used by potential batterers that can escalate to violence are so common among Muslim families that they are not seen as threats to the family's existence; minimizing the victim's complaints, denying the abuse, and blaming the victim, isolating the victim from family and friends, intimidation, so-called "joking" about marrying a second wife, and emotional abuse such as name calling and degrading remarks in the presence of her children or guests.

While none of this behavior is consistent with the teachings of the Qur'an or the Sunnah of the Prophet Muhammad, few parents ever make the mental connection between this behavior and abuse. In fact, many abuse parents will say they are just "maintaining the discipline of the family." In most cases, after an episode of violence, the abuser says he is sorry, may ask for forgiveness, and promises not to repeat the behavior. Women may stay because they hope for change, still love the person, or are afraid of losing their children; they often leave only when they perceive imminent danger to their children.

Sadly, all research proves that children from abuse homes are equally affected permanently whether or not they are victims themselves. Maria continued to be confused about her relationship as she tried to sort out her Islamic duties, what was best for her son, and her own feelings. The Imam pointed out that Islamically she should stay away from her ex-husband, and said that he did not know what she expected from him, since she had not followed his advice. When an incidence of abuse or violence is reported to someone in the Muslim community, the general response is to avoid "interfering" in family affairs.

Some Muslims believe it is the man's Allah-given right to abuse his wife and children in any way he sees fit. Others, like the Imam in Maria's community, recognize the behavior as Islamically unacceptable, but have no training in the areas of domestic violence counseling, and do not know how to intervene effectively and legally. Many Imams, though, blame the situation on the wife. Most people just hope the problem will go away. When it does not, the entire Muslim community suffers; the existence of abuse convinces a community that they are ineffective and unable to protect women. Maria fell back into silence about her own experiences, but presented the sisters with information about Sisters of Peace, a group of Muslim women in Philadelphia organized to combat domestic violence in their community.

Under no circumstances is violence against women encouraged or allowed. The holy Qur'an contains tens of verses extolling good treatment of women. Several specifically enjoin kindness to women. These verses make it clear that the relationship between men and women is to be one of kindness, mutual respect, and caring. Some verses, where Allah calls men and women "protecting friends of one another," refer to the mandated atmosphere of mutual kindness and mercy in the marital home (30:21; 9:71).

Others show disapproval of oppression or ill treatment of women. Surah two, ayah 231 condemns taking women back after a separation in order to hurt them; Surah four, ayah 15 specifies taking an oath against a wife rather than doing violence to her if a husband suspects adultery; Surah four, ayah 19 prohibits forces marriages; Surah four, ayah 29 prohibits deliberately causing a wife suspense or insecurity; Surah five, ayah 92 removes the legal effect from oaths against wives made in anger; and Surah 17, ayat 90-91 require the fulfillment of oaths, verbal agreements, and commitments.

Even in the case of divorce, spouses are instructed to bring an arbiter from each side of the family to attempt reconciliation (4:35). If this fails, the instruction is to get back together with dignity and fairness, or to part on good terms (2:229 and 231). Anyone who violates the limits set by Allah is labeled a "transgressor" in the Qur'an. Added to these verses is the inescapable fact that the Prophet vehemently disapproved of men hitting their wives, and that he never in his entire life lit any woman or child. In the Prophet's last sermon, he exhorted men to "be kind to women-you have rights over your wives, and they have rights over you." He also said, "Treat your women well, and be kind to them, for they are your partners and committed helpers," and at a different time, he said, "The strong man is not the one who can use the force of physical strength, but the one who controls his anger" (Bukhari).

Very important are those verses that give women the right to self-supervision. Surah five, ayah 44 instructs believers to, "Have no fear of people; fear Me." Surah 33, ayah 35 promises heaven to men and women who individually guard their chastity (or modesty)." In the abusive mindset, all of these verses and hadith are ignored, and males misquote two specific verses and one hadith to justify complete control of females. The worst interpretations go so far as t assert that a woman is mentally, emotionally, psychologically, and spiritually permanently disabled, and is prone to immorality, putting her in constant need of male supervision.

The most abused verse is ayah 34 of Surah four: "Men are the protectors and maintainers of women because Allah gave them more to the one than the other, and because they support them from their means. So devout women are extremely careful and attentive in guarding what cannot be seen in that which Allah is extremely careful and attentive in guarding. Concerning women whose rebellious (nushooz) you fear, admonish them, then refuse to share their beds, then hit them; but if they become obedient, no not seem means of annoyance against them.

For Allah is Most High, Great." This translation charges men with the task of financially and physically protecting and caring for their wives and families, since Allah has made men physically stronger than women, which is the interpretation of most scholars. Women, in return for that care, should be careful in guarding their fidelity and morality at all times when no one can see them in obedience to Allah. Instructions are then given regarding women who rebelliously ignore Allah's commands about sexual fidelity and become sexually disloyal to their husbands.

The husband is instructed first to admonish his wife (talk to her), and then to refuse to share her bed. Should those measures fail, the last instruction is often translated as "hit her," (or "lightly tap her," when the sunnah of the Prophet is considered). Some translators assert that it is incorrect to translate the word "hit" at all, based on the Prophet's lifelong abhorrence of hitting women, seen in his statement, "Never hit the handmaids of Allah" (found in the hadith collections of Abu Daud, Nasa'l, Ibn Hibban, and Bayhaqi), and in his instructions in his last sermon where he restrict striking to a light tap (ghayr muharrib - without causing pain) only if the wife has become guilty of nushooz, obvious immoral conduct. The term nushooz is applicable to men as well (4:128).

The wording of this verse emphasizes the woman's obedience to Allah's desires, and not to those of another human being, but those who misinterpret this verse would assign men the duty of being eternal surveillance police over their wives. This verse has been so misunderstood that it is not uncommon for husbands to prevent their wives from going to the corner store, to attend births, deaths, or marriages, to see doctors, seek education, or even to visit their parents without express permission. This verse has also been used to underpin the mistaken belief that the qawwama of men as protectors and maintainers of their wives not only implies unquestionable obedience to men as individuals but also that only men may lead women in any aspect of life whatsoever on any level.

In short, this verse has been used as a tool of control and abuse completely opposed to the Islamic foundation of marriage and family. Another misused verse is ayah 53 of Surah 33: "O you who believe, enter not the dwellings of the Prophet for a meal without waiting for the proper time...and when you ask of them (his wives) anything, ask of them from behind a curtain. That is purer for your hearts and their hearts...it is not for you to cause annoyance to the messenger of Allah, nor may you ever marry his wives after him. That in Allah's sight would be an enormity."

The verse is obviously directed at Muslim men describing their property conduct only with the wives of the Prophet. It continues, however, to the main reason that some Muslims believe that men and women must be separate in all spaces, and an excuse for some men to claim that all public space belongs to men alone. This is erroneous. The instruction relates only to the wives of the Prophet, and to proper behavior in the Prophet's house. Those who want to apply this verse to all Muslim women never assert that all Muslim women may not marry after the deaths of their husbands (although in practice, that is exactly what is expected of women in some Muslim societies according to their un-Islamic customs).

Confining women to the kitchens of their houses during dinner parties, relegating women to back rooms with inadequate or absent audio hookup in most mosques, or worse, banning women from mosques, and bans by political authorities in some countries against women going to school, all come from warped interpretations of the previously mentioned verses. A hadith often used in the control of women reads: "Women, when they travel a far distance, should have a muhrim with them." At the time of the Prophet, traveling even 40 miles could be very dangerous since roads were full of bandits and law consisted of each tribe's different rules and regulations. Rule of law that crossed tribal boundaries, and was consistent with a new concept in 7th century Arabia introduced by Islam.

Today women can travel halfway across the world by airplane in 19 hours, and remain safely among large groups of people at all times. Yet this hadith continues to be sued, even by a few Muslim leaders in large US cities, to prevent Muslim women from going from one city to another, from one part of the city to another, or from leaving the doorways of their apartments, alone. The real question is, did the Prophet practice, encourage, or even condone surveillance and control behaviors towards women? He never did. Knowing this, it is up to each individual Muslim, as husband and wife, as extended family member, or as community member, to shape morally, ethically, psychologically, and physically sale and healthy society where families can raise happy and contributing members of society.

Let there be zero tolerance for abuse and violence against women! The words of a famous ad campaign state, "There's no excuse for domestic violence." If we hold this in mind, the future for battered women will be a positive one. Research shows that the more we are exposed to violence against women, the less we are upset by it. Muslim women need to improve their knowledge of their own faith, and then reclaim their right to define themselves in the light of the Qur'an and the Sunnah, instead of by customary practices, traditions, extremist viewpoints, or those who believe Muslim women need to be saved from themselves.

Families need to maintain open lines of communication between all of their members; regular family meetings where everyone is allowed to express themselves without any recriminations are helpful. Marriage must be seen as a partnership, and marriage contracts should specify a commitment to an abuse, free and violence-free family. The parents must ask of their children only that which is good and which conforms to Qur'anically based concepts. Extended families must stop covering up abuse, violence, and incest in the name of "preserving the family honor." Above all, the family, like the individual must keep Allah as its focus.

The Family Violence Prevention Division in Canada this year published a full report on family violence. Of great significance to Muslims is the need they identified to "reconceptualize power in a way that distinguished between creative and violating power and that more directly expands the focus on power to move beyond power dynamics in individual relationships to power structures." This thinking should be taken from the personal level to the global level. Communities need to see individual cases of family violence in the light of the nature of the global power structure, and that of the community as a whole, to discover whether the community power structure is actually promoting a license to batter.

Imams must be protectors of women's safety by example, avoid blaming wives, and recognize when they do not have the expertise to truly help women who are battered. Community members should be encouraged to obtain profession training and degrees in counseling. The community is responsible to develop protocols for handling problems of domestic violence, network with existing Muslim and non-Muslim agencies that can provide training or referrals, and set up safe houses for battered women and children.

At least twice a year, each mosque or community center should present an Abuse and Domestic Violence Awareness Program for Muslim Families that will teach risk identification, abuse and violence identification, safety planning for possible situations, safety planning for unsupervised visits by a batterer, problem solving techniques, and information on counseling available for battered women and their families. Muslim community activists, lawyers, and counselors should meet in each city to develop protocols addressed to their specific community which will allow for early identification of abuse and a willingness to deal with the situation in order to protect the victims from further abuse or victim blaming. Wherever possible, shelters and Muslim family service agencies should be put into place.

In 1993, the North American Council for Muslim Women was the first national Muslim organization of any kind to discuss Abuse and Violence Against Women and Children during a national convention. In 1995 in Plainfield, Indiana, and the following year in Chicago, the Islamic Society of North America held conferences for social service providers that addressed several subjects including family counseling, divorce and children's issues, and the last one was attended by over 200 providers.

WORKING WITH IMMIGRANT WOMEN

Immigrant women are a diverse group and include women who have lived in the United States for one month, as well as women who have lived here for forty years. The immigrant woman who contacts you for help may have entered the United States as a refugee fleeing persecution in her country of origin, as a relative with family members in the United States, as a student, as a tourist, or as a worker seeking better economic conditions. Shelters sometimes are concerned about the legal or funding consequences of serving battered immigrant women, particularly undocumented immigrant women.

Some shelter providers mistakenly believe that it is unlawful to provide services to undocumented women. However, non-profit organizations are explicitly exempt from verifying immigration status as a condition for providing services. Further, any non-profit or government domestic violence services program or shelter that denies assistance to immigrants who are undocumented is violating the Attorney General's order requiring that services "necessary for the protection of life and safety" be provided without regard to immigration status and is violating civil rights and fair housing laws.

In general, immigration status is not relevant to a battered immigrant woman using your program's services. The fact that a woman may not be a U.S. citizen or lawful resident should not affect your ability to provide her with services. Her immigration status is only relevant for you to know if it may protect her from abuse, through knowing the risks she may be facing, and helping her become a permanent resident if she is eligible. To help a battered immigrant woman, you do not need to be an expert in the technicalities of immigration law. Your role as an advocate is to empower her by knowing the range of her options, and helping her find the assistance she needs. However, you should consult an immigration lawyer if you have determined that the victim's immigration status is uncertain.

Newly arrived battered immigrant women whose immigration status is not permanently established - because they are undocumented, conditional residents, or here on visas - have special needs. Typically, their batterers control and manipulate their unsettled immigration status as a means of keeping them in abusive relationships. These women experience the complex intersection of domestic violence with their immigration status. Their option to reside legally and permanently in the United States may have been restricted by domestic violence. Your role is to learn about possible options, assist battered immigrant women in accessing them, and respect the decisions they make. It is up to the immigrant woman to decide whether she wants to reside in the United States or return to her country of origin.

POWER AND CONTROL TACTICS USED AGAINST IMMIGRANT WOMEN

This version of the Power and Control wheel, adapted with permission from the Domestic Abuse Intervention Project in Duluth, Minnesota, focuses on some of the many ways battered immigrant women can be abused. The Immigrant Women Power and Control Wheel is available in both English and Spanish.

In recent years, family violence has become a prominent area of social research. However, no comprehensive studies have detailed the scope of this crime within Aboriginal communities. As well, scant documentation exists analyzing the attitudes and perceptions of victims, their abusers and the community at large within the Aboriginal context. In 2006, the Ipsos-Reid research firm prepared a report entitled "Aboriginal Women and Family Violence" for Indian and Northern Affairs Canada.

The research project on which the report is based studied the attitudes and opinions of Aboriginal women, and the professionals who work with them, on the issue of family violence, specifically intimate partner violence against women. This report is a condensed version of the larger report. The following aspects of the issue are addressed in this report:

- The importance of intimate partner violence compared to other issues facing women in Aboriginal communities – that is, perceptions of incidence and severity of violence;
- Causes of male violence against women in Aboriginal communities, including opinions on the role of factors such as poverty, familial experience, parenting skills, substance abuse, familial and community indifference, and gender stereotyping;
- Consequences of male violence against Aboriginal women – in terms of the effects on the emotional, physical and financial status of the victims and the effects on children, extended families, community relationships and the abuser;
- Sources of help for Aboriginal women who experience violence (such as shelters, crisis centres and social services) in terms of accessibility, privacy, safety and reliability;
- Resources available for the families of both victims and abusers, including educational preventative initiatives and long-term counselling;
- Gaps in resources and community supports needed to end male violence against Aboriginal women; and Perceptions

of effective ways to disseminate information and provide assistance to families experiencing this form of violence.

This research was designed to capture information from two categories of respondents: Aboriginal women and those working with them (or first responders). With regard to the first category, a series of eight two-hour focus groups were held, each with 10 First Nations and Métis women, in the following locations: Prince Albert, Saskatchewan Val-d'Or, Québec Prince George, British Columbia Sydney, Nova Scotia Focus group participants were evenly divided between First Nations women living on reserve, and First Nations and Métis women living off reserve.

With regard to the second category of respondents, professionals working with Aboriginal victims of intimate partner violence, telephone interviews were conducted with 15 key informants. These key informants, or "first responders," included police (both the Royal Canadian Mounted Police and those employed by provincial governments), health care workers, social workers, and crisis centre staff from Aboriginal communities across Canada, both on and off reserve. More specifically, five of these first responders worked with Inuit women in the North; the remaining 10 worked with First Nations women living on reserve and in urban centres in Southern regions across Canada.

Despite the fact that no effort was made to recruit victims of violence, many participants in the focus groups had personal experience with intimate partner violence. While intimate partner violence is perpetrated in many ways, physical and emotional abuses were the two most common forms described by the participants.

INCIDENCE AND CAUSES

Confirming other research findings, first responders expressed the perception that there is a higher incidence of intimate partner abuse in Aboriginal communities than elsewhere. Although many factors are perceived as root causes of violence (loss of identity and way of life, continued impact of residential schools, a "learned cycle," etc.), nearly all participants pointed to drug and alcohol consumption (by both parties) as an aggravating factor.

CONSEQUENCES

All participants identified a variety of physical, psychological, financial and social consequences of male violence against Aboriginal women. A common view expressed by women within Aboriginal communities and among first responders is that community sanctions are mild, and those delivered by the corrections system are inconsequential. Although some laws and policies allow police officers to lay charges against a perpetrator without the consent of the victim, neither victims of violence nor first responders feel that relevant laws are adequately applied.

All participants in this study called for the imposition of increased accountability on perpetrators of violence and reform of the justice system to allow for more punitive measures. Nevertheless, some first responders see reason for optimism in what they perceive to be a gradual opinion shift among Aboriginal leaders, some of whom are beginning to condemn male violence against women.

Focus group participants, on the other hand, had mixed perceptions of community progress in this regard. Although some feel that community opposition to male violence may be increasing, others worry that unless steps are taken to develop greater awareness and accountability, abuse may simply go further underground within the still prevalent culture of secrecy surrounding this issue in Aboriginal communities.

Key resources discussed include: On reserve and in settlements: informal networks of family and friends; health care professionals (nurses); Health Centre referrals to off reserve and urban resources, including counselling, shelters and other victim service programs; and police. In urban centres: informal networks of family and friends; crisis centres and shelters; hotlines; Friendship Centres; and counselling services.

The use of such resources and services, however, is compromised by: low awareness of them; their distance from the home community; the lack of transportation; poor relationships with the police; lack of faith in the effectiveness of the resources; lack of privacy in communities and the consequent shame about accessing resources; complex relationships among the victim, the abuser, their families and other community members; and the desire to keep the family intact at all costs (because of fear of the unknown and of losing face, as well as the possibility of losing one's children, home and assets).

Although community-based resources would be ideal, smaller reserves and Northern settlements often do not have the means to sustain crisis centres or shelters, and all respondents noted that privacy and safety are significant concerns. Locating services and resources in close proximity to communities would be appropriate if residents also had access to adequate transportation and if the resource services were staffed by experienced and well-trained personnel. However, respondents raised concerns about the qualifications of staff, and the low numbers of Aboriginal personnel (especially the police) staffing such services in some communities.

Even when Aboriginal personnel are recruited for policing among Aboriginal people, respondents felt that their presence does not guarantee that women will be treated in a culturally sensitive manner. In addition, respondents suggested that women need to be helped to become more aware of the resources that are available. Women who live on reserve and in small settlements have a particular interest in receiving information without having to seek it out, given the chronic lack of privacy in such communities.

Furthermore, although the Internet can be useful to a small minority of people, it is only a supplement to other means of acquiring information. Most Aboriginal women would not think to look to the Internet, given the low incidence of computer ownership and web access. Not a single first responder mentioned the Internet as a likely candidate for future educational or support initiatives. Instead, suggestions from participants regarding communications include the use of: local papers; local radio; directories of services; advertising and educational programs in schools; advertising through Friendship Centre bulletins; inserts in government mass mailings; and integrating information about male violence against women into regular women's meetings, as a means of educating women about this issue.

The following points were suggested as potential means by which both Aboriginal women and first responders may become better informed about and assisted in dealing with the problem of male violence against Aboriginal women: Increased funding for resources to assist Aboriginal women victims of male violence, encompassing:

Educational programs to teach Aboriginal women about healthy "relationships Short-term and long-term housing for victims"

Short-term and long-term counselling for victims "Counselling and provision of basic resources (e.g., food and clothing) for "children Interim financial assistance for victims"

Affordable transportation to available services "Emergency 24-hour, 7-day crisis hotlines 24-hour, 7-day access to assistance from first responders within reasonable proximity to communities. Increased convenience and privacy in reporting acts of violence on reserves and in settlement communities

Cultural sensitivity training for all first responders (police, health care professionals, educators and others who directly assist women victims of intimate partner violence or otherwise work with communities to reduce the incidence of such violence)

Strong incentives or mandatory training for community leaders to ensure that they treat the issue of male violence against women as a high priority and a serious community-wide problem School-based activity to teach Aboriginal children about the issue and to reach out to parents A "piggy-back" use of existing programs (such as Friendship Centres and medical facilities) or government sponsored mailings (such as regular mailings of payments) to provide information on this issue and spare women from having to seek it out Encouragement of word-of-mouth dissemination of information about coping with and stopping such violence

Training for personnel dealing victims of abuse about privacy issues and the consequences of failing to respect the confidentiality of women dealing with this sensitive issue in communities with tight and overlapping familial ties Both short-term and long-term assistance and relapse prevention for abusive men, including:

Educational programs, including community-based education on the issue "Substance abuse programs".

Job training and job-search assistance "Mandatory participation in community-based education programs as part of "treatment and counselling for perpetrators, with immediate, predictable and reliable punitive consequences for repeat offences or failure to participate Long-term engagement with perpetrators by the corrections and parole" systems, including following release, to facilitate long-term change.

This should include: Development of Aboriginal community-based support programs for men a Development of sentencing circles and application of the principles of a restorative justice to foster culturally sensitive means of determining consequences for acts of violence and to develop a sense of individual and community responsibility for the issue of male violence against Aboriginal women.

MALE VIOLENCE AGAINST ABORIGINAL WOMEN

Incidence and Severity of Violence against Women in Aboriginal Communities Respondents identified intimate partner violence as a major problem facing Aboriginal women. Focus group participants described abuse as verbal and physical, sometimes having severe emotional and physical effects and sometimes causing death. First responders typically deal with multiple acts of violence in any given month, with estimates ranging from a few to more than 300, depending on the size of the community.

Several women made a point of saying that violence can go both ways. Some participants see violence against women as having dissipated somewhat in recent years. This decrease may be reflective of gradually shifting attitudes about the acceptability of such abuse. Other participants suggest that, while abuse continues, abusers may now take greater care to conceal it. The Victims and the Perpetrators: Common Characteristics First responders point to a few factors that are often shared by women victims of intimate partner violence.

Many come from violent homes and low self-esteem is thought to be a common characteristic of these women. Many have substance abuse histories, although substance abuse may be more the result of the violence than a preceding factor. Foetal alcohol syndrome among women victims of violence was also mentioned. Low education levels, poverty and being of a young age are also thought to characterize women victims – although first responders are also quick to point out that there are many exceptions. Others said that victims include women from all levels of education and income and all ages.

First responders also identified many of these characteristics for male perpetrators. Substance abuse problems, in particular, are almost universally considered to be a characteristic of abusive men. A domineering attitude toward women is also common. Finally, a lack of self-esteem (seen to stem from the loss of traditional roles and identity, and sometimes from direct or indirect experience with the residential school system) was mentioned as a characteristic of abusers. Of course male violence against women does exist outside Aboriginal communities.

However, a series of important characteristics that contribute to this type of violence exist in higher proportions within Aboriginal communities, including poverty and its correlates (limited education, substance abuse) and the "legacy impact" that residential schools have had on traditional gender roles and family structure across generations. Each of these adds a layer to the likelihood of Aboriginal women experiencing intimate partner abuse. Drivers for Male Violence against Aboriginal Women Most focus group participants felt that among the main drivers of (or factors that explain) male violence against Aboriginal women, alcohol and drug abuse rank very highly.

First responders said that, in the long term, substance abuse contributes to other problems such as the breakdown of the family and an increase in poverty, which in turn feed back into the cycle of violence. In those communities in which access to alcohol is controlled, occasional bingeing is more problematic. Poverty itself is also seen as a contributing factor. First responders explained that this is not only because of the inherent difficulty of living in poverty but also because of the complexities involved when men are unable - or in some cases unwilling - to provide for their families and take advantage of women who are able to hold down jobs.

Violence may also be nurtured, in part, by the economic insecurity of men and the lack of financial independence among women. Focus group participants explained that these factors can lead to disputes over finances and how to deal with poverty. They can also promote insecurity and low self-esteem on the part of the victim and abuser, as does the frustration resulting from the boredom and monotony associated with being unemployed in a small community. Participants echoed the perception of first responders that loss of the traditional way of life (and identity) is also a contributing factor.

This loss is seen to be exacerbated by the related erosion of the traditional role of the male within the community and household, and the legacy of residential schools. Both the abuser and the victim may have attended, or had parents who attended, residential schools where abuse took place. On the matter of residential schools, there seems to be some difference of opinion between first responders and women who took part in the focus groups. Some first responders point to the residential school experience as a contributing factor to intimate partner violence, but this was not generally considered to be a major problem, at least for current generations.

They felt that the residential school experience may, however, have contributed to the poor parenting skills of the victims and perpetrators of intimate partner violence. Focus group participants were much more likely to stress the impact of the residential school experience on the victims and perpetrators of male violence against women. They believe the residential school system has had ripple effects on family structure and parenting skills across decades, while first responders were less likely to directly link male violence against women with residential school experience.

A lack of parenting skills can also contribute to violence. Participants suggest that abusers may have had a violent upbringing by parents who were poorly equipped for the job; as a result these men grew up with a faulty understanding of the impact of violence on their own children. Participants think that violence is a learned behaviour: both the victim and/or the perpetrator, having grown up in violent homes, learned to associate violence with love. For them, violence may be seen as normal, perhaps even inevitable and unpreventable.

According to first responders, intergenerational experience with family violence goes hand-in-hand with poor parenting skills and poor relationship skills in contributing to male violence against Aboriginal women. Community indifference, reinforced by sexist attitudes about women's role in precipitating acts of violence, can be a further contributing factor. Some first responders think it is less a matter of sexist attitudes than simple resignation to what appears to be an irresolvable issue.

Some first responders were reluctant to ascribe significance to such contributing factors, suggesting instead that there is no excuse for the behaviour and that a stereotypical attitude of male dominance is at the root of the problem. So first responders and the women they assist may have different perceptions of the issue of male violence. In other words, the women and their communities may be less able to view the issue with clarity or resolve, having yet to fully come to believe that male violence against women is inexcusable.

THE IMPACT OF MALE VIOLENCE AGAINST ABORIGINAL WOMEN

When Violence Occurs Focus group participants said that, in the short term, women often turn to family and friends, particularly on reserves and in small Northern settlements where other resources may not exist. Other women may leave the community on their own, with the help of the police, family and friends, and/or a crisis centre worker. Temporary assistance and accommodation can be found at crisis centres and shelters in some communities, and these resources can provide a needed sense of safety, albeit only temporarily.

In the longer term, the women frequently return to the relationship and the home, following a "cooling off period" that is characterized by a temporary shift of power in the relationship (also known as a cyclical "honeymoon" period). According to focus group participants, there are many factors that may lead a woman back to an abusive relationship, including distance from extended family, children and friends; lack of financial resources or job and life skills to enable her to cope outside her home community; and, often, simply a profound sense of loneliness.

First responders point out that available supports and services are certainly not accessed every time women experience an act of violence against them. Instead the resources may be used as a last resort. Barriers to Reporting Violence Aboriginal women face a wide variety of obstacles – psychological, social and logistic – to reporting acts of violence against them and in seeking help and legal recourse. Focus group participants said that when violence occurs, it must be very severe – often nearly fatal – before the woman will report it to the police or leave the home. First responders agree that often by the time women call the police, they have suffered a series of incidents of escalating violence culminating in what is often a severe beating.

Reporting is compromised by distance from police and support resources, by what is often a poor relationship with the police, and by fear of reprisals. The fear of reprisal is a significant barrier for any woman considering reporting an act of violence to the authorities. Acts of reprisal, or the threat of them, may come from not only the abusive husband but also from members of his family; these relatives often exert pressure on the woman to leave the incident unreported and to return to the relationship.

First responders also expressed an appreciation of the concern about reprisals. Few participants were aware that laws and policies exist in most provinces to allow police to lay charges in cases of intimate partner violence without the consent of the victim. Moreover, many felt that the police were unsympathetic, ineffectual and sometimes cynical about the often-recurrent cycles of male violence against women and the apparent reluctance of some women to help themselves by reporting the matter, pressing charges or leaving.

Focus group participants suggest that police may tire of women who seem unwilling or unable to help themselves. There seems to be a kind of vicious circle at play here: these perceptions mean that many women have little faith in the efficacy of reporting an act of violence to the authorities because they have little faith in the authorities' ability or willingness to act effectively. Furthermore, allegiance to and dependence on an abusive partner sometimes leads women to attempt to protect the partner from the legal consequences that police can set in motion.

Among the first responders, police confirmed the cycle of cynicism that other participants described. They agree that, after a while, cynicism does grow among their members, feeding into the belief that there is little they can do in the long term to fix the problem. Women's expectation of police cynicism may itself contribute to a distrust of police, and to a reluctance to seek assistance or follow the recommendations of the attending law enforcement officer – the very behaviours that in turn increase police cynicism.

Another barrier to reporting acts of violence is the fear of losing children to child welfare authorities when violence in the home is disclosed. Focus group participants explained that one cannot assume that friends or members of the extended family will be able to take in women and their children who wish to flee an abusive man. Some first responders noted that, in the past, children were often removed from the home when police were called to respond to a violent incident, and although the approach has shifted in many communities – to keeping children with parents wherever possible – many still have this fear.

Although first responders now strive to preserve and support family units as much as possible, they note a common perception among Aboriginal families, more or less historically justified, that losing children to social services is a distinct possibility following a report of violence, and that getting the children back may be very difficult. Another significant barrier is, simply, shame.

Not surprisingly, participants reported that violence negatively impacts on the victim's self-esteem and sense of security. They also felt that victims often blame themselves and conceal the violence from others as best they can to avoid the stigma that is attached to being a victim of intimate partner abuse. Some participants said that a "code of silence" prevents many victims from disclosing abuse outside the family unit. Turning to alcohol or drugs as an escape is seen to be a common coping mechanism. Participants also described women's concern that their parenting is affected by the experience of violence.

Women may feel that they have nothing left to give to their children emotionally or physically – after dealing with violence. Some participants said that women feel a huge sense of failure, betrayal and hurt when the children side with the abuser against them. A few participants said that the sense of failure is often accompanied by feelings of hopelessness when patterns of male violence and abuse emerge in subsequent generations, reflected in the behaviour patterns of both victims and perpetrators.

According to first responders, the impact of intimate partner violence on women is primarily felt in their physical and emotional health. Respondents generally rate these as the most serious consequences of violence. For some, the consequences for emotional and mental health radiate into other areas of their lives, impacting the ability to function normally at work, or in their role as parent, or within the community in general. The impact on the woman's social relationships can also be quite serious.

Poverty Impacts

Participants talked about women being trapped by their sense that violence in a relationship is normal and may represent love. They are also trapped by their lack of knowledge about options and access to information and resources to deal with the problem. Participants living on reserve were especially likely to indicate a poor understanding of what "healthy" relationships are and especially unlikely to have had access to relevant information and resources. Fear of the unknown can keep women from seeking help, as can fear of losing a home and income.

Some first responders suggest that the financial impact of violence can actually be less of an issue than it might at first appear, given the higher employment levels among Aboriginal women and the fact that, at least for First Nations women, housing can sometimes be provided by the Band. Nonetheless, most acknowledge that the potential financial consequences certainly play a part in determining Aboriginal women's reactions to male violence. This is of particular concern if the woman does not reside in her own community.

The Impact on Family Members

There is a clear sense that the impact of inter-parental violence on children is a serious consequence of such situations. In the short term, their school performance may fall and substance abuse can become an issue. Children are scared and scarred by the violence, and eventually violence becomes a behaviour that they themselves learn. This may be the most feared impact – that of children replicating the behaviours they have observed. One woman spoke of her dismay at seeing her child and the neighbourhood children playing "grown-ups" by pretending to stagger around drunk.

For first responders, the impact on the children is particularly egregious. In addition to the direct short-term impact on emotional and physical health, in the long-term, the future parenting and relationships skills of children are at stake. Another consequence of the conflicts that stem from violence is tension between parents and children. Children's loyalties may be torn between their mother and father, and being taken from the family home to a shelter can lead them to inadvertently re-victimize the woman by blaming her for the situation. The effects on other family members can also be serious.

They may have to take in or financially support victims of violence and their children. The safety of extended family members may be compromised. Other family members, friends and even neighbours may be drawn into the conflict and seek to punish or protect the abuser. Some relationships with friends and extended family members come to be characterized by frustration when the victim refuses help. First responders agree that the consequences are serious for the family unit as a whole. The breakdown in expectations and roles, the lack of trust and the soaring resentment involved in family violence can negatively affect generations of a family.

First responders also point to the complexity of family relationships in small communities, where abusers and victims are well known to all, and extended families can be drawn into conflicts. Privacy concerns are fundamental, with a general sense that in such small inter-related communities everyone knows everyone else's business. The Impact on the Perpetrator When asked about the male perpetrator, participants expressed the view that they had often been victims of violence themselves and that it was typically a learned behaviour.

Some felt that, in the short term, the perpetrator often felt remorseful about the violence. Focus group participants see police as reluctant to deal with or to remove the man from the scene or to charge him with an offence. Occasionally participants mentioned racist attitudes among police, including some Aboriginal officers. Some even speak of friendship and familial ties between police and abusers that compromise the objectivity with which victims are treated. In response to a question about what usually happens to the abuser, first responders mentioned a variety of legal proceedings that can take place as a result of a victim reporting the violence.

Legal sanctions can range from a night in jail to a sentence of several months or more, depending on the severity of the incident. In some communities, alternative treatment-based programs are an option for those who plead guilty. However, it is recognized that reporting is much less frequent than the violence itself and that many offences go unpunished. Treatment programs and jail terms are viewed by many as insufficiently punitive to discourage future violence, even if the offender is genuinely remorseful at the time. Logistically, imposing consequences on the man can be very difficult in some communities, particularly in more isolated areas.

For fly-in communities in the North, residents' access to the criminal justice system is often remote and infrequent. According to first responders, this can discourage victims from pursuing charges against the perpetrators because of the difficulty of physically reaching the courts and the length of time between the incident and any trial that ensues. In many cases, women victims of violence and their abusers return to the same home long before any legal repercussions are felt. Furthermore, the geographical obstacles to women obtaining legal representation can inflate the fear of reporting acts of violence and of losing custody of children.

That is, it may take exponentially longer for a woman in such an isolated community to find a lawyer to help press charges or to regain custody after an incident. On reserve, especially the smaller reserves, as well as in isolated Northern settlement communities, enforcement of restraining and other protective orders becomes very difficult. The perpetrator is often allowed to stay in the home while the women and children are forced to leave. Furthermore, the legal consequences are seen as insufficient and not in keeping with the severity or impact of the crime. This perception is likely derived from personal experience, word-of-mouth or an inadequate understanding of existing abuse related laws and legislation.

Participants also suggested that victims of violence, or their families and friends, occasionally resort to vigilante justice, and that this might be more effective than the legal consequences. Most first responders agree that it is usually the victim who moves out of the family home when violence occurs. Nonetheless, there are at least some communities in which the perpetrator is encouraged to leave, particularly when legal proceedings are instigated. Within the larger community, however, participants said that there is little responsibility or accountability assigned to the perpetrator. People are aware of the violence but "tend to their own business."

Among first responders, there was a clear view that the community sanctioned the violence to some extent. First responders suggest that in many Aboriginal communities, male violence against women is seen by some as an unpleasant but inevitable aspect of the relationship between a man and a woman.

Some stated that even Band Council leaders are not universally innocent. In terms of community sanctions, there has been little for the abuser to fear. However, first responders also point to encouraging signs that attitudes are shifting within their communities. Violence against women is gradually becoming less socially acceptable, and community leaders are beginning to favour educational initiatives that spread this message. Nonetheless, currently, little stigma is attached to the man as an abuser.

For Victims and Their Children Knowledge of support services and resources was lower among women who live on reserve, and there was a sense that there was not a wealth of available resources (with the exception of Val-d'Or). Nonetheless, participants were able to list a variety of resources for women victims of intimate partner violence. A number of participants had personal experience with these resources and some spoke approvingly of the way they were treated and the support and security they were given.

The most commonly cited resources were: transition houses, women's shelters or crisis centres (municipal, non-profit or associated with a church); and crisis hotlines. Services provided by such facilities include: temporary accommodation and assistance with longer-term housing; financial assistance; counselling services for victims and children; life skills courses; security and safety; drug and alcohol treatment and counselling (although there was uncertainty about the adequacy and allocation of these services); exposure to and companionship with other victims; and transportation. Some participants decried what they feel is a tendency to refer them from program to program without any longer-term solution.

First responders also described some resources specifically designed to deal with intimate partner abuse, such as special courts that deal only with incidents of family or intimate partner violence. Programs that work hand-in-hand with such courts often allow perpetrators to receive help prior to sentencing. In some places, a special Aboriginal constable has been able to develop a good relationship with the community over time. This relationship allows for a higher level of comfort in dealing with the police. Most first responders thought that these services were accessed by women victims of male violence much of the time, when they actually choose to seek help or report the incident.

However, the frequency with which women choose not to report acts of violence means that these services are probably underutilized in relation to the actual incidence. On the other hand, it is important to note that the demands on these services are often at or over capacity. Should the many unreported incidents and unmet needs be reported, they could further overwhelm existing resources. For the Perpetrator Knowledge of resources for abusive men was low among focus group participants.

Many felt that the men are reluctant to seek help, for reasons that include: a low sense of accountability or responsibility for acts of violence; a need to be seen to control the family; implications for the family and his personal reputation; expected financial impact; concern for privacy; inability to express personal thoughts and feelings with others; distance from resources; and lack of resources, particularly outside the criminal justice system. Focus group participants felt that men would change their abusive behaviour patterns only if the consequences of their acts were severe (e.g., losing the family or receiving criminal charges and imprisonment). For those men who do wish to change, participants recommended accessing support groups, education and counselling services.

However, participants suspect that men only agree to participate in these programs when faced with a court order, not because of a sincere desire to change. Information on Support Resources Participants said that the main sources of information on support resources are: posters in health facilities or elsewhere in the community; "word-of-mouth"; the telephone book; and brochures or pamphlets. As mentioned above, reference to web-based resources was almost non-existent. First responders said that a primary channel for information should be the schools. Stopping the inter-generational cycle of violence by educating children at a young age that violence against women is not acceptable is seen to be crucial.

Funding and Management of Resources for Aboriginal Women Knowledge was mixed as to how the resources for victims of violence are managed. Many participants were aware that governments help fund the support services, although some expressed skepticism about government commitment to women's needs. Fewer understood that charities and fundraising also play a role. Although it is important that Aboriginal people are involved in the creation and provision of services and resources to victims, participants also see professional expertise, empathy and direct personal experience as significant in terms of funding and management of resources.

Views on the management of resources were varied. Some focus group participants perceive a lack of transparency and accountability and suspect there may be problems of favouritism or corruption. Clearly, community leaders do not always enjoy the whole-hearted trust of all members of the community. Many participants believe that neutral, uninterested individuals should have control over managing resources. Few First Nations participants favoured placing funds directly into the hands of the Band Council, suggesting instead that a "third party" should administer the funds. Gaps and Problems in Resources Focus group participants believe there is a lack of resources in their communities.

Many victims feel cut off or abandoned by their community, and a sense of loneliness resulting from leaving to seek help may drive them to return to the abusive situation. Participants mentioned the need for nearby accommodation for their children while the mothers are receiving counselling or other treatment off reserve. Support services may only provide short-term accommodation, counselling and security, leaving women vulnerable in terms of ongoing support and physical safety. In some communities, services are offered only on a 9:00-5:00 basis or are located in a remote area and may therefore be inaccessible at the time abuse occurs. In addition, the police (RCMP) may be hours away.

Often they are also associated with racism; with favouring the perpetrator over the victim; and with simply not caring. In some communities as well, available resources provide little follow-up or after-care, leaving victims without long-term support or an ongoing guarantee of safety. (Other focus group participants did note, however, that some centres provide a tracking service for several months to ensure that women are financially stable and that their children are all right.) In some communities, available resources have limited admittance quotas. Focus group participants have found that women are occasionally turned away without receiving assistance. As well, available resources often do not employ Aboriginal staff.

Focus group participants suggest that non-native staff leave them feeling less comfortable than if they were able to deal with Aboriginal counsellors and social workers. This discomfort is caused by cultural and linguistic differences as well as a sense of displacement that accompanies their moving to an urban community. First responders also acknowledge there is often a lack of Aboriginal staff, particularly among police officers, and this can be discouraging for Aboriginal women seeking help for this sensitive matter.

They also note, however, that hiring Aboriginal staff in small communities may mean that the victims would be related to the staff, thereby compromising client privacy. Some first responders point to the culture shock that some Aboriginal women experience when they leave their home community to seek help. This is often most acute for Inuit women from isolated communities in the North. Crisis centre and counselling service staff may also include women who do not have first-hand experience with male violence.

Participants have perceived judgement and a lack of sympathy among some women staff of crisis and counselling services. Some participants, on the other hand, praise the available resources that do employ culturally sensitive women who have themselves experienced male violence. In addition, childcare and transportation services may be sporadically available or unreliable, so women who leave reserves or small rural communities to arrive on their own in the city may be at an increased risk, especially if they are hitchhiking or adjusting to life on the street. Among focus group participants from Prince George, this is considered to be a particularly important issue, given that region's proximity to the "Highway of Tears."

First responders cite a similar variety of barriers to women accessing the resources available to them. They also note that a lack of staff training can be a barrier for some potential clients who perceive inexperience at some service agencies. According to participants, Band and community leaders are not adequately engaged in the issue of family violence generally. Lack of trust – in both service providers and other members of the community – is a major obstacle to women reporting and acting on abuse. First responders working with First Nations women living on reserve also see the lack of involvement in dealing with the issue by the Band leaders and the rest of the community as problematic.

The lack of engagement can lead women to believe that their community is not interested in the problem. However, others point to encouraging signs that the tide is turning, with Band leaders and community members becoming more aware that male violence against women is unacceptable.

Publicity and Awareness

Many communities have already launched a variety of educational and awareness raising efforts to encourage women to report violence. Focus group participants suggested several methods by which awareness of resources can be increased and violence against women can be discouraged; for example, publicizing names of offenders, educating children about all forms of family violence, expanding available resources and changing funding allocations.

Education

Among focus group participants, education is a particularly preferred means of interrupting the cycle of violence. It can involve teaching adults to respect each other within relationships, and training children to understand that violence is unacceptable. Providing opportunities for teenagers to socialize in a sober environment is also seen as potentially very helpful. Most first responders also strongly support the call for better education about how to deal with this issue, both for the women victims of male violence and for the next generation.

Many suggest educational initiatives in the schools that are attended by the children of women at risk, in order to prevent the development of a new generation of abusers and abused. Others think it is really an issue of community education, of teaching Aboriginal communities to be self-sufficient and to treat each other honourably.

Specialized Workshops and Programs

According to first responders, a variety of initiatives are in place to encourage reporting and prevent violence against Aboriginal women. Some victim services centres conduct workshops to raise awareness and teach Aboriginal women how to deal with and prevent violence against them. Others have created special programs and courts to deal with violence against women.

Cultural Sensitivity Training

According to focus group participants, existing resources, such as crisis centres, should be expanded to reflect more sensitivity to Aboriginal women.

Gender Balance in Community Influence

Focus group participants also suggest that more opportunities should be provided for women to hold positions of influence within the community. For instance, men dominate First Nations Band Councils, and participants think that allowing First Nations women to participate in Band and community decision-making would help to prevent abuse.

Criminal Justice Consequences

Some focus group participants raised the possibility of more punitive criminal justice measures. Enforcing sentences and "peace bonds" is seen to be particularly important; some women point out that men are frequently able to dismiss the seriousness of the problem because the criminal justice consequences are light.

A lack of consensus exists among first responders on the criminal justice aspect of this issue. Some suggest that harsher punishment from the courts is needed, but others believe that a more restorative and less punitive approach is called for. Sentencing circles, as a method of engaging the community and discussing the many issues, consequences and grievances related to interpersonal abuse, are considered by some to represent a particularly fruitful approach.

Funding

Women who fear losing shelter and the financial ability to care for their children are less likely to report abuse.

Providing funding for women to purchase goods and services and pay for housing is thought to be a particularly useful way to encourage them to report and act on incidents of violence. In addition to the logistical benefits of such funding, the psychological impact of knowing such a safety net exists would be extremely helpful.

First responders strongly suggest that insufficient financial resources constitute a significant part of perpetuating the problem. They call for increased numbers of crisis centres and services, and for having the justice system more closely focused on the problem. Ultimately, however, the consensus rests on the need to dramatically increase educational programs, both in communities and in schools, as the key to resolving the problem of male violence against Aboriginal women.

The findings of this study point to several challenges in providing assistance to both the Aboriginal women who experience intimate partner violence and the perpetrators of this violence. They include the extensive prevalence and severity of violence in the community, as well as the long-term effects on children in terms of learned behaviour. Providing explicit information and educational initiatives for all family members, not just parents and children, is essential to ending male violence against Aboriginal women.

These educational initiatives should address the matter of "what a healthy relationship looks and feels like." Many victims and perpetrators of violence lack a basic understanding of what constitutes a healthy or loving relationship. Within the focus groups, women who had "turned their lives around" indicated that information they had received about how a healthy relationship works helped them understand how to break away from the cycle of violence. Clearly, it is necessary to introduce and support such norms, not just for individuals who are experiencing intimate partner violence, but for the entire community.

An approach that raises awareness among members of the whole community - including victims, perpetrators and community leaders, as well as the general public - is recommended for dealing comprehensively with violence against women in the long term. In particular, participants felt that a "culture of victimization" should not be treated as an excuse within Aboriginal communities - neither for committing abuse nor for accepting it as normal. Instead, it is believed that an increased sense of community and individual responsibility for the safety and security of Aboriginal women should be fostered.

However, even when information is available to women suffering in an abusive relationship, it can take time and repeated exposure for this information to be absorbed and for women to act on it. In many cases it takes an accumulation of violent incidents to finally push a woman to overcome the barriers to seeking help. For other women, evidence of the effects on children can be an important impetus to their seeking help. Because children are often adversely affected by male violence against women, they represent a key audience for educational materials.

Trust is an especially important issue within Aboriginal communities. It takes time to develop trust, but the process can be facilitated in a crisis situation by a friendly and familiar Aboriginal face. In the opinion of some respondents, it can be further enhanced by knowledge that the helping professional has had personal experience with violence. Nonetheless, focus group participants expressed mixed views about the need to have Aboriginal staff managing crisis facilities.

Women who do not live on reserve are more likely to give priority to expertise and personal experience. By contrast, women who live on reserve tend to think that an experienced Aboriginal woman would be better equipped to deal with Aboriginal women - and be more trustworthy. It was the consensus of all respondents that funding, tools and resources are required to provide the means and the opportunity for women to look beyond the cycle of violence and rebuild their lives.

Aboriginal women believe that financial help, access to affordable housing and transportation to enable them to access services that provide education and assistance, counselling and life skills education, are the ideal means by which to approach this problem. While community-based resources may be optimal, they may not be realistic or sustainable in smaller communities. In those communities, reliable, convenient and affordable transportation to a nearby safe shelter that offers accommodation for their children is of prime importance.

The inadequacy of the criminal justice response is also a key area seen to be in need of reform, especially with regard to what is felt to be the current leniency of sentencing and insufficient engagement with the issue by the correctional and parole systems. At this point in time, given the rare ownership of computers within Aboriginal communities, web-based resources are not effective forms of information. Rather, crisis phone lines, posters in community centres and schools, brochures and direct mail were suggested as effective means of providing information about violence to women and their partners.

5

Militarization, Violence, Development and Women

Indigenous women from various parts of Asia gathered in Baguio city, the Philippines, on 5-8 March 2004 for the second Asian Indigenous Women's Conference (AIWC). This gathering was held 11 years after the first AIWC. About a hundred people, including observers, from 13 countries participated. There were no Ainu women participants. The author participated on behalf of an Ainu woman. The conference was organized by the Asian Indigenous Women's Network and Tebtebba, and hosted by INNABUYOG-CWERC (Cordillera Women's Education and Resource Center).

DEVELOPMENT, MILITARIZATION, AND ANTI-"TERRORISM"

A major issue in the conference was the link between globalization and development and its effect on indigenous women in Asia. In the Cordillera (Philippines), indigenous vegetable growers have been badly hit by the influx of cheap vegetables from China and other countries. A participant from Yunnan, China reported that the policy of the Chinese government forces indigenous farmers to produce cash crops. But only a handful succeeded in it. Many are increasingly being pressured to abandon their communities and migrate to cities in order to survive.

With the entry of "suicide seeds" or other genetically engineered seeds of high yielding varieties marketed by transnational corporations, indigenous women farmers are now losing the role of keeper of indigenous seeds. They now have to buy seeds, which is an added drain on their already limited cash. These cases show a common pattern of the market economy penetrating indigenous communities resulting in the loss of subsistence economy and more dependence on cash income. This situation leads to greater economic gap between rich and poor within the community and the collapse of mutually beneficial traditional social system. In this process, distinct cultures undergo significant transformation.

This process greatly affects women. It was reported that in many parts of Asia, indigenous women used to have an important role in resource management and production in the traditional economy. However, as the market economy penetrates the communities and women's roles are no longer valued, their status in the community declines. Large-scale infrastructure projects such as dams are undertaken in indigenous peoples' lands without their consent. In the Philippines, most of the large-scale dams have been built or planned in indigenous peoples' territories. In India, it is reported that 40 to 50 percent of those who were displaced by development projects are indigenous peoples.

The Doyang Hydro Electricity Project in Nagaland, India is a case in point. The dam was built on Doyang River in 1983 and 30,000 indigenous people were affected. They (the Nagas) lost their land and traditional ways of living which depended on the forest and wetland resources. They became wage laborers, while their community systems and social fabric were affected. A second phase of the project is proposed and they fear that the destruction of the indigenous communities will continue. Development in the form of tourism transforms indigenous peoples' lands into national parks and protected areas. Many of these projects have military support to suppress people's opposition. The most obvious cases can be seen in Burma.

Militarization of indigenous peoples' territories is one of the common issues facing indigenous peoples in Asia. Military power is used not only to violently suppress indigenous movements for self-determination and autonomy (such as in Nagaland), but also to promote State-sponsored or private transnational corporation development projects. Militarization deprives indigenous peoples of freedom of movement, destroys their environment and gives rise to sexual violence against women and girls. Another serious issue related to militarization is the increasing labeling of legitimate indigenous movements as "terrorists" in the "war on terror" after 11 September 2001.

In the Philippines, after the US government added the Communist Party of the Philippines and its military wing New People's Army (NPA) to its Foreign Terrorist Organizations list, the Philippine government undertook military offensives against the NPA and the indigenous communities suspected of supporting it. In India, many indigenous peoples organizations fighting for their rights to land and resources have been labeled as "terrorist" organizations under the Prevention of Terrorism Act enacted after 11 September 2001. The author reported on the situation and concerns of Ainu women, particularly the Ainu Communal Property Case.

This case, filed in 1999, questions how the Ainu communal property has been managed under an 1899 law on the Ainu people. There is a suspicion of misuse of the communal property by the Governor of Hokkaido who is given the responsibility to manage it. The litigation is considered as one of the efforts towards restoring Ainu's right to their land and resources. It became very clear in the conference that globalization, development and militarization go hand in hand to hinder indigenous peoples from achieving self-determination and full enjoyment of their legitimate rights.

TRADITION AND CULTURAL DEVELOPMENT

The conference also took up a wide range of other issues including women's rights, reproductive rights/health, violence against women, and women are organizing. The participants reported that under customary practices women usually play a central role in preserving the land and forest resources and thus their status in society is relatively high. Indigenous customary laws and practices worked favorably for women in many cases. In the Cordillera, violence against women used to be a communal concern and various interventions by the community were useful in preventing violence or persuading the men from resorting to violence.

With the deepening westernization of the society, however, violence against women became private matter and no longer subject to communal intervention. Also, indigenous women used to have control over forest resources which helped guarantee their relatively independent and higher status in the community. Due mainly to the imposition of the modern land registry and forest management systems, women have lost this important role. These examples suggest that it is desirable to maintain, rather than dismantle, the traditional economy and value systems, and the customary laws and practices in order to keep the women's status high and protect their dignity.

On the other hand, there were reports about traditional practices that women want abolished. In some indigenous societies, the "bride price" system in marriage is now functioning as if "women are being bought." A Maing participant from Thailand said that after marriage she was forced to pay back through her labor the cost of her huge wedding ceremony. Male child preference is strong in some ethnic groups, such as the Hmong in Thailand, and in the Chittagong Hill Tracts of Bangladesh. In the Chittagong Hill Tracts, women are pressured to give birth to two or more male children. If they fail, the husband divorces his wife and/ or takes another wife.

In sum, the destruction of traditional indigenous systems and the shift to modern values and legal systems often lower women's status in society and lead to violation of their rights. On the other hand, changing certain traditional laws and practices that work against the interests of women, should not mean that other systems and cultural aspects that the women themselves want to preserve should also be destroyed. The participants expressed pride in transmitting their distinct culture and values to future generations. To label them as "victims of tradition" is wrong.

A Nepali participant explained that when a marriage system that allows a woman to marry all the brothers of one family in an ethnic community in Nepal was subjected to Western feminist criticism, the women in the community strongly felt shame and lost confidence in themselves. Women without self-confidence "will not become agents of change in the social institutions they want to abolish," she pointed out.

EMPOWERING INDIGENOUS WOMEN

In response to the need to protect and/or recover the traditional important role of indigenous women, the second AIWC recommended to the indigenous people's organizations and movements the following:

Empowerment of Indigenous Women for Leadership:

Empower indigenous women to exercise our life skills in health, education and decision-making and to play our important roles in our families, communities and the indigenous peoples' movement.

Carry out gender-sensitivity programmes within indigenous organisations and communities.

Strengthen indigenous women's participation in all aspects of leadership and governance. Special meetings, leadership training as well as other training courses and exposure programmes should be organised.

In terms of participation, a quota for women should be allocated, and when projects or meetings are going on, nursery facilities should be provided.

Women will be encouraged to take up decision-making positions, after gaining the necessary confidence.

The role and perception of women should not follow stereotypes and women who are qualified and experienced should be selected as leaders.

Leadership by indigenous women will have an impact on the way the indigenous people's organizations and movements operate. It will also supplement the ongoing effort to establish indigenous women's organizations in many countries in the region.

FUTURE NETWORKING IN ASIA

In the past 11 years, organizing of indigenous women in Asia has considerably advanced. In Indonesia, indigenous women's network called Aliansi Perempuan Adat Nusantara, or Indigenous Women Alliance of the Archipelago (APAN) was created in 2000. In Bangladesh, 11 indigenous women's organizations participated in Hill Tracts NGO Forum that was established in 2000. In Nepal, 8 indigenous women's organizations are organized and 9 more are planned. At the sub-regional level, South Asian Indigenous Women's Network was established in 2003. The conference decided to activate sub-regional and regional networking of indigenous women in Asia. It successfully ended by adopting the Baguio Declaration.

If they are to survive, there are two specific challenges that indigenous peoples must overcome: the protection of their cultural identity and the preservation of their relationship with the land. Both of these are jeopardized when indigenous territories come under military attack, whether by state or non-state armed forces.

The militarization of indigenous territories tears at the social fabric of the community at large, divides families and has particularly devastating effects on women. It is disturbing that some indigenous groups´ numbers have been so reduced that they are at risk of disappearing altogether.

UN Security Council Resolution 1325 acknowledges that in armed conflict situations, most victims are civilians and not combatants. Among those civilians, women and children account for the vast majority of those badly affected. In fact, women and children constitute nearly 80% if the world's millions of refugees and internally displaced persons. In Asia, the militarization of indigenous territories has taken on new shapes and dimensions over the past decades.

Not only are a growing number of indigenous communities living in areas affected by armed conflict - such as the case of several states in Burma and in North-East India as well as in West Papua, Mindanao, Tibet, Kashmir and the Chittagong Hill Tracts - but many indigenous territories are also affected by military troops that have been deployed to protect the implementation of large-scale development projects. Militarization is closely linked to "development aggression." As many governments push for their own development plans and projects, they neglect to obtain the Free, Prior and Informed Consent of the communities affected, and uses militarization to intimidate or eliminate resistance from indigenous communities.

The United States' "war on terrorism" has been used by many national governments to justify militarization or the increase of military operations. Under the label of terrorism, human rights can be easily curtailed. Such human rights violations can occur not only on the ground due to the presence of militarization, but they also occur at the policy level where financial allocation for the so-called war on terrorism has drastically increased in recent years, thus having an impact on the budgets of other government priorities. At the regional level, the Association of South East Asian Nations (ASEAN) adopted a Convention on Counter-Terrorism at its 12th Summit in January 2007.

Human rights violations under militarization can be carried out by State or non-State actors. State actors can take the form of a military regime (like in Burma) or the soldiers of a democratic state's armed forces deployed or based in conflict areas. Governments sometimes use trained paramilitary groups or militias. Non-State actors can include armed groups (insurgency, pro-independence, revolutionary, commandos, etc.) fighting the national government or they may be at war with other armed groups. Private corporations in indigenous territories often hire and arm their own security forces.

IMPACTS OF MILITARIZATION ON INDIGENOUS WOMEN

The militarization of indigenous lands affects women in disproportionate or different ways from men. In the past decade some progress has been made in documenting and publicizing sexual violence against women in conflict zones, which has been described as the extension of battlefields onto women's bodies. Even when human rights violations affect the whole community, the impact on indigenous women is different from the impact on men. Violence against indigenous women can take several forms, which can lead to the violation of their civil, political, economic, social and cultural rights, having a devastating impact on their physical, psychological and spiritual integrity as well as on their communities.

RAPE AND SEXUAL VIOLENCE

Armed groups regularly employ strategies that target women, notably sexual violence. Rape continues to be used as a weapon of war by armed forces. Numerous reports document the widespread and systematic use of rape by Burmese military rulers against indigenous women from Burma. Young girls and elderly women are not spared. The experiences of indigenous women in Vietnam, Laos and Cambodia in the 1960s and earlier resonate in the present day experiences of indigenous women in Bangladesh, Burma, Indonesia and the Philippines who have been subjected to harassment, torture, rape, humiliation, forced prostitution, pregnancies as a result of rape, and compulsory servitude.

It is not uncommon for women to be raped in view of the community or in front of their families. When women survive these types of attacks, they may be further victimized by domestic violence or their husbands may divorce them in accordance with cultural norms. Social stigma often results, particularly if a pregnancy occurs. Members of armed groups often coerce young women into becoming their "girlfriends" in order to obtain information about the community or to involve them in the conflict by having them act as messengers or even recruiting them into their forces.

Sometimes, under pressure from insecurity and poverty, indigenous women become involved with military personnel as a way of seeking security for themselves or their families. However, in most cases the military personnel are transferred to other locations and the woman is abandoned. This situation has become so common that it prompted the participants of the second Asian Indigenous Women's Network (AIWN) Congress to consider this emerging phenomenon as another way in which indigenous women are dishonored and humiliated.

OCCUPATION OF TERRITORIES

Communities with ongoing contact with armed groups almost inevitably have increased problems with drugs, voluntary or forced prostitution, alcoholism, domestic violence and other problems that have long-lasting effects in the community. Militarization in these communities often curtails economic activities, the entry of food supplies and basic social services as well as disrupts children's education.

In Bangladesh, Jumma women cannot take their products to the market, for fear of abuse and violations. Men take over the sale of products and as a consequence, indigenous women's freedom of mobility is impaired and they lose control of their own incomes. In other cases, they have nothing to sell, as the forests are completely under the control of the military while the agricultural lands are under the control of the Bengali settlers, or in the case of Burma, women are prevented from going to their fields.

DISPLACEMENT

Most of the time the militarization of indigenous territories forces entire communities to flee for their safety. Fleeing the militarized areas does not, however, necessarily provide security for women; in fact it often makes them more vulnerable to trafficking, prostitution, rape or other types of physical abuses. The primary role of women in many indigenous communities is to provide food and water for their families.

When their communities are displaced, they find themselves without food, shelter or protection, forced to abandon not only their homes, their crops and belongings but also places of spiritual significance. This displacement can be devastating for indigenous women in particular, who are left feeling impotent and unable to provide for their families. Internally displaced persons (IDPs) are also vulnerable to a myriad of other issues such as the uncertainty of livelihood, family disintegration, the loss of customs and traditions, and unhealthy living conditions.

IDPs may move temporarily to a nearby community, hide in the forest for years, and attempt to re-establish their community in another location migrate to cities or eventually leave for neighbouring countries. When people migrate to urban centres, they often lose contact with other community members and begin to lose their traditional practices. It is not uncommon for women to migrate alone with their children and then they are forced to find a way of making a living in an environment that is foreign to them and lacks their traditional support system.

LOSS OF IDENTITY

One of the significant impacts of displacement on indigenous women is the loss of identity they experience. Whether they flee to relocation sites, refugee camps or other areas outside of their traditional territories, women lose their social, cultural and spiritual sites and cannot fulfill their traditional roles in the community.

Communities begin to disintegrate, and traditional ceremonies and customary activities cannot be performed. When this occurs, how can indigenous women maintain their identity, and transmit their culture to the next generation, especially to young girls?

Key recommendations from the International Conference on Conflict Resolution, Peace building, Sustainable Development and Indigenous Peoples, organized by the Tebtebba Foundation (Indigenous Peoples' International Centre for Policy Research and Education) in December 2000 include:

The need to create awareness among indigenous peoples and the public at large on the important role played by indigenous women in conflict resolution and peace building, and the need to document their efforts in different parts of the world;

The promotion of effective participation of women at all levels and stages of peacemaking processes;

The encouragement and support (including training, technical and financial assistance) for women to build capacity and to seek decision-making positions, and the need to build mechanisms which will enable women to have access to such positions whether in the traditional or modern governance systems;

The forging of networks and linkages with other women's organizations and networks at all levels in their respective region and internationally; and

The urgent need for international agencies, NGOs, indigenous peoples and the donor community to include gender in their analysis of conflict and peace building processes and in the assessments done on the economic, social, political and cultural situation pre- and post-conflict.

PORTRAIT OF INDIGENOUS WOMEN IN INDONESIA

The Indonesian Archipelago hosts more than 1000 different ethnic and sub-ethnic groups, and as many languages. Such diversity means that it is a challenge to have a clear picture of the situation of indigenous peoples in general, more so to get a true overview of the situation of indigenous women in Indonesia. This is particularly true because Indonesian women are invisible in Indonesian statistics. They are not acknowledged in any government statistics related to health, justice, education, poverty or violence. However, despite this diversity, or perhaps because of it, indigenous women in Indonesia share one common element: they have to face a double marginalization: as indigenous peoples and as women.

The first factor of this marginalization is due to the fact that indigenous women are affected by the issues that touch indigenous peoples. In Indonesia this means that indigenous peoples are limited by government policies that do not acknowledge their rights to their traditional lands and natural resources. As a result of each problem affecting indigenous peoples, indigenous women face issues which affect their everyday lives.

For example, if an indigenous community is displaced because their land has been granted by the government to a logging or plantation company, it is the women who have to walk longer distances to fetch water, find food and medicinal plants.

The second factor of this marginalization is that in general, as women, they do not have access to decision-making at any level, including within their own communities and in many cases within their own homes. Important decisions that influence the future direction of the community and family are done without involving women. At the community level, according to most hukum adat (customary law), the division of roles and labour of men and women in indigenous communities are quite clear.

The role of women is linked to productive and reproductive work (e.g. finding water, working in the gardens and rice fields, giving birth and taking care of the family), while men hold more dominant roles in the community, such as political positions at all levels (for example in adat institutions, farmers groups, youth associations or others). In some indigenous communities, however, important roles and positions in decision making and leadership are held by women. This is the case in the Dayak Sikung community in West Kalimantan, the Toro Community in Central Sulawesi and the Toraja Community in South Sulawesi.

COMMON ISSUES

Indigenous women in Indonesia face several common issues such as the disregard for their basic human rights, linked with their civil, political, economic, social and cultural rights. Indigenous women are denied access to decision-making processes which has direct impacts on their interests. This often results in problems related to health and education, as well as violence.

For indigenous women, the main causes of their health problems are a shortage of health services, a lack of information about family planning and contraception as well as the disappearance of natural medicines because of the destruction of their environment and natural resources.

The most significant health problem is related to the reproduction and the maternal mortality rate. According to the United Nations Children's Fund (UNICEF), for every 1000 births, four women die. In Papua more than 10 indigenous women die for every 1000 births. Indigenous women face increasing violence because of the implementation of private companies which employ militias and trans-migrant workers, facilitate the sale of alcohol and increase prostitution in the areas where they operate.

Moreover, women from indigenous communities whose lands and natural resources have been taken away have very few other options other than to work abroad or on other islands as transmigrant workers. Transmigration is also an issue that increases violence against indigenous women, as there are many cases of murder, sexual harassment, rape, and disappearances of indigenous women who have become trans-migrant workers.

THE INDONESIAN LEGAL SYSTEM AND INDIGENOUS WOMEN

Despite the fact that Article 28I (2) of the Indonesian Constitution states that every person has the right to be free from any discrimination on any grounds and the fact that

Indonesia has ratified CEDAW, as well as the International Covenant on Civil and Political Rights and the International Covenant on Economic, Social and Cultural Rights, both of which contain non-discrimination and gender equity clauses, Indonesia still has some national laws that discriminate against indigenous women. The following are just two examples:

Marriage Act (No. 1, 1974)

The Marriage Act rigidly divides roles between men and women: "The husband is the head of the household and the wife is the housewife", (Article 31(3)). For indigenous women, this article legitimates the domination of men in the family and in the community. It also means that it is even more difficult for indigenous women to be recognized as legitimate leaders in Indonesian Law, even if they are recognized in some hukum adat. This Act restricts women's activities to the household and keeps them far from decision-making.

Religion

Despite the fact that the 1945 Indonesian Constitution states in Article 29(2) that "The State guarantees all persons the freedom of worship, each according to his/her own religion or belief", a Religious Ministry Instruction (no. 4, 1978) ignores this and recognizes only the five major religions of Islam, Christianity, Catholicism, Buddhism and Hinduism, ignoring the existence of indigenous beliefs. This makes it technically illegal for indigenous peoples to perpetuate their traditional culture, customs and beliefs.

In March 1999, more than 250 indigenous representatives from all over the Indonesian Archipelago met in Jakarta to share experiences and discuss their concerns at the First Congress of Indigenous Peoples of the Archipelago. AMAN (Aliansi Masyarakat Adat Nusantara – The Indigenous Peoples' Alliance of the Archipelago), was created as a result of this Congress. AMAN is an independent civil society organization that acts as a forum for the indigenous peoples of Indonesia. It is the only national indigenous organization that also constitutes a network of indigenous organizations at the provincial and regency levels.

Although indigenous peoples are partially recognized under Indonesian Law, the Indonesian government does not politically acknowledge indigenous peoples' rights or existence. Consequently, AMAN works on the issues of indigenous collective rights concerning lands and territories, as well as natural resource management and the right to self-determination. Since the Third Congress of the Indigenous Peoples of the Archipelago held in March, 2007, AMAN has a directorate specifically working on indigenous women's issues.

The directorate recognizes the importance of the work done by indigenous women at the community level, and therefore aims to involve indigenous women locally through the formation of community-based indigenous women's organizations. The directorate will also pursue the recognition of indigenous women at all levels, an increase in the resources that are available to indigenous women, the involvement of indigenous women in the planning, implementation and evaluation of policies at all levels as well as greater awareness among indigenous women of their rights as women and as indigenous peoples.

DEVELOPMENT AGGRESSION AND INDIGENOUS WOMEN IN INDONESIA

Article 33, paragraph 3 of the 1945 Indonesian Constitution states that: "The earth and water and nature contained within are controlled by the Country and are utilized for social prosperity". Since the Soeharto era, the Indonesian Government has continued to interpret this Article as Country ownership (rather than control) of the land and natural resources in Indonesia. This has meant that the government has allowed land and resources to be taken from indigenous peoples. In the name of development, the country has and continues to transfer land ownership to private industrial enterprises such as mining companies, industrial timber companies, forest concession holders and other industries without implementing the process of Free, Prior and Informed Consent.

Government policy-making regarding the conservation of natural areas also bypasses indigenous peoples. Human involvement in the management of natural areas is not allowed, nor are people allowed to occupy them. To reinforce support for development programs, the Government passed regulations on foreign investment in Indonesia in 1967. These regulations made it easier for foreign investors to invest their capital in Indonesia. For the funding of these development projects, the Indonesian government relied on foreign capital from International Financial Institutions such as the World Bank and the Asian Development Bank.

The statistics regarding land loss and the destruction of natural resources are overwhelming. Since 1950, approximately 70% of primary forest in Indonesia has been destroyed (Forest Watch Indonesia). This is the result of large-scale commercial forest felling for forest concessions and industrial timber plantations. This is aggravated by illegal logging in primary forests which contributes 70 to 80 % of wood production in Indonesia (Friends of the Earth, Indonesia). Equally disturbing are mining statistics.

According to a report by The Mining Network, 35 % of land in Indonesia has been allocated for extractive mining. In 2004, a total of 890 contracts were given to mining companies in Indonesia for activities such as large scale mining of minerals, gold, coal and others found in primary forest regions. The government's attitude toward natural resource management produced policies that did not support management systems based on traditional wisdom. In addition to this, the presence of large-scale industries in the management of these natural resources affected the cohesiveness of indigenous communities, including social, economic, and legal practices as well as traditional institutions.

The shift in control over natural resources as a result of the presence of large-scale industry has changed the nature of management systems from community based to individual-based. Not only have indigenous peoples lost their land rights and the right to manage their territories, but the social systems that managed the functions and roles of indigenous women in natural resource management have also been affected. Women had specific roles and functions within their communities, such as the management of medicine crops and non-timber forest products. The opening of forests resulted in women losing medicinal sources, which forced a change from traditional medical treatments to more modern medical treatments. This resulted in a change in the political positions of indigenous women in their communities.

The capitalist and patriarchal work systems of industry have disrupted the social structures that traditionally defined women's and men's roles. This has caused discrimination against indigenous women. For example, for those women who have little choice other than to work in such industries, they are paid less than men and have fewer opportunities to obtain strategic and decision-making positions. Women are usually employed as domestic or cleaning attendants. In addition to this discrimination, women also face increased threats of violence due to the military being hired to 'protect' the mines or plantations.

Poverty

Indigenous peoples who have traditionally relied on nature to provide them with all of their requirements such as food (plants and animals) from the fields and forests, fish from the rivers and seas, and sources of clean water, suffer from poverty when they are denied control and access to land and natural resources.

The systematic impoverishment of indigenous peoples has occurred through the transfer of land and natural resource ownership, resulting in the loss of indigenous peoples' livelihoods. To survive, indigenous women have come to depend on their husband's income or, in some cases, have had to find paid work to increase the family's income. In many cases the family's income is not enough to cover the requirements for everyday life, including education and health.

Health Issues

Pollution of bodies of water and land resulting from disposal tailings and the use of fertilizers and pesticides has caused serious health problems for indigenous women. These poisonous chemicals enter the land, bodies of water and fields as well as plants that are used by indigenous peoples every day. Women's domestic roles expose them to such chemicals in the land and waters and can cause serious health problems. Women also get sick from the animals they eat because the animals have been infected from the contaminated water and land.

HIV/AIDS is also becoming a serious health issue for indigenous women. For example, in Timika (Papua), the PT Freeport mining company has provided infrastructure such as nightclubs and motels which have encouraged migration (trans-migrant workers, military personnel) as well as the sex industry. Prostitution involving indigenous women has increased and as a result, HIV/AIDS has become an issue in indigenous communities. Infected indigenous women are marginalized by their husbands and communities, creating social problems in addition to health problems.

Sexual Violence

Indigenous women who work in mining and plantation companies responsible for the loss and destruction of indigenous lands and natural resources often experience discrimination, even sexual violence. For example, in PT Kelian Equatorial Mining (KEM) in East Kalimantan, there have been several cases of sexual harassment of indigenous women by PT KEM workers at all levels in the company hierarchy. According to Mining Network, 17 out of 21 legal cases reported between 1987 and 1997 have been for sexual harassment, rape or sexual intercourse under psychological pressure from PT KEM employees on indigenous women working in the company.

The Asian Indigenous Women's Network (AIWN) and the Indigenous Peoples' Alliance of the Archipelago (AMAN: Aliansi Masyarakat Adat Nusantara), in partnership with Rights & Democracy have prepared this information kit to highlight the work of indigenous women who are acting at the local, national and international levels to have their rights respected. As a number of challenges lay ahead in the Second Decade of the World's Indigenous Peoples (2005-2014), it is an appropriate time to explore not only the issues that have an impact on indigenous women in Asia, but also to bring to light the strengths and hopes of these women.

The kit proposes possible avenues for action to enable indigenous women to take full advantage of legal instruments, and international fora and mechanisms that may be useful in furthering their rights. Indigenous women have always been part of their peoples' struggles at all levels: locally, nationally and internationally. In spite of their immeasurable contributions to society, indigenous women are still victims of a double marginalization that is a result of them being women and being indigenous. They are disproportionately affected by extreme poverty, trafficking, illiteracy, lack of access to ancestral lands, non-existent or poor health care and violence in the private and the public spheres.

Over the last two decades the situation of indigenous peoples worldwide and the violations of their human rights has become a key issue in the international arena. This increased attention is reflected in several activities at the level of the United Nations: the establishment in 1982 of the Working Group on Indigenous Populations (WGIP), the proclamation by the General Assembly of the International Decade for Indigenous People (1995-2004), the establishment of the Permanent Forum on Indigenous Issues in 2000, the creation of a Special Rapporteur on the Situation of Human Rights and Fundamental Freedoms of Indigenous People in 2001, and the proclamation of a Second International Decade for Indigenous People (2005-2014).

While it is true that the First International Decade of the World's Indigenous People, which ended in 2004, created several spaces, including the 1995 World Conference on Women in Beijing, which allowed for greater participation by indigenous peoples at the international level, the situation of indigenous peoples still requires the attention of the international community. For example, the First International Decade did not stem the exodus of thousands of indigenous people pushed off their lands by the "development" of others (mining and oil companies, land settlement), by armed conflict or famine.

Indigenous women inevitably pay a higher price when there is displacement and dislocation, whether they remain behind in the communities that men have deserted or flee to cities where they find themselves isolated from their family and cultural networks. They usually suffer the most from the violations to the integrity of their peoples and family, and are prime targets for violence resulting from the militarization of their territories. Indigenous women in Asia were particularly active during the first International Decade of the World's Indigenous People.

At the local level, they built and strengthened their own community organizations and allied themselves with others to form networks. AIWN played the lead role in bringing together indigenous women from all over the world during the Beijing World Conference on Women in 1995. The Beijing Declaration of Indigenous Women has become a framework for understanding the situations, perspectives and issues of indigenous women. There are other networks presently working on these issues, including the Gender Desk of the Asian Indigenous Peoples Pact (AIPP), and the Asia-Pacific Indigenous Youth Network.

The Second Decade of the World's Indigenous People began on January 1, 2005. Its five main objectives are relevant to indigenous women:

i. Promote non-discrimination and inclusion of indigenous peoples in processes regarding laws, policies, resources, programmes and projects;
ii. Promote the full and effective participation of indigenous peoples in decisions which affect their lifestyles, land and culture as well as considering the principle of free, prior and informed consent;
iii. Redefine development policies that are culturally appropriate;

iv. Adopt targeted policies, programmes, projects and budgets for the development of indigenous peoples with an emphasis on indigenous women, children and youth;

v. Develop strong monitoring mechanisms and enhance accountability at the international, regional and national levels regarding the implementation of laws, policies and operational frameworks for the protection of indigenous peoples.

Several activities have been scheduled for the Second Decade, including the adoption of the United Nations Declaration on the Rights of Indigenous Peoples at the international level, strengthening regional cooperation between international and regional human rights mechanisms, and at the national level, further development of activities in cooperation with States, United Nations country offices and indigenous peoples to improve the human rights situation of indigenous peoples.

These sheets can be used in various contexts: during training sessions with organizational leaders, as materials for capacity-building sessions, to promote the regional network and anytime there is a need for information on the situation of indigenous women. They can help to further discussion by providing information and asking questions and raising issues relevant to indigenous women. They also include useful references for further information and suggestions for action.

Militarization anywhere in the world is a difficult problem to deal with; South Asia is no exception. History tells us that countries in the region have undergone considerable periods of economic exploitation and social repression, whether under feudal or colonial rule. After independence, locally established regimes in these countries also turned to ruthless methods of social control-often relying on the police and military-to maintain power. The region therefore shares a common harsh history in terms of bloodshed and deprivation of civil liberties, although the degree of harshness may vary depending on time and place.

Misconceived notions of hope often mean that frank discussions of difficult problems are discouraged. Instead, it is suggested that discussion focus on positive aspects so as to sustain hope, rather than reveal the complexities of any issue. Attempts to generate positive attitudes detract from our responsibility and participation in solving the problem. They also facilitate looking at the world through rose-tinted glasses.

This is not the real world however, which is particularly important when dealing with difficult societal situations. Contributing to the resolution of these requires serious attempts to first understand the problems, which may, at first glance, appear to defy any solution. With regards to militarization, if we are unwilling to look into the difficulties faced by people living in such situations, it is not possible for us to participate in finding a solution. Therefore, no apology is needed in presenting the difficult aspects of South Asian life today.

EXPERIENCES OF AVERAGE CITIZENS ARE IMPORTANT

While it is possible-and even legitimate in certain contexts-to discuss peace, security and development on a grand, theoretical level, when the concern is resolving problems, it is essential to focus on how they affect ordinary citizens. This should, in fact, be the entry point to understanding the problems themselves. It is therefore appropriate to briefly discuss the difficulties facing one of the participants for this conference, Mr Santha Fernando. Santha is well known to ecumenical and civil society organizations. He was stopped at the Sri Lankan airport on his way to this meeting, and has been detained under anti-terrorism laws for more than five days now. We have learned that a detention order has been issued by the Ministry of Defense to detain him for 30 days, which makes any application for his release in court futile.

Santha Fernando is a person of whom would be said, "He would not hurt a fly". And yet, he has been detained under charges of terrorism. Under ordinary law, any arrest must be based upon a reasonable suspicion of having committed a particular offense. What is the basis of any reasonable suspicion of Santha Fernando committing an act forbidden under the anti-terrorism law? There is obviously nothing of the sort, as those who arrested him are fully aware. We thus have a peculiar kind of arrest; an arrest for which there need not be any reasonable grounds. Only a declaration of the arrest is needed, in the face of which there is nothing the arrestee or his relatives can do.

This is an exercise of power in the most absolute sense. Representations have been made by those with high social standing on his behalf, including bishops, lawyers and international organizations, all to no avail. Santha's place of detention is not any regular prison, which in Sri Lanka are harsh institutions. It is the TID (Terrorism Investigation Division), notoriously known as the 'fourth floor' and infamous for harassment and torture.

Even if Santha Fernando himself has not been subjected to torture, he would have heard the screams and stories of others exposed to violence. A young Sinhalese journalist arrested and held in the TID for a short time was a changed man. He had not been tortured, but he saw and heard what was happening. After his release he did not even want to talk to anybody about his experience, as it had so thoroughly shocked and disturbed him. Detention in such a place is already enough punishment.

It must then be asked, what is the detention for, and what is the punishment for? Through the experience of Santha, someone known to us, we can understand what is faced by the tens of thousands of persons subjected to such arrest and detention, which has become a common occurrence. Everyone knows one or more persons who have faced such situations. It is necessary for us to take note of these experiences and participate in creating a relevant collective discourse. It is from this perspective that we should view the issue of peace, security and development.

The common heritage of a unique servant-master relationship within the South Asian culture is another issue that we need to keep in mind during this discussion. What makes this relationship unique is the lack of physical chains binding South Asia servants, unlike the black slaves of the

United States and elsewhere. In contrast, South Asia developed a comprehensive scheme of internalizing servanthood.

The chains are inside the minds and hearts of the people themselves. Their instincts have been shaped in such a way as to reproduce habits of faithful service to masters, even with smiling faces. This continues today, mostly through the institution of caste and other modes of internalized branding and degrading of humanity. A recent novel, The White Tiger by Aravind Adiga, portrays this servanthood graphically:

The greatest thing to come out of this country in the ten thousand years of its history is the Rooster Coop.

Go to Old Delhi, behind the Jama Masjid, and look at the way they keep chickens there in the market. Hundreds of pale hens and brightly coloured roosters, stuffed tightly into wire-mesh cages, packed as tightly as worms in a belly, pecking each other and shitting on each other, jostling just for breathing space; the whole cage giving off a horrible stench - the stench of terrified, feathered flesh. On the wooden desk above this coop sits a grinning young butcher, showing off the flesh and organs of a recently chopped-up chicken, still oleaginous with a coating of dark blood. The roosters in the coop smell the blood from above. They see the organs of their brothers lying around them. They know they're next. Yet they do not rebel. They do not try to get out of the coop.

The very same thing is done with human beings in this country. Watch the roads in the evenings in Delhi; sooner or later you will see a man on a cycle-rickshaw, pedaling down the road, with a giant bed, or a table, tied to the cart that is attached to his cycle. Every day furniture is delivered to people's homes by this man - the delivery- man. A bed costs five thousand rupees, maybe six thousand. Add the chairs, and a coffee table, and it's ten or fifteen thousand. A man comes on a cycle-cart, bringing you this bed, table, and chairs, a poor man who may make five hundred rupees a month.

He unloads all this furniture for you, and you give him the money in cash - a fat wad of cash the size of a brick. He puts it into his pocket, or into his shirt, or into his underwear, and cycles back to his boss and hands it over without touching a single rupee of it! A year's salary, two years' salary, in his hands, and he never takes a rupee of it. Every day, on the roads of Delhi, some chauffeur is driving an empty car with a black suitcase sitting on the backseat. Inside that suitcase is a million, two million rupees; more money than that chauffeur will see in his lifetime. If he took the money he could go to America, Australia, anywhere, and start a new life.

He could go inside the five-star hotels he has dreamed about all his life and only seen from the outside. He could take his family to Goa, to England. Yet he takes that black suitcase where his master wants. He puts it down where he is meant to, and never touches a rupee. Why? Because Indians are the world's most honest people, like the prime minister's booklet will inform you? No. It's because per cent of us are-caught in the Rooster Coop just like those poor guys in the poultry market.

The Rooster Coop doesn't always work with minuscule sums of money. Don't test your chauffeur with a rupee coin or two - he may well steal that much. But leave a million dollars in front of a servant and he won't touch a penny. Try it: leave a black bag with a million dollars in a Mumbai taxi. The taxi driver will call the police and return the money by the day's end. I guarantee it. (Whether the police will give it to you or not is another story, sir!) Masters trust their servants with diamonds in this country!

It's true. Every evening on the train out of Surat, where they run the world's biggest diamond- cutting and polishing business, the servants of diamond merchants are carrying suitcases full of cut diamonds that they have to give to someone in Mumbai. Why doesn't that servant take the suitcase full of diamonds? He's no Gandhi, he's human, he's you and me. But he's in the Rooster Coop. The trustworthiness of servants is the basis of the entire Indian economy. The Great Indian Rooster Coop. Do you have something like it in China too? I doubt it, Mr Jiabao. Or you wouldn't need the Communist Party to shoot people and a secret police to raid their houses at night and put them in jail like I've heard you have over there. Here in India we have no dictatorship. No secret police.

That's because we have the coop. Never before in human history have so few owed so much to so many, Mr Jiabao. A handful of men in this country have trained the remaining 99.9 per cent - as strong, as talented, as intelligent in every way - to exist in perpetual servitude; a servitude so strong that you can put the key of his emancipation in a man's hands and he will throw it back at you with a curse. You'll have to come here and see it, for yourself to believe it. Every day millions wake up at dawn - stand in dirty, crowded buses - get off at their masters' posh houses - and then clean the floors, wash the dishes, weed the garden, feed their children, press their feet - all for a pittance. I will never envy the rich of America or England, Mr Jiabao: they have no servants there. They cannot even begin to understand what a good life is.

Now, a thinking man like you, Mr Premier, must ask two questions. Why does the Rooster Coop work? How does it trap so many millions of men and women so effectively? Secondly, can a man break out of the coop? What if one day, for instance, a driver took his employer's money and ran? What would his life be like? The answer to the first question is that the pride and glory of our nation, the repository of all our love and sacrifice, the subject of no doubt considerable space in the pamphlet that the prime minister will hand over to you, the Indian family, is the reason we are trapped and fled to the coop. The answer to the second question is that only a man who is prepared to see his family destroyed - hunted, beaten, and burned alive by the masters - can break put of the coop. That would take no normal human being, but a freak, a pervert of nature.

A few centuries ago, many enlightened persons talked about educating these servants and assisting them to be free from such restraints. Nearly all countries of South Asia saw various movements for education, and even attempts to provide opportunities to break this internalized servitude. Many generations of such work has had its impact. The servants have begun to wake up and to want to walk away from their servant hood. Their masters however, have not had the enlightenment to end the master-servant bondage and begin a mutual relationship on the basis of humanity and equality. Rather, they have turned to their guns to suppress servants who no longer want to be servants.

This situation, in which servants-the larger sectors of society-demand a fundamental change to the traditional political, social and economic relationships, is the essential background to militarization in the region. Any discussion on peace, security and development must give serious consideration to this historical conflict and the present state of contest by the underclass. This contest is likely to continue until an effective solution is found, by way of social and economic rearrangements recognizing the equality of all. Mere legal recognition of equality, while the basic master-servant relationship remains unchallenged, is of little use.

Having discussed some background and relevant factors to today's militarization within the region, let us look at a few incidents that indicate the impact of militarization on collective social behavior in different South Asian countries. These impacts include kidnapping, the loss of legal protection, the undermining of civilian policing, the loss of importance of the individual and the lack of respect for women, among others.

Kidnapping is a widespread problem in several countries. The extent of the problem is India is suggested by a photograph of a group of young children holding placards with slogans such as, "Kidnapping Uncles, do not kidnap us". This photo comes from the state of Bihar, known for the complete collapse of its rule of law and basic institutions. As a result, kidnapping for ransom has become a common occurrence, causing much parental anxiety.

The photograph of a six-year-old girl in Sri Lanka, amidst her classmates, was published in the media after she was kidnapped from school. Within hours of her kidnapping, some persons contacted her family in town, as well as her father who was employed in the Middle East. They demanded a ransom of 30 million rupees. Two days later, Varsha's body was found in a drainage ditch with her throat slit.

To make matters worse, although the Sri Lankan police arrested two persons suspected of involvement in Varsha's kidnapping, they both died in police custody, precluding any public trial into the case. Not only did the police fail to protect her, they also failed to find her after the kidnapping, and they denied the rights of the family and the public to know what happened by summarily killing the suspects.

There has been considerable discussion about the frequent practice of kidnapping in Bihar as well as Sri Lanka. Businessmen, professors and many other persons have been kidnapped for ransom. Kidnapping also occurs for revenge or intimidation. It is also used as a political tool to harass or blackmail individuals wishing to leave certain political parties or engage in 'disloyal' activities. Frequent kidnappings of this manner create a certain psychological state amongst society. People become wary of independent thought, free speech, or even any initiative to assist others, in the fear of being kidnapped.

Frequent kidnappings are a symptom of the breakdown of social relationships as well as the institutions of rule of law and democracy. In these circumstances, kidnappings will be accompanied by extrajudicial killings, physical harassment of all types, the grabbing of private property, and illegal occupation of land. Under a rule of law system, many safeguards to individual rights are built into the legal structure. The practice of arrest and detention for instance, is subject to specific procedures to prevent any abuse of power. To further ensure that these procedures are followed, lawyers are legally entitled to intervene on behalf of the individual. An individual may not be aware of all relevant legal provisions, or may be afraid to assert their rights in the face of state officers who have the power to use force. Effective interventions by lawyers are therefore an essential component of protection.

When a society becomes militarized, the lawyer's role is minimized and may even completely disappear. This was noted in the March 2009 report of the UN Special Rapporteur on the situation of human rights in Myanmar: "None of the prisoners with whom the Special Rapporteur spoke had been represented in the court by legal counsel. Many of them did not even know the definition of the word 'lawyer'."

Although Burmese lawyers may wear black coats and ties like their counterparts in former British colonies, in reality they have little capacity to protect their clients. In effect, lawyers in Burma are a mere decoration. Their incapacity leaves their clients at the mercy of those who arrest and detain them. The situation of the role and authority of lawyers in Burma differs only slightly from other South Asian countries, where lawyers complain of being ignored for a variety of reasons.

The increase in militarization drastically reduces the legal space available for consulting lawyers. Emergency regulations and anti-terrorism laws-known by different names in different countries-allow for long periods of detention with limited access to lawyers. Often the possibilities for bail under such laws are also limited, leaving lawyers with little to do by way of applications to courts. Moreover, courts themselves do not have the power to adjudicate on the legality of such detentions.

Not only does militarization increase the possibilities of-and decrease the safeguards against-arrest and detention, it also dispenses with fair trial in large areas of the law. In particular, those charged with offenses under 'special laws' are given no trials at all. Guilt and innocence is decided not by the courts, but by the police, military and other parts of the defence establishment. The disposal of fair trial further limits the space for lawyers to protect individuals, however unfairly they may be treated.

When court powers are diminished, it is made clear that the real decision makers are these other authorities; they are the ones to be approached for necessary matters, not the courts. This realization inevitably leads to widespread corruption. The relatives of a detainee for instance, may try to obtain his release by paying bribes to officers involved in the detention or with relevant connections. In these circumstances, lawyers willing to engage in such behavior become more wanted than those relying on professional abilities. Many lawyers complain that would-be clients first inquire into their connections to the authorities, before seeking their assistance.

It has been said that you know the value of lawyers only when they no longer exist. This is true in many parts of South Asia today; lawyers with real powers ensured by law are largely extinct. The absence of a legal profession capable of effective protection serves to enhance militarization. Authorities therefore take extraordinary steps to attack and intimidate lawyers. Many lawyers appearing in cases against the ruling regimes are killed or suffer other grave attacks. Lawyers have had grenades thrown into their homes, their offices set on fire, or their names listed in government websites as traitors for making representations in courts on behalf of alleged terrorists.

A law student attended a lecture regarding the prevention of corruption given by a senior lawyer. The senior lawyer mentioned many ways of avoiding corruption. The junior lawyer asked a question at the end of the lecture: "Sir?" he asked, "When I join a chamber to practice law - which is soon I expect- if I am given some money by my senior lawyers to carry to the judge, what I do?"

Complaints about corruption within the judiciary are heard throughout Asia. The increase of such complaints coincides with the increased use of emergency and anti-terrorism laws suspending the operation of normal laws. In fact, the greater the takeover by the military, the greater the possibilities for corruption and the link between militarization and the increase of corruption among the judiciary is related to the undermining of the separation of powers.

Under militarization, not only does the power shift to the executive, but the executive itself begins to come under military pressure. This change undermines the judiciary. Even though externally the courts may exist as before, internally there are substantive changes. As with lawyers, those judges used to strict professional habits may find themselves making room for more ambitious and adventurous individuals ready to forsake justice for their own interests.

Militarization impacts the local policing system in many ways. Most importantly, once the police are called upon to assist the military, civilian policing habits are undermined. Searching a home under normal criminal law for instance, requires police to obtain a warrant from a magistrate, to use minimum force, and to maintain proper reports regarding all events. Military searches are of a different nature however. They include heavy arms and many personnel, and inhabitants are told to surrender or be fired upon. In other instances, the police and military are used as secret death squads. Such operations are carried out with no regard to the law.

Military operations are often accompanied by impunity, while police actions are controlled by the law. When the police begin to work within a military environment though, they also acquire a taste for impunity. A key function of the police is to investigate crimes, and yet under militarization of the police, routine criminal investigations are among the first to deteriorate. This is because police officers become too busy in other operations, such as providing security to politicians, to carry out criminal inquiries.

Furthermore, the police are often required to create obstacles in cases where the state itself is directly or indirectly involved; they are told to disrupt complaint receiving mechanisms, to intimidate witnesses, or to tamper with the official records. They may even receive instructions-from political sources or their own superiors-not to investigate. All this serves to land honest officers in conflict, while generating the attitude that the pursuit of integrity is nothing but a way to get in trouble.

Ultimately, police officers learn to use their uniforms as a means to make money. It is far from uncommon in South Asian societies to learn of illegal arrest, detention and the fabrication of charges by the police, merely to earn some profit. The police begin to associate with criminals, developing shares in brothels and the illicit liquor and drugs trade. They then pose a serious threat to citizens. Security is impossible when the police themselves become instruments of insecurity.

Militarized environments expose women to serious forms of dehumanization. One of our own conference participants quoted a Tamil woman from Sri Lanka saying, "I don't to be born a Tamil and even more I do not want to be born a woman". The atmosphere is one of male domination, with the corresponding images of men enhancing their power with guns. On the roads and at checkpoints, women are often humiliated by vulgar language and behavior. Rape also becomes a common feature. The military allows a permissive atmosphere with regards to women to encourage men and youth to stay put in their assigned locations and duties. Encouragement of sexual adventures is also part of 'keeping up morale' among the armed forces. Many stories of girls abducted for sexual abuse and thereafter killed are thus heard in South Asia.

Apart from such direct abuse suffered by women at the hands of the military, they must also deal with problems affecting their loved ones, such as their husbands, fathers, brothers and sons being killed or attacked. Women heading families are a common feature in militarized societies. Under these circumstances, women face a twofold punishment.

Firstly, in a society where economic powers are unfairly vested in men, their loss severely affects the economic life of women. Secondly, they must also bear the emotional loss of arbitrarily losing their men folk. Public debates regarding conflict and civil war in South Asia rarely discusses the consequences to women. As a result, a considerable amount of suffering is unrecognized and undocumented, even as it leaves a social impact. Life within society becomes bleak when large numbers of women are exposed to grave suffering, frustration and depression.

When the Sri Lankan Secretary of Defence was questioned about the assassination of well-known journalist Lasantha Wickrematunge by a BBC correspondent, his quick response was, "When thousands are being killed, does the killing of one person matter?" When media reports of killings are heard daily for years, sensitivity is diminished. One more killing does not seem to make any difference. If a society is to remain sane however, a great sense of outrage must be expressed on the issue of life and murder. The loss of such outrage signifies an extremely negative transformation, both morally and psychologically. It also creates further space for killings to occur.

Any rule of law system is formed around the importance of the individual. Every wrong against an individual is of prime importance in the development of civil and criminal law. To define an act a crime means that it is a wrongful act against an individual and society will take notice and offer just retribution. When these crimes are no longer matters of importance, the very foundation of criminology is undermined. This can only signal the abandoning of criminal justice. Once criminal justice is abandoned, society is left in a situation where no collective control can be exercised on people's behaviour. Individuals can then no longer rely on collective support or protection.

The emergence of extrajudicial punishments is rooted in this loss of collective control and support. Mob justice is one such punishment, where people themselves decide on the punishments for whoever they find as alleged culprits of any offense. Proof of guilt and proportionality between crime and punishment are of little significance in these cases. More important is a sort of psychological satisfaction that something is being done against crime, which will intimidate others.

Another form of extrajudicial punishment is that meted out by the police or military, whereby persons are killed during or after their arrest. In different countries, this practice has different names-encounter killings, crossfire killings or self-defence killings. Just as the life of an individual ceases to be a matter of importance, so threats to private property are also of no importance. Theft and land grabbing are common complaints in South Asia today. Legal redress for such wrongs is as difficult as redress for personal wrongs.

Civil law requires that dealings on properties and transactions be based on contracts. For this, it is essential that contracts can be enforced. When militarization undermines the law and courts can no longer inspire confidence to hold individuals to what they have agreed, the certainty of contracts is in question. The performance of obligations becomes dependent on who has greater force or authority at their disposal; in other words, those with police or military connections.

The same can be said regarding the law relating to tort. The system of compensation for negligent actions on the part of the state or private sector acts as a deterrent when effectively implemented. When those in power are beyond the challenge of the law, negligence cannot help but spread. A public health system left in the control of individuals not subjected to legal scrutiny for instance, can lead to negligence in the purchase of medicine, storage of medicine, the treatment of patients, record keeping relating to treatment and many related matters.

Once collective consensus on basic social norms and standards has been destroyed over a lengthy period of militarization, significant damage is caused to society's memory and language.

This is well demonstrated in the experience of South Asia. South Asian societies for instance, no longer have a concept of a public officer who will not abuse power. While this can be somewhat attributed to abuse of power under feudal and colonial rule, significant losses have occurred from achievements made in the 19th and 20th centuries. Many juridical notions developed after enlighten-ment in Europe were brought to South Asia.

The transformation of medieval systems of social control to a process of reason is a significant human accomplishment. The development of jurisprudence and legal practices on the basis of rational principles rather than the whims of those in power is not just 'a western affair', but the triumph of humanity. Such development requires enormous effort in any society. It involves the education of generations of people on these notions, as well as the practices required to uphold them; educating civil servants, the intelligentsia and the population as a whole is no small matter. The introduction of these systems in most South Asian countries happened during colonial times, or with colonial influence.

Inevitably, colonial interests conflicted with a rational system of justice and rule of law, which meant that only partial transformations occurred. This meant that post-independence, new ruling regimes had to undertake several unaccomplished tasks if they wanted to see the functioning of effective justice and law systems. However, the new governments in South Asia faced such overwhelming responsibilities that they paid little attention to the development of a rational system of justice. Instead, they were consumed by the need to win popular votes. In the contest for power, they lost sight of society's long term interests.

The first casualty of emerging crises within the new nations was the limited system of justice administration. Modifications to the system in order to deal with immediate problems largely resulted in the removal of basic protection mechanisms and the erosion of rule of law foundations. Militarization emerged from such a background, and began to undermine weak justice systems that could not withstand the pressures of the military. The narrative of how this happened in different South Asian countries is a sad tale of how the struggle to base the administration of justice on rational notions of jurisprudence was abandoned.

The failure of certain practices in society will inevitably lead to a lack of knowledge about them. When the judiciary no longer stands against the wrongdoings of the executive, people will forget what the independence of the judiciary, or the separation of power means. In the same way, words and concepts lose their original meanings. With the change of relationships, there is also a change in the meaning of words. 'Judge' may begin to signify someone who rubberstamps the diktats of the government and a cynic who allows justice to be subjected to the rules of the marketplace.

A 'policeman' can be seen as a terror and someone who could engage in any kind of immorality without suffering any consequences. A 'trial' can become a mockery; a show trial. Legal procedures, held at one time as strict rules ensuring fair play, are now trivialities to be dispensed with by anyone, at anytime. The loss of the memory of a rationally functioning justice administration is accompanied by a change in the associated language. This will affect social attitudes. People will begin to lose respect for relationships based on laws. The acquisition of goods and power by whatever means, emerges as a legitimate social ideal. The crudest forms of selfishness cease to be considered socially denigrating.

If we compare militarism with democracy (even in the third world sense), we find:

The source of legitimacy in a democracy is a constitution based essentially on the separation of powers. This is true even when it does not abide by any of the basic principles of liberal democratic constitutionalism.

For militarism, the source of legitimacy is the capacity to use force; the gun itself is the legitimacy. The use of the gun is not subjected to any overriding rules or monitored by institutions. Under militarism, if there is a constitution at all, it is just a paper on which the military ruler or clique can incorporate whatever they wish.

In a democracy, the entire system is subjected to the rule of law. This implies that:

Laws arrived at by consensus are above everything else.

The implementation of the law is subjected to a process laid down in the law itself.

The rulers, like everyone else, are subjected to this law and process.

In any study of the change from a democratic state to a militarized one, we may notice the following stages:

i. Initial resistance in varying degrees towards militarization.

ii. A lessoning of democratic and legal resistances, and the serious weakening of the voices of the middle class.

iii. The virtual disappearance of any legal forms of resistance or opportunities for such resistance.

iv. Under militarism, the ruler is above the law. This means that carrying out his orders need not be subjected to any process; the ruler can decide on whatever way his orders are implemented.

v. The military's increasing grip on society is accompanied by a gradual displacement of reason.

vi. The idea of building consensus on the basis of reason is displaced with blatant forms of propaganda that create the impression of artificial consensus.

The distinction between truth and the absence of truth is made relative to the extent that all rules of language and discourse to convey meanings become irrelevant. Words can have whatever meaning given to them at a particular moment.

Facts and figures lose significance, creating a 'no-fact zone'.

Accountability:

Auditing ceases to be a matter of significance in the military context, while in the democratic context almost everything centers on accounting and auditing

Militarization gradually removes the distinction between public and private. This applies to property ownership as well as decision making.

Morally and ethically:

Under militarization, the absolute prohibition against murder ceases to be significant; murder becomes a lesser evil. In this way, murder becomes a way to settle disputes and to threaten individuals.

The cheapening of life extends to other areas such as personal and family relationships. Moral abuse becomes normal even in relationships where guardianship is involved.

Reformers who wish to improve things are uncertain of where to begin or whom to rely on for support.

Distrust towards others is the norm.

Powerlessness becomes the excuse for compromise, no matter how morally unacceptable.

The way out

The only way out of such militarization is to:

Develop the capacity to understand the shock and shame suffered under these circumstances, as well as collective shock and shame. In the aftermath of WWII in Germany, people suffered various illnesses, resulting in the famous book, 'The Inability to Mourn - principles of collective behaviour' by Alexander and Margarete Mitscherlich. Individual and social recovery was dependant on the capacity of the people to admit their plight and mourn, and thereby find the path back to recovery.

Raise fundamental issues relating to public and legal institutions. Although public confidence in justice mechanisms may have been lost, recovery requires bold attempts to discuss these issues.

Document every incident of abuse and develop databases and information centers for this purpose. Elie Wiesel, the Nobel Prize laureate, recalled the advice of the Rabbis at the height of the holocaust, when they told people to make records of everything they see happening to others or themselves. The literature that survived through this provided the basis for later reflection and helped the recovery process legally, socially and spiritually. One remarkable piece of this nature is the Diary of Anne Frank. There is no alternative to dedicated documentation of injustice and abuse. The night, when it comes, causes havoc-but faithful records of that havoc is an essential component for the recovery of the conscience.

6

Problems of Violence Against Women

In all societies, to a greater or lesser degree, women and girls are subjected to physical, sexual and psychological abuse that cuts across lines of income, class and culture. Poverty, marginalisation and certain aspects of women's identity, such as their race or ethnicity, can also leave some women more vulnerable to violence. While men also experience violence, women's lower social status puts them at particular risk and the number of cases of violence against women continues to grow at an alarming rate.

The 1992 UN Declaration on Violence against Women, the first international human rights instrument to address the issue, contains this definition:

'The term "violence against women" means any act of gender-based violence that results in, or is likely to result in, physical, sexual or psychological harm or suffering to women, including threats of such acts, coercion or arbitrary deprivation of liberty, whether occurring in public or private life'.

Some women experience domestic violence in the family at the hands of an abusive partner or relative. Others face sexual harassment in the workplace. In some countries, women are subjected to harmful traditional practices which can leave them scarred or severely traumatised, or may be force to marry at an early age, increasing their vulnerability to abuse. Women may also be forced into prostitution by traffickers and, in times of conflict, it is women who are most likely to be the target of sexual violence, especially rape. And abuse is not just physical, but may also be emotional, sexual or psychological.

Womankind believes that violence against women is an abuse of their fundamental human rights, including their rights to health and freedom from torture. Aside from the physical, emotional and mental toll on women, violence prevents women from participating fully in society. Violence limits women's access to resources, such as land, water and food and their ability to participate in activities such as work, education, travel and community meetings.

Violence against women also carries economic costs for both the individual and society. While the cost implications are difficult to assess, some of the costs include missed work, health care for survivors, emergency shelters and legal procedures to bring perpetrators to justice. For these reasons, violence against women constitutes a major obstacle to development, peace and security.

Womankind believes that discrimination and unequal power relations lie at the heart of women's greater vulnerability to violence and that addressing the inequality that is deeply entrenched in all societies must be central to our responses to the issue.

Throughout history, violence has been used as a way of controlling women, both within the family and the wider society, and reinforcing their subordinate position to men. There are a number of cultural, social and political factors which perpetuate and exacerbate the problem. Factors such as cultural norms, military tactics, negative media images, social pressures on men to express their 'masculinity', inadequate laws to prohibit violence against women, government complacency and the absence of educational programmes to address the causes and consequences of violence.

Equally, the issue of violence against women cannot be separated from other important issues affecting women, such as HIV/AIDS. For example, women who are raped in South Africa are being killed when they disclose their HIV positive status to the rapist.

What is Womankind doing to tackle the problem of violence against women? Efforts to enable women to gain control over their lives and their bodies are at the heart of Womankind's work to reduce violence against women. Through our partners, we support the development of local strategies and responses to violence against women that include counselling and support services for survivors of violence, education and awareness-raising to reduce tolerance and increase knowledge of the causes and consequences of violence, as well as research, advocacy and lobbying of decision-makers with the power to change laws and policies to benefit women.

The forms of violence that we respond to and the types of responses may differ from country to country but in each instance, we encourage women and men to work together and to involve the wider community in order to bring about lasting change in attitudes and behaviours. We also bring partners together to share information about lessons learnt and new strategies and to use this information to inform future planning and to shape the views of decision-makers.

For example:

In Ghana, WOMANKIND supports Community-based Action Teams or COMBATs to find local solutions to the problem of domestic violence. Our partners are also part of a wider coalition that has lobbied the government to pass a law prohibiting violence against women.

In Peru, WOMANKIND supports organisations providing a range of services to women survivors of domestic violence, including legal advice and representation, counselling and a help-line. They also conduct research and advocacy work aimed at changing public attitudes towards violence against women.

In the UK, we have developed an educational programme to reduce violence against women in the next generation. Based on the findings of an initial piece of research, the programme has developed materials that can be used by teachers to explore and develop young people's attitudes towards violence, sexual identity and relationships.

In addition to our country programmes, WOMANKIND is also lobbying for improvements in current policies and practices to tackle violence against women and raising awareness of the issue, both in the UK and at the international level. For example:

In 2003, WOMANKIND produced a 'shadow' report which it submitted to the CEDAW Committee. This UN body monitors government's implementation of the UN Convention for the Elimination of Discrimination Against Women, the only global convention governing equal rights between women and men. The report focuses on violence against women and is a tool to push the UK government for stronger measures to tackle different aspects of violence in the UK, including rape and sexual assault, trafficking and the sex industry, domestic violence and harmful traditional practices, such as female genital mutilation and forced marriage.

Each year, as part of the international 16 Days of Activism Against Gender Violence Campaign, WOMANKIND promotes the link between local and international work to end violence against women by supporting the awareness-raising activities of a range of African women's organisations. The 16 Days period symbolically links November 25th, International Day Against Violence Against Women with December 10th, International Human Rights Day, to emphasise that violence is a violation of women's human rights.

Violence against women is a persistent and ongoing problem in Canada and around the world. It affects women's social and economic equality, physical and mental health, well-being and economic security. Decision-makers require a clear understanding of the nature and severity of social problems in order to develop effective responses.

In 2002, the Federal/Provincial/Territorial Status of Women Ministers released Assessing Violence against

Women: a Statistical Profile. The Profile introduced a number of violence indicators that are intended to monitor changes over time, serve as benchmarks, and highlight emerging problems. This updated edition revisits these indicators, expands upon them, and assesses the current situation. According to the Beijing Platform for Action adopted at the Fourth United Nations World Conference on Women in 1995:

> Violence against women is an obstacle to the achievement of the objectives of equality, development and peace. Violence against women both violates and impairs or nullifies the enjoyment by women of their human rights and fundamental freedoms. The long-standing failure to protect and promote those rights and freedoms in the case of violence against women is a matter of concern to all States and should be addressed.

The Beijing Platform for Action also emphasized the importance of reliable statistical data in understanding violence against women and recommended that work be done to:

> promote research, collect data and compile statistics, especially concerning domestic violence relating to the prevalence of different forms of violence against women, and encourage research into the causes, nature, seriousness and consequences of violence against women and the effectiveness of measures implemented to prevent and redress violence against women.

Canadian governments have made important advancements in the availability of statistical data to describe the dimensions and nature of violence against women, the impacts and consequences, societal responses and supports for victims, and women's use of criminal justice and other services. This document summarizes these data within a framework of indicators on violence against women.

Until recently, researchers and statistical agencies often gathered statistics generically, compiling data on violence regardless of the gender of victims or offenders. This approach contributed to the development of general programs that addressed violence in society as a whole. Social program and policy developers have identified instances where programs for Canadians as a whole often fail to consider the effect of gender. As an example, federal employment assistance programs are often only accessible to Canadians who work full-time or who can take full-time training. Analysis of data by gender reveals that while one-third of Canadian women voluntarily working part-time reported doing so in order to care for their children, only 4% of men gave this as a reason.

Women's traditional role in society as caregivers often limits their ability to access programs intended for all Canadians. Generic programs meant to address violence against all Canadians risk failing to adequately address women's experiences of violence. Gender-specific data can pinpoint those areas where the need for support services is different for women and men. It is also important to further disaggregate data (for example, by race, ethnicity, age, sexual orientation, socioeconomic status or ability) in order to fully understand the situation of different groups of women.

Data that are made available by gender demonstrate the specific risk areas for men and women and highlight the need for targeted programs to address violence for each gender. Men's and boys' experiences of violence are different than women's and girls' in important ways. While men are more likely to be injured by strangers in a public or social venue, women are in greater danger of experiencing violence from intimate partners in their own homes. Women are also at greater risk of sexual violence. The fear of violence is more pervasive for women and can prevent them from taking part as full citizens in their communities.

In addition to the negative effects for women themselves, the violence women experience at the hands of their intimate partners can have profound effects on their children. Children who are exposed to violence in the home suffer from emotional trauma, have poor educational outcomes, and are at increased risk of using violence to solve problems. Women experiencing violence from intimate partners are sometimes forced to flee their homes with their children, which can result in unstable living situations and additional negative impacts on children.

Worldwide, violence against women is an impediment to women's equality. According to the United Nations Population Fund (2005):

> Gender-based violence is perhaps the most wide-spread and socially tolerated of human rights violations. It both reflects and reinforces inequities between men and women and compromises the health, dignity, security and autonomy of its victims.

The 1995 Federal Action Plan for Gender Equality emphasized the interconnections between equality and not only gender, but other personal characteristics:

> Barriers to equality are rooted in long-standing attitudes and traditions not only about women, but also about race, age, sexual orientation, disability, colour, etc. In particular, the life situations of women outside the dominant culture-women with disabilities, Aboriginal women, women from visible minorities, elderly women, lesbians, lone mothers, women in poverty-are quite different from the mainstream.
>
> For them, the path to equality has been, and continues to be, even more difficult. Equality for all women will come about only as these attitudes, imbedded in the workplace, educational institutions and the family, are challenged and begin to change. To achieve true equality, actions must be taken that adjust for the differences in experiences and situations between women and men, and among women, and that correct the systemic nature of inequality.

The Action Plan further defines the concept of "substantive" equality, which acknowledges the systemic and structural nature of inequality. It recognizes that both freedom from discrimination and positive actions are required to arrive at equal outcomes. To achieve gender equality, the social structures that govern the relationship between men and women will need to give equal value to the different roles they play, as parents, as workers, as elected officials and others;

to foster equal partnership in the decision-making process; and to build a just and equitable society.

Definitions of violence against women vary broadly depending on the objectives of a particular research study or policy, and on the source of the data being used. The United Nation's 1993 Declaration on the Elimination of Violence against Women, which was signed by Canada, provides a very broad definition that has been accepted by the international community:

Any act of gender-based violence that results in, or is likely to result in, physical, sexual or psychological harm or suffering to women, including threats of such acts, coercion or arbitrary deprivation of liberty, whether occurring in public or in private life.

Violence against women shall be understood to encompass, but not be limited to physical, sexual and psychological violence occurring in the family, including battering, sexual abuse of female children in the household, dowry-related violence, marital rape, female genital mutilation and other traditional practices harmful to women, non-spousal violence and violence related to exploitation; physical, sexual and psychological violence occurring within the general community, including rape, sexual abuse, sexual harassment and intimidation at work, in educational institutions and elsewhere; trafficking in women and forced prostitution; and physical, sexual and psychological violence perpetrated or condoned by the State, wherever it occurs.

The Canadian Criminal Code has no specific offence of violence against women or spousal assault. Code provisions that most commonly apply to cases of violence against women include the offences of assault, sexual assault, criminal harassment, threats of violence, forcible confinement and homicide. For the most part, the statistical data presented in this publication were derived from Criminal Code definitions. Types of abuse addressed in this report include the following:

Physical violence, including threats of violence, hitting with fists or weapons, with or without physical injury, is the most commonly understood form of abuse. All forms of physical violence are crimes under the Criminal Code.

Sexual violence is any form of non-consensual or forced sexual activity or touching, including rape. All forms of sexual violence are crimes under the Criminal Code. The term "sexual assault" encompasses a wide range of criminal acts ranging from unwanted sexual touching to sexual violence involving weapons, and is categorized according to three levels of severity. The term "sexual offence" refers to the three levels of sexual assault as well as other sexual offences which are designed primarily to protect children.

Psychological or emotional abuse includes insults, humiliation, put-downs and yelling, and extreme (often unfounded) jealousy. These are not crimes under the Criminal Code, but are often effectively used to control and intimidate intimate partners. It also includes harming pets and damaging property, which are crimes under the Criminal Code.

Financial abuse (also referred to as economic abuse or material exploitation) includes restricting access to family resources, inheritance or employment opportunities, or to seize pay cheques. Unless theft, fraud or some form of coercion is used, financial abuse is not a crime under the Criminal Code.

Spousal abuse refers to physical or sexual violence or psychological or financial abuse within current or former marital or common-law relationships, including same-sex spousal relationships. The broader category of intimate partner abuse encompasses spousal violence and violence committed by current or former dating partners.

Spousal assault is measured according to the Criminal Code and includes physical or sexual assault and threats of violence.

Spousal homicide refers to the killing of a marital or common-law partner and includes first and second degree murder and manslaughter.

Criminal harassment/stalking are obsessive behaviour directed toward another person. It can involve persistent, malicious and unwanted surveillance, and invasion of privacy that is a constant threat to the victim's personal security. Criminal harassment is an offence under the Criminal Code.

Trafficking in persons is a crime under the Criminal Code. It is not addressed in this publication because of the absence of data in this area. Trafficking is the use of deception, coercion or force to recruit, move or hold a person in order to use or exploit that person against their will for the sex trade or forced labour. The US State Department, in their Trafficking in Persons Report 2005, estimates that 600,000 to 800,000 persons are trafficked across international borders each year and approximately 80 percent are women and girls. The majority of transnational victims are trafficked into commercial sexual exploitation. These estimates exclude millions of persons who are trafficked within their own national borders (US State Department 2005).

Spouses and ex-spouses include legally married, separated and divorced persons as well as common-law spouses and ex-spouses. Also includes same-sex spouses.

Intimite partners and ex-partners include spouse and ex-spouse, and current or former dating partners.

The indicators of violence against women are organized into five themes in this report:

1. Prevalence and severity of violence against women

These indicators can help governments take stock and assess whether efforts to reduce violence against women have made a difference. Although they cannot detect whether specific programs and services have directly affected the level of violence, indicators describing the prevalence and severity of violence against women can show changes that happened at the same time as prevention and intervention efforts were underway. These indicators also help plan the delivery of services and modifications to policy and programs.

2. Impact of violence against women

These indicators monitor the impacts and consequences of victimization, including physical consequences such as injury, medical attention, hospitalization, emotional impacts, and broader societal-level impacts such as the economic costs of violence.

3. Risk factors associated with violence against women

    Identifying factors that increase the risk of victimization is important for both intervention and prevention efforts. To target resources, stakeholders need to know who is at risk of what types of violence and in what situations, and who is vulnerable to multiple, chronic and ongoing victimization. Knowledge about risk factors can also help to focus prevention efforts and social service supports on sub-groups of the population that have the greatest need.

4. Institutional and community-based responses

    Tracking how governments and community organizations have responded to violence against women will help address questions about the types of services available and how the availability of services has changed over time.

5. Use of services by victims

    These indicators help identify how victims use services and what the barriers to obtaining help might be.

The 2002 publication, Assessing Violence Against Women: A Statistical Profile, included a sixth type of indicator: public attitudes and perceptions. While tracking societal attitudes on violence against women remains an important task, few jurisdictions have updated these surveys since 2002. This report therefore focuses on the five indicators for which current data are available.

In addition, the Federal/Provincial/Territorial (F/P/T) Status of Women Ministers felt that the situation of violence against Aboriginal women and women living in the territories warranted specific sections in this document. Recent statistics confirm what other small scale studies have found: Aboriginal women in Canada are at significantly higher risk of spousal violence than other segments of society. For the first time, residents of the three territories (Yukon, Northwest Territories and Nunavut) were interviewed for the 2004 General Social

Survey (GSS) as part of a pilot test and results show that women who live in the territories also experience higher levels of violence. However, due to undercoverage of Aboriginal people, residents of rural or remote areas and those whose mother tongue is not English or French, estimates of violence in the territories must be used with caution.

On the international stage, Canada has been taken to task for the persistent disadvantage faced by Aboriginal women in education, employment and physical safety. The lack of detailed statistical data on violence against Aboriginal women has been identified as an impediment to addressing the causes of violence and ensuring access for Aboriginal women to the justice system. The focus on Aboriginal and Northern women's experiences of violence in this publication makes a contribution toward the goal of providing improved data for policy making.

BENEFITS AND LIMITATIONS OF INDICATORS

Violence indicators have many potential benefits. They can:

i. Increase understanding of the severity and prevalence of acts of violence against women;
ii. Enhance awareness of community and government responses to violence;
iii. Serve as a "red flag" for governments and non-governmental organizations by highlighting emerging issues;
iv. Assist in policy-making, planning and resource allocation;
v. Help identify possible points of intervention by examining factors associated with a heightened risk of violence;
vi. Together with other tools and information, contribute to an evaluation of efforts to reduce violence;
vii. Act as a catalyst for further scientific inquiry and research.

Despite these advantages, readers need to be aware of the limitations of statistical indicators, including the undercounting of victims due to the very personal nature of these experiences. In addition, while indicators may highlight problems, they cannot prescribe solutions. Nor do they necessarily show cause and effect without also taking into account other social and demographic factors. Due to jurisdictional differences in the way policies and services to victims are organized, caution must be used when making comparisons across provinces and territories. For example, police charging policies vary among jurisdictions - some jurisdictions have pre-charge screening by prosecutors while others do not. The way victim services are organized by jurisdictions also varies due in part to resource availability.

In recent years, the importance of involving men in achieving gender equality has been highlighted within the United Nations system, international and civil society organizations. There has been a growing recognition that the role of men is crucial in changing unequal power relations. In particular, involving men in movements to end violence against women, focusing on men's roles and responsibilities and emphasis on men as part of the solution to combat violence against women has gained increased attention in the last several years.

Many innovative initiatives have been developed and organized to engage and involve men in the struggle to end violence, such as gender- and violence against women sensitization workshops for men, police trainings, and awareness raising activities or campaigns targeted at and led by men who repudiate violence against women. In this regard, UNESCAP organized a "Sub-regional Training Workshop on Elimination of Violence Against Women in Partnership with Men" in December 2003 in New Delhi for Government officials and civil society representatives working on eliminating violence against women. The two papers in this publication and the inventory of organizations and initiatives were prepared for this training workshop. They are aimed at highlighting ideas, concepts, policies, approaches and strategies for a greater involvement and engagement of men to eliminate gender violence.

Gender-based violence is one of the greatest blocks to development worldwide. Consequently, it is of highest priority for many development organizations and the United Nations system. Across South Asia, some of the highest rates of gender violence are being reported - and in some of its most malicious forms such as honour killing, trafficking, acid attacks and prison rape. Ending gender-based violence requires a cohesive combination of effective laws, social policies and fundamental transformation of the beliefs and practices of institutions and individuals. This chapter discusses the relationship between gender-based violence and gender norms for men and to outline some of the ways in which progress can be made to reduce violence in South Asia with a focus on men's roles and responsibilities.

MEN, VIOLENCE AND GENDER

Compared with women, men, especially young men, are overwhelmingly involved in all types of violence. It is mostly men who commit acts of personal violence - against women and girls, as well as towards other men and boys. Men are also most often implicated in other types of "organized" or institutional violence as victims and perpetrators of violence. Around the world and in South Asia, militaries consist of only men or mostly men. Men fight more than women – in wars, in the home, schoolyard, and on the street. It is primarily men who are drafted into jihadi, nationalist or separatist movements or who perpetrate acts of terrorism. In general, men use weapons more than women, and are imprisoned and murdered more than women.

It is also a fact that, in general, men control more resources and wield more power than women. Violence and being a man seem to go hand in hand. As do violence and seeking and retaining power. But that is not to say violence is a natural condition for men, or a natural part of being a man. Nor is it to say that all men are in positions of power. Men are taught to use violence, and at times are encouraged to use it. Violence is culturally and politically sanctioned, both implicitly and explicitly in different ways. This chapter is focused on gender-based violence, which can be argued, is intricately connected to all other types of violence. Gender-based violence is rooted in the structural and the personal.

At the structural level it is grounded in patriarchy - a system that positions men over women (and other men) and instills a sense of entitlement and privilege in many men. Patriarchy is also linked to the social, cultural and legal contexts that permit for gender-based violence including, for instance, systems of class, caste, dowry and fundamentalism of all sorts. But at the personal level, gender violence is also based on the pressures, fears and stifled emotions that underlie many of the dominant forms of manhood espoused in different settings. Added to this are the individual experiences of violence for individuals - learning and experiencing violence from the family, the media, the community and or other institutions.

One short definition of gender-based violence is any form of violence used to establish, enforce or perpetuate gender inequalities and keep in place gendered orders. In other words, gender-based violence is a policing mechanism. It is rooted in the gender discourses of masculinity and femininity (prescribed norms and definitions of what it means to be a man or a woman) - and how men and women are positioned vis-à-vis one another and other groups of men and women. Gender- based violence is mostly men's violence towards women and girls, but it can also be violence toward other men and boys (in the form of bullying, baiting, violence against homosexuals or transsexuals, sexual abuse, etc.).

Gender-based violence takes many forms - physical, sexual, and emotional abuse, as well as restricted freedoms and rights, coercion and/or threats. Gender-based violence cuts across culture, class, caste, religion and location - no one is immune to its devastation. It incapacitates families and partnerships and the ability for many to relate to themselves or others with love, compassion or respect. It spreads fear, pain and self-loathing - inhibiting the basic rights of adults and children alike. In a macro sense, gender-based violence restricts the achievement of development, peace, and freedom. As such, it is a major contributor to global poverty – in both the income and human definitions of the term.

One reason the term "gender-based violence" is useful is that it helps ground violence firmly in gender and allows for a careful analysis of the gender socialization processes surrounding men and women. It also highlights the connections between gender-based violence and other types of violence used as "policing mechanisms" to keep social hierarchies in place and to perpetuate inequality – such as the violence behind racism, the caste system and bigotry. Thus, to ground violence more firmly in gender, a deeper understanding of men's gender is in order.

THE USES OF MASCULINITIES

It is not easy for men to articulate their fears, give words to rising anxieties in their heart. What comes more easily is violence, not always but often. Just as men's roles and responsibilities are often missing from the phrase "violence against women and girls", far too often men have been conspicuously missing from conversations around gender. This near invisibility of men's gender is part of the privilege men gain as a "dividend" of patriarchy. In general, men as a group benefit from gender inequalities; it is to men's benefit to keep the means of their privilege hidden from critical examination.

One way to bring men's gender into focus is through the examination of masculinities. Masculinities are different definitions concerning what it means to be a man in different cultural contexts around the world. The plural form "masculinities" conveys that there are many definitions of being a man and that these can change over time and from place to place.

This plural form also suggests that men are constantly negotiating differing positions within social hierarchies – and this multiple positioning affects men's relationship to injustice and violence. In recent years, there has been more and more academic work focused on men and masculinities. This academic work starts from the basic premise that men and masculinity are different notions entirely. Men are biological creatures - each individual uniquely different - whereas masculinities are stories or "discourses" about men and how they ideally should behave in a given setting.

Men are human beings, and as such are social and gendered beings. Explorations of masculinities help clarify men as gendered beings, and also help with the understanding of the varying ideals about manhood that inform men's behaviours and how these are related to the use of violence. Examining masculinity and the role it plays in society is not simply an analytical exercise, but has widespread implications for the effectiveness of programmes that seek to end violence and improve economic and social outcomes in every country in the region.

In addition to the plurality of masculinities across South Asia and the world, there are also repeated notions about being men; dominant or "hegemonic masculinities". To understand this concept in simple and personal terms one may ask, "What should an ideal man look like? What do societies expect first and foremost of men? What are boys taught in schools, through the media and social institutions, in communities and in families in terms of how they should perform and what they should achieve as men? Some common denominators around South Asia - in fact some of the shared characteristics of dominant masculinity around the world - describe men as strong, breadwinner, attractive, protector, leader, and decision maker.

These characteristics apply both within the household as well as in public - heterosexual and sexually successful. An ICRW report on masculinity in Rajasthan shows that men's roles and responsibilities are largely understood through the three main roles of provider, protector and procreator. The performance of these roles and responsibilities is a critical factor in men understands of masculinity. As the report shows, 99.8 per cent of men agreed that these roles and responsibilities are an essential part of masculinity, and 66 per cent of the men ranked them as the most essential aspect of masculinity.

In many instances, there is an implicit assumption that men must be ready to use violence to successfully achieve these roles. At other times men are explicitly encouraged to use violence in the name of protecting or fulfilling these roles. Yet across South Asia as in other regions no less, no man can fully live up to all of these ideals, at all times throughout the lifecycle. This is even more evident in the context of societies built upon a complex of privilege and inequality, and added with the compilations and flux wrought by economic and social globalization. And yet many men see no alternative but to struggle to live up to these ideals, despite inevitable failures or stacked odds. This crisis of masculinity or "paradox of men's power" as one author describes it, is one of the root causes of gender-based violence.

At the same time they are trying to live up to ideals of dominant masculinity, men are indoctrinated into violence as a means of asserting their perceived positions as men. "If you ask men about their experience of power, most probably you are going to hear experiences of powerlessness, insecurity and instability - all situations that can lead to confusion and ultimately to violence". Men struggle with these dominant notions of masculinity in both the public and private parts of their lives. If men do not "succeed" as masculine in the public domain - through status, economic gains and/or security - violence may occur in the private sphere in the form of intimate partner violence.

"For all castes and religions, domestic violence is frequently is linked to men's failure, either real or perceived, to fulfill masculine roles. Such failure is compounded when wives react to a husband's failure by challenging his misconduct. Both the failure itself and the wife's challenges, which undermine his masculinity, make the husband feel humiliated". Feelings of pressure and insecurity cut across class as well.

As one contributor to a UN DAW online discussion relates: My husband and I are both young urban professionals educated and reasonably well-off and may be described as well-to-do in Dhaka Society today. But in spite of coming from families where both parents have been educated and where higher education of the girls in the family have been encouraged, I can see that my success and being outgoing often becomes a source of worry for my partner, especially when his career is not going so well. It seems whatever I do I must always be subdued and never outshine him. This seems to be an inherent insecurity in males not only in the Bangladeshi society but I am sure in a lot of other societies too.

Understanding masculinities as socially constructed also means that men are not merely passive that are being shaped by "society" or "culture". Men and women are active in producing gender discourses and acting them out. Patriarchy and other systems of inequality are a backdrop to gender-based violence, but individual men are responsible for their violence. Both women and men are part of the problem when they teach and reinforce strict gender roles that allow for violence - especially violence against women and girls - to exist in their communities.

One man from the Pakistani/Afghani border region tells how, "on my wedding night, my grandmother came to me and said, 'tonight you must beat your new wife, or she will never respect you' - but I felt that I did not want to beat her, in my heart I felt that I wanted to love her". On the other hand, being socially constructed means that there many "masculinities" and multiple options of behaviour for individual men and women. Across and within the countries of South Asia there are countless variations of the masculine. From Bollywood film stars to Bhutanese monks, from Pashtuns to Singhalese, from rural to urban and from young to the old there are innumerable notions and articulations of being a man.

Many men are not violent, some men are actively seeking to end violence and there are countless cultural messages and examples of masculinity that encourage peaceful engagement with the world. Exploring masculinities helps to expose men's gender and to highlight the socialization process (of boys into men) in terms of teaching men to use violence and the sanctioning of violence in general. Conversations about masculinities can also help individual men reflect on the various costs to them of playing out dominant masculine roles and to help highlight the benefits of alternative constructions of the masculine.

A SPECTRUM OF POSSIBILITIES FOR WORKING WITH MEN

Significant strides have been made over the last few decades towards reducing gender-based violence in many parts of the world. There are local, national and international laws, conventions and agreements that define gender-based violence and legislate against those who use it. There is more public education, awareness and acceptance of the problem and more institutions acting in accordance of the laws. In addition, there are now more shelters around the world and trained service providers to care for survivors of violence, and even some services to council those who use violence, or to give them counseling before violence is used. Many of these efforts are now more informed by a clearer understanding of men and masculinities.

Historically, violence prevention work has been driven by and focused on women. Women still need to be center stage in terms of empowerment, equality and safety. Yet in terms of violence prevention, men have a responsibility to play a much greater role. Men are key power brokers, decision takers and change makers - and men are the ones most implicated in gender-based violence. Fortunately there are concrete examples of the different ways in which men can become part of the process of overcoming gender-based violence. Men's roles in and responsibilities for ending violence are manifold.

They range from men changing their relationships with their intimate partners to male-dominated institutions changing the way they function in order to better confront issues of gender and power. Men in Madurai wear white ribbons to mark the International Day for the Eradication of Violence against Women. NGOs in Bangladesh, work with men in rural communities through popular education workshops. In Pakistan, some male lawyers and judges have connected with one another to set precedents for convictions of perpetuators and to advocate for the rights of "accused" women susceptible to honour killing. One way to help map these entry points for engaging men is to categorize them at different levels of work namely the policy, public, and the personal level.

PUBLIC POLICY AND LAWS

Examples of policy work include both men as partners in advocating for better laws around gender-based violence and ensuring those laws recognize the roles and responsibilities of men. Policy work is much more than appropriate national legislation on violence against women or reporting on CEDAW or other international conventions. Policy around gender-based violence is also concerned with basic rights and poverty reduction – in short ending violence is not a standalone issue. For example, policy initiatives in the health (ending the spread of HIV/AIDS), education (more gender-sensitive curricula that includes men), finance (gender budgets and cost surveys on violence) and labour sectors (ending gender segregation in employment), can also be part of a cohesive national violence prevention effort that includes men and boys.

Gender-based violence is now being understood more as a public issue, not a private/silent matter – and thus it is treated as public health policy issue. Many national health agencies, like the Center for Disease Control in the United States, have discrete offices or programmes on ending violence against women and are funding prevention initiatives working with men. Also, across the world, public policies to help end the spread of HIV/AIDS have been solidly connected to both masculinities and ending gender-violence. NGOs in many countries are working with education ministries to devise core curricula for gender studies, explicitly including men as well as women.

In terms of finance policy, in New Zealand for example, the Ministry for Women undertook a national cost/benefit analysis – measuring the costs of gender violence incurred by the government – finding that the cost of violence was greater than the revenue earned from the country's largest import - wool. Other cost of violence studies are also being undertaken by the Inter-American Development Bank in Latin America. "Economic arguments" highlighting the public costs (from incarceration, medical expenses, loss of work, trials, etc) can be compelling for some policy makers, especially when gender-based-violence is understood as a major block to national development and poverty reduction.

Other sets of policy examples encourage more gender equitable behaviours in men such as caring for children and sharing of household responsibilities. In Scandinavia and other parts of Europe, paternity-leave and flexible work childcare laws, legislated and adhered to nationally, encourage men to take time off for child care. The connection here is that much research indicates the more time men spend in child-rearing activities, the less likely they will commit acts of family violence.

THE PUBLIC SPHERE - ORGANIZATIONAL PRACTICE AND PUBLIC AWARENESS

Laws and polices mean little if institutions and cultural contexts are enabling environments. Overall work in the "public sphere" aims to make gender-based violence accepted as a public issue, to build the capacity of institutions to more effectively deal with the problem, and to ensure men play a role in speaking out against violence and working for better, more equitable institutions. Organizations in general play a pivotal role between the individual and their societies at large - and are key for gender transformation.

The literature on the gendered nature of organizations suggests that, as organized sites and arrangements of power, they typically reflect and reinforce the social hierarchies and inequalities of power that structure the lives of individuals. In most organizations, as in most societies, such power is male. This is true for public agencies and development organizations as well - all of which have special responsibilities to set the standards with firm sexual harassment policies, more gender balance at management levels and flexible work/care policies that encourage more men to engage in child care.

In Islamabad, an NGO called Rozan is conducting gender violence sensitization workshops with the police to help transform the way that institution thinks about and responds to gender-based violence. These workshops focus on gender implications in both the personal and professional aspects of police men and women's lives - and help the individuals see the connections between the two. In another example, a leader in Pakistan's National Medical Association works at raising awareness on the issue of violence against women and girls through campaigning, sending postcards to policymakers (depicting victims of acid attacks) - and this work is amplified by his position within the national organization.

Finally, the White Ribbon Campaign is a widely known public awareness effort engaging men around violence prevention. White Ribbon mobilizes men to speak out against violence against women and, in doing so, helps men examine their own attitudes and behaviors. Today there are forms of white ribbon activities in many countries including India. In Canada thousands of schools and workplaces participate in the annual White Ribbon Days, which last 16 days beginning from November 25.

THE PERSONAL DOMAIN

Improvement in laws and institutions is necessary for ending violence, but positive change is also needed in the ways that individuals perceive of and behave towards one another and themselves. At the personal this level involves the transformation of gendered relations, perceptions and beliefs within households and among individuals. Projects that deal with men who use violence have traditionally been seen as the space to work towards personal transformation. But in effect, any moment individuals, families or community groups are gathered is an opportunity for discussing personal perceptions and beliefs. Examples of projects at this level include peer counseling and awareness raising around gender and violence through other entry points such as health and community development projects.

As mentioned above, Rozan serves as a good example of a project that works at the personal level to transform an institutional culture. These connections between the personal and political are vital for prevention. As one participating police officer commented, "Before this workshop I was a violent husband and police officer. Now I try my best not to abuse power at my home or office. Now I even help my spouse in domestic work". Another example - Instituto Promundo in Rio de Janeiro, Brazil - coordinates a peer outreach programme called the Guy-to-Guy Project, which trains young men from low-income communities to work with other young men in promoting sexual and reproductive health and preventing gender- based violence (Barker – UNDAW 2003).

SOME ENTRY POINTS FOR THE SOUTH ASIAN CONTEXT

Across South Asia, different countries and cultural contexts have different starting points and opportunities for work towards reducing gender-based violence. What might work in one context will not in another at any particular point in time because perceptions of how they are engaged as partners vary widely. While the evidence of effective ground level work for and by men to overcome gender-based violence in South Asia is sparse, there are some examples of promising initiatives including those mentioned above. As the region is a vast mixture of cultures, classes, castes, beliefs, religions and languages, the task at hand is to identify and utilize the various possible entry points that are culturally appropriate across the diverse settings.

As noted, violence prevention polices can stretch far beyond specific laws around domestic or sexual violence. In South Asia there is certainly room for improvement in anti-dowry laws, laws of "evidence", inheritance and property ownership laws, labour laws and setting percentages for women in governing bodies - to name a few. Countries across the region also need better legal frameworks that protect women and create a greater dis-incentive for perpetrators of violence. National laws need to be strengthened and enforced, and international commitments need greater backing. Even when there are strong laws in place (such as Sri Lanka's anti-rape laws) violence is not reported or acted upon due to lack of precedent or awareness around the law, fear and shame and/or public humiliation on the part of victims (or for her partner) and/or other cultural norms. In many South Asian contexts, as in other parts of the world, there is a complex mixture of civil law, sharia and/or religious based laws and cultural norms that comprise the local "legal" setting.

To identify potential for men's involvement in prevention through the legal - one is then obliged to explore civic, cultural and religious realms. "There is no substitute for expanding the contexts in which supportive, pro-feminist, gender alive practices are talked about and circulated" (Chopra 2003 p. 7). There is a strong potential in work with men in local religious and cultural institutions. Imams, priests, monks and local civic leaders wield broad influence, can serve as positive non-violent role models and can make the connections between local beliefs and more peaceful homes and communities.

Both Syed and Shah describe NGOs in Pakistan who work with imams of different mosques and sects, community leaders police and judges. Hayward (2000) describes how many men in South Asia are concerned with the way religion is used for political purposes - including being used as rationales for the subordination of women. The men interviewed relate, "All religions are against violence, those who do not obey the religion carry out various types of violence." Or "We have to differentiate between religion and tradition. Since religion has been diverted into a superstitious tradition, women have been considered as "inferior creatures". No such things exist in Islam" (Hayward 2000).

Men may also be engaged around the issue of shifting economic roles for men and women necessitated by keeping their households economically sustainable. Women need greater economic opportunities for empowerment and freedom – and to help end violence. But South Asian realities such as economic migration (for men and women) and increased formal and informal employment for women are forcing men and women to think and act differently in terms of traditional gendered divisions of labour within the household and the public sphere. Openly discussing these changes, and showing the benefits of more flexible divisions of labour may offer a space to engage men in discussions about gender and violence that are highly relevant to their own lives.

"Men within families are fully aware of the critical nature of women's earnings and I have rarely come across instances where the nature of work has been downplayed by men. However, patriarchal controls, duties and power are being re- negotiated under these unpredictable times and families are being re-organized along lines which are still not clear to the participants…the legitimacy of the patriarchal discourse around masculinities might have been chipped away in the developments we are witnessing but the exercising of power remains very much in place and is probably the next bastion to be cracked open" (Roy – UNDAW 2003).

These changes in work and roles within families and the wider labour market are occurring at different rates within and across the South Asian countries – rural versus urban areas and so on – but one major indicator for acceptance of new behaviours is youth. To give one example, "where micro-credit is been made available for women of working class households to begin small, home based industries (either through government or NGO initiative) gender dynamics within households have undergone a perceptible, though still restricted, change. Younger men in particular – sons, brothers and nephews – become employees of women who run these small household businesses.

The investment of the younger men in affirming male dominance does not vanish. But it does vacillate between treating the woman "business head" as a boss on the one hand and on the other as a woman who now needs help to complete her home-oriented responsibilities" (Chropra - UNDAW 2003).

Young people represent great potential for remaking the world in a more peaceful and equitable fashion. Young men and women are still learning, practicing and "trying out" their sexuality, their attitudes and behaviours towards relationships and society. More engagement and partnerships with youth is an obvious and necessary way forward for violence prevention.

There is also potential to engage men in their various roles as fathers, sons, husbands and brothers. Men as fathers often express great care and concern for the safety and well being of their daughters, as do sons for their mothers. Using these relationships as entry points to talk more broadly about gender roles and violence is a common strategy. But in South Asia, there are specific roles for men in families that can also be seen as potential entry points for these conversations. As Chopra points out, "women in Indian families count their fathers and brothers as key partners throughout the period of pregnancy, childbirth and continuing care of their children. This dual orientation (toward the father and the husband) is important for women precisely because they can evoke their rights vis-à-vis both sets of men".

Finally more research, understanding and public awareness around men, masculinity and violence are needed throughout the region. Some public awareness initiatives include the White Ribbon Campaign in Madurai, Tamil Nadu and Men against Violence and Abuse (MAVA) based in Mumbai which conducts awareness raising programmes geared towards gender justice. MAVA releases a yearly publication, Purush Spandan, in collabouration with Purush Uvach - a similar group in Pune. There is also a growing interest in and academic study of the diverse examples of masculinities in South Asia. In 2002 in India, for example, there has been a "traveling seminar" on masculinities moving through six universities in the country (organized by Rahul Roy with the support of UNIFEM). There is also a post Masters level course "Theorizing Masculinities" in the sociology department of the University of Delhi (taught by Dr. R. Chopra).

Men are the main agents of violence in the world. It is also clear that widespread patterns of masculinity, or definitions for what it means to be a man, support this violence. Yet many men are not violent, and there are alternative patterns of masculinity that are displayed by and open for men. South Asia, a broad and intense amalgamation of cultures and practices, offers specific openings for engaging men around violence prevention. Some of these openings include engaging men as policy makers, public service providers and civic and religious leaders. But ultimately policy and institutional transformations also require fundamental changes among individual perceptions, beliefs and behaviours of men - men who are fathers, sons, husbands and brothers.

The police officer attending gender sensitization workshop in Islamabad makes the connections between gender roles in his own family and the police force's failure to effectively address men's violence against women. Connecting issues and experiences in this way is critical if men are to become more effective partners in changing the attitudes, behaviours and conditions that create gender-based violence. To work towards transformation and gender justice, not only are stronger partnerships that include men essential, but also more cohesion is needed across the various levels of work described above. Ministries should talk to one another to establish consistent messages and goals of policy. NGOs can form stronger coalitions for violence prevention to coordinate efforts and share resources.

Local and international NGOs and the United Nations System can play a key role in educating policy makers and providing strategies to address priority prevention issues. At the community level, service providers and local leaders should also coordinate efforts. The examples of working with men to end gender-based violence bring to light some guiding principles that can be identified and incorporated into new initiatives. For example, a clear conceptual framework of gender-based violence is needed, one that makes the connections between men, gender and violence, and brings men firmly into the prevention equation.

Such a conceptual framework includes an understanding that some models of masculinity encourage violence and restrict men's choices and safety.

Following from this is the notion that ending gender-based violence presents benefits for men as well as women and children. These benefits include more choice in how to behave, relate to others and form more productive relationships within families and the community. There are economic benefits as well, for the productivity of households, communities, institutions and businesses. Related to the benefits is the understanding of the unique positions, needs and motivations of boys and men. Rather than categorically blaming and shaming men, or using normative language not connected to men's experience of both power and vulnerability, programmes should start with a more holistic understanding.

Not all men use violence, and not all men are privileged in the same ways by gender hierarchies. Those men that stand up as advocates for women and for ending gender-based violence are at times ridiculed and are often lonely voices – more efforts should be made to support and connect them. In South Asia attention also must be paid to specific cultural contexts and interventions should be nurtured that work to enhance positive cultural norms. Interventions that appear to be "top down" or "foreign" have a high likelihood of failure. As one author puts it "some NGOs which are working for the rights of women have no appeal for the common people, including women, because through their conduct they give an impression that they are strangers to the society" (Shah – UNDAW 2003).

Another view argues that "policies that engage with existing practices building on them while simultaneously orienting them toward expanded contexts have a better chance of becoming culturally incorporated that those that operate from above and outside (Chopra – UNDAW 2003). Cultural competency includes working from the ground up, identifying local traditions, norms and masculine characteristics that are conducive to ending violence – while at the same time not allowing for "culture" to be an excuse for the violence of individuals. And finally, an additional guiding principle is connecting ending gender-based violence with other social development goals such as public health, social justice and poverty reduction.

At the project level, this requires a macro vision of anti-violence work that is connected to overall social development in the community. At the institutional and governmental level, this entails making clear and strong the connections between ending gender-based violence, men's responsibilities to this end, and the achievement of national and international commitments such as the Millennium Development Goals and Poverty Reduction Strategy Papers.

INVOLVING MEN IN ELIMINATING VIOLENCE AGAINST WOMEN

The role of men in ending gender-based violence, and working in partnership with men has become an important aspect in the movement to end violence against women. United Nations entities, NGOs, community based organizations, activists and researchers have begun to realize that it is crucial to involve men and that men need to be part of the solution to combat violence against women. This report intends to highlight the good practices and activities of organizations and networks that work with men to end violence against women.

In addition to United Nations programmes, Rozan, an NGO in Pakistan, the Fiji Women's Crisis Centre, the Man's Action to Stop Violence against Women (MASVAW) network in India, the Cambodia Men's Network and the White Ribbon Campaign all provide unique examples of ways to involve men in the movement to end gender-based violence. Gender-based violence and violence against women is a human rights, public health, and gender issue. It is the most oppressive and pervasive violation of women's human rights and an impediment to achieving gender equality, as well as promoting development and peace. World-wide, it is estimated that one out of three women has been beaten, coerced into sex, raped or otherwise physically abused.

Violence affects women in all societies, regardless of culture, region, ethnicity, religion and economic status. The causes for violence against women are a complex combination of cultural, legal, economic and political factors, yet it is a generally accepted view that violence against women is the result of patriarchal ideology, values, and norms, unbalanced power relations, as well as strict divisions of labour, socialization processes, and cultural customs and traditions. Poverty and low socio-economic development further exacerbate the problem. In the Asian and the Pacific region, strictly defined gender roles, discrimination and gender inequality result in an environment rife with violence against women. Recent years have shown a notable increase in all forms of violence against women in the South Asian region.

Although great advances have been made in the international context regarding legal frameworks, mechanisms and policies to protect women from violence, challenges remain in effective implementation of these laws and standards. Gender-based violence is a complex phenomenon that requires a multifaceted response by the United Nations, governments, NGOs, practitioners, and community based organizations.

ROLE OF THE UNITED NATIONS

The United Nations has been at the forefront of protecting women's rights and efforts at eliminating violence against women. The Convention on the Elimination of all Forms of Discrimination against Women (CEDAW), commonly referred to as the "international bill of rights of women", covers a vast array of women's economic, political, social, cultural and civil rights, and has been ratified by 174 member countries. Unfortunately, only 56 Countries have ratified the Optional Protocols to the Convention, which include inquiry, communication and investigation procedures.

The Beijing Declaration and the Beijing Platform for Action is the most comprehensive document outlining pronouncements and recommendations on twelve critical areas of concern, of which violence against women is one. The Platform for Action categorizes violence against women as an obstacle to the achievement of equality, development and peace, and calls on all governments to place priority on initiatives to eliminate all forms of violence against women. The United Nations Commission on Human Rights in 1994 appointed a Special Rapporteur on violence against women to collect and analyze comprehensive data on violence against women in member states, and recommend measures aimed at eliminating violence at the international, national and regional levels.

Radhika Coomaraswamy, UN Special Rapporteur on violence against women until 2003, presented yearly reports on the issue of human rights and violence against women, and made explicit and specific recommendations on how governments should take action to eliminate violence against women. The United Nations Declaration on the Elimination of Violence against Women, adopted by the General Assembly in 1993, defines violence against women as "any act of gender-based violence that results in, or is likely to result in, physical, sexual or mental harm or suffering to women, including threats of such acts, coercion or arbitrary deprivation of liberty, whether occurring in public or in private life."

This encompasses "physical, sexual and psychological violence occurring in the family and in the general community, including battering, sexual abuse of children, dowry- related violence, rape, female genital mutilation and other traditional practices harmful to women, non-spousal violence and violence related to exploitation, sexual harassment and intimidation at work, in educational institutions and elsewhere, trafficking in women, forced prostitution, and violence perpetrated or condoned by the state." Feticide, infanticide, honour killings and sexual slavery, sati (widow-burning), marital rape, dowry-related abuse and acid-throwing are included in this definition.

THE ROLE OF MEN

In the last decade, the role of men in ending gender-based violence, and working in partnership with men has become an important aspect in the movement to end violence against women. United Nations entities, NGOs, community based organizations, activists and researchers have begun to realize that it is crucial to involve men and that men need to be part of the solution to combat violence against women. There is a variety of valid arguments for the importance of involving men.

Men are not only the predominant perpetrators of violence against women, but their decision-making roles and power in the economic, political and social spheres necessitate their commitment to eradicating violence against women. An important aspect of the significance of involving men in efforts to eliminate violence against women is that men hold higher positions of power and decision-making in most communities in the world, making it crucial to garner their support and commitment in ending violence against women. In addition, it is in men's interest to eliminate violence against women, because violence directly affects them, whether as witnesses, relatives, victims, and perpetrators.

Men need to be involved in efforts to eliminate violence against women due to the socialization processes that support men taking on dominant behaviors toward women that allow them to exert power and control over women, as well as feel entitled to be privileged over women. Men need to be involved and incorporated because only then will the message spread that men need to take responsibility for their actions, choose not to use violence, and develop alternate norms of 'masculinity'. Cooperation, partnership and dialogue between women and men must be fostered in order to create alternatives to violence and foster environments that nurture peace and development.

Men should also take collective action against violence against women in order to encourage other men to get involved and to show that it is a sign of strength to fight violence, instead of a sign of weakness. In addition, working with men to end violence should be viewed as part of an overall goal of achieving gender equality, meaning that working with men is complimentary to empowering women and achieving gender equality as a whole.

THE UNITED NATIONS AND THE ROLE OF MEN

The role of men in promoting gender equality and eliminating violence against women has been highlighted in several United Nations documents and declarations. These include the Beijing Declaration, adopted during the Fourth World Conference on Women in 1995, where participating governments expressed their determination to encourage men to participate fully in all actions to end violence against women. In its recommendations to eliminate violence against women, the Beijing Platform for Action states, "Men's groups mobilizing against gender violence are necessary allies for change" Further, the Beijing Declaration and Platform for Action emphasizes the importance of working in partnership with men and involving men in all actions aimed at achieving gender equality.

At the International Conference on Population and Development (ICPD) held in Cairo in 1994, participants agreed that "men play an important role in achieving gender equality, since in most societies, they exercise preponderant power in nearly every sphere of life, ranging from personal decisions regarding family size, to all levels of political and program decisions". Lastly, at the forty-second session of the Commission on the Status of Women, governments were asked to encourage and support men's initiatives to prevent and eliminate violence against women and girls, and one of the themes for the forty-eighth session of the Commission on the Status of Women in 2004 will be the role of men and boys in achieving gender equality.

The role of men, and a focus on including men in sexual and reproductive health and HIV/AIDS prevention, has also gained increased attention in the last several years by many United Nations bodies and international organizations. UNFPA, UNAIDS, as well as organizations such as Engender Health and the Population Council have developed programmes and projects involving men and focusing on male responsibilities in reproductive health and HIV/AIDS prevention. One of the first United Nations initiatives involving men in regards to violence against women was the UNESCO Women and Culture or Peace program, which held an expert group meeting in Oslo 1997 on "Male Roles and Masculinities in the Perspective of a Culture of Peace".

This meeting was convened to address issues of masculinity and explore ways in which changing norms of masculinities is important in working toward peace and an end to violence against women. Participants at the meeting agreed that the transformation from a culture of violence to a culture of peace is dependent on the development of more egalitarian and partnership-oriented forms of masculinity, as opposed to traditional forms premised on dominance, authority, control and force.

The UNESCO Women and Culture of Peace programme's objective was to promote gender-sensitive socialization for non-violence and egalitarian partnerships with a special focus on young men and boys, and to organize conferences, educational campaigns and training projects to achieve elimination of violence against women. The UNESCO publication Male roles, Masculinities and Violence: A Culture of Peace Perspective was the first United Nations publication to focus on the direct involvement of men in ending violence against women.

In 2002, the United Nations International Research and Training Institute for the Advancement of Women (UN INSTRAW) developed an e-mail based seminar discussion series called "Ending Male Violence -Net" to provide a forum for United Nations bodies, practitioners, NGO representatives, activists and university professionals to discuss men's roles and responsibilities in ending gender-based violence. This seminar series drew nearly 600 participants worldwide who discussed lessons learned, and shared good practices, experiences and ideas about men's roles and responsibilities and how to involve men in combating violence against women.

A set of working papers titled Partners in Change: Working with Men to End Gender-Based Violence was subsequently published by UN INSTRAW in collaboration with UNDP. UN INSTRAW maintains an extensive collection of resources, summaries of the seminar series, contacts and working papers on men's roles and responsibilities in ending gender-based violence on its WebPages. In 2002, UNIFEM South Asia, in collaboration with Zonta International, organized the exhibition "Men and Masculinities" to coincide with the 16 days of activism on violence against women in New Delhi. UNIFEM, UNICEF ROSA, Zonta International and Delhi University collaborated on a multi-disciplinary approach pilot intervention that involved photography, research and a travelling seminar, bringing together activists, experts and NGOs to foster partnerships and plan activities against violence involving men.

A comprehensive publication titled From Violence to Supportive Practices: Family, Gender and Masculinities in India was published by UNIFEM in conjunction with this project. The United Nations Division for the Advancement of Women (DAW) in cooperation with ILO and UNAIDS, held an Expert Group Meeting on "The role of men and boys in achieving gender equality" in October 2003. This meeting is part of the Division's preparation for the forty-eighth session of the Commission on the Status of Women, which will address the role of men and boys in achieving gender equality as one of its themes.

The objectives of the meeting were to:

Analyse approaches and strategies that have so far successfully focused on the role of men and boys in achieving gender equality in different parts of the world;

Identify persistent obstacles and challenges to men's and boys' full participation in efforts to achieve gender equality; and

Determine the value of gender equality for men and any benefits for men and boys that may result from greater equality between women and men, considering a wide range of issues relevant throughout the lifecycle.

UNESCAP organized a four-day sub-regional training workshop on "Elimination of Violence against Women in Partnership with Men", in December 2003 in New Delhi, India.

The training workshop gave focus to the South Asian Association for Regional Cooperation (SAARC) countries. The goal of the training workshop was to increase the capacity of the participants to promote policies, and to design and implement measures and activities to end violence against women in partnership with men. The training workshop, which involved three participants including one NGO representative and two Government officials from each country in the SAARC region, will focused on:

Sharing good practices regarding men's roles in ending violence against women, and

Developing guidelines on strategies and techniques to incorporate men's involvement in ending violence against women.

The workshop included presentations on good practices involving men, sessions on how to design awareness- raising activities targeted at men and boys, and how to design workshops aimed at changing male behaviors and attitudes in order to promote male advocacy to end violence against women.

NGO: WHITE RIBBON CAMPAIGN

The organization White Ribbon Campaign (WRC) was established in Canada in 1991 to advocate for men to speak out and organize against violence and specifically violence against women. It is the largest men's network and educational organization promoting men's collective action to end violence against women. The objectives of WRC are to help foster a society free from violence against women; to encourage reflection and discussion that lead to personal and collective action among men; and to urge men to take responsibility to work with women to end men's violence. WRC's activities include organizing global white ribbon campaigns during the "16 days of activism to end violence against women" that begins each year on 25 November, the International Day for the Eradication of Violence against Women.

The White Ribbon Campaign also organizes educational campaigns in communities and schools, support local women's groups, and advocates on issues of violence against women in public policy. The White Ribbon Campaign proposes to:

Make young and adult men aware of the repercussions of violence against women in their own lives and those of other men and to put forward proposals for changing attitudes and behaviour towards women;

Integrate young and adult men into the campaign, turning them into active participants capable of passing on the campaign's goals to other men;

Publicize the campaign as widely as possible and spread awareness of the facilities already in existence for dealing with violence against women;

Involve shapers of public opinion by way of the mass media in the effort to publicize the campaign; and

Encourage public policy at municipal level that strengthens the development and sustainability of action taken in this area.

The work of this organization has now spread beyond Canada, Europe and the Scandinavian countries to many other regions, including countries such as Brazil, India, Japan, Vietnam and Africa. In China, for instance, a visit by one of the founding members of the White Ribbon Campaign, Michael Kaufman, sparked the creation of China's first men's group dedicated to eliminating violence against women.

MEN'S PROGRAM AGAINST VIOLENCE AGAINST WOMEN

The Fiji Women's Crisis Center (FWCC) is a leading NGO providing legal advice, crisis counseling and medical services to women and children victims of violence, as well as community education and public advocacy on violence against women. The organization documents and conducts research on programmes and responses to violence, and is well-connected to a global network of organizations working against violence against women. In 2002, the Fiji Women's Crisis Center implemented a three-year initiative "Men's

Program against Violence against Women", with support from the Fiji Government Taskforce on Violence against Women.

The project commenced with a training workshop for male advocates from the police force, religious groups, education and religious institutions, as well as the welfare, health and legal fields. The men were selected based on their potential influence in the community and workplace as advocates against violence against women. The training encouraged men to realize the consequences of violence against women, and included gender awareness raising activities, activities to explore male attitudes towards women, as well as individual self-exploration exercises. The definitions, dynamics, effects and myths around violence were explored, and emphasis was placed on the cultural and religious aspects of violence.

According to one of the facilitators of the training, a crucial aspect of the training was the men's self-examination, which involved examining their own and society's attitudes and how violence is perpetuated by these attitudes. At the workshops, the men committed themselves to personally become advocates in efforts to end violence against women. The commitments included the following:

Accept that women are equal; reflect the equality of men and women through our behaviour and attitudes;

Re-educate sons and daughters that men and women are equal;

Advocate in religious groups, youth groups and men's groups, that violence against women is a crime that must be eliminated;

Create awareness with men in the community, workplace and social groups on the facts of violence against women;

Be actively involved and supportive of all Government and NGO programmes that promote the elimination of violence against women; and

Take reference from members of the women's movement when conducting work in the area of violence against women.

The men also prepared personal plans of actions which are monitored by the Fiji Women's Crisis Center through personal contact, and the FWCC planned follow-up trainings to examine various men's programmes and to develop counseling skills to deal with male perpetrators. Several of the men also joined the FWCC and the Taskforce in conducting seminars in other locations, while others continued with advocacy efforts on an individual level in their communities. This programme is being replicated in 11 other countries in the Pacific, and in August 2003, the first "Advocacy Training for Men against Violence against Women" was held in Vanuatu, in collaboration with the Vanuatu Women's Center and the Pacific Women's Network against Violence against Women.

Realizing the importance of awareness raising campaigns targeted at the general public, the FWCC produced pamphlets targeted at men, community education tools and TV ads as part of a media campaign against violence against women. The FWCC also conducts training on gender issues, violence against women, as well as women and armed conflict and human rights to the military and the police force.

The military training aims to provide officers with advisory and counseling skills in order to help their military personnel with family problems. The FWCC initiatives to address and involve men are exemplary due to the participatory aspects of the workshops, the aim to replicate the programme in other regions, the focus on men examining their own attitudes and beliefs, and the organization's collaboration with both the government and other local community organizations. The follow-up actions to maintain contact with the male participants of the training, as well as the focus on harnessing the participants' advocacy in their own communities are also very effective strategies.

ROZAN: POLICE TRAINING AND THE WHITE RIBBON CAMPAIGN

Rozan, an NGO in Pakistan, works with men as a conscious strategy to end violence against women. Rozan conducts training and sensitization workshops on emotional health, gender issues, violence against women and children, as well as self-growth and life skills workshops for communities on self-awareness, facilitation and communication skills, attitudinal change exercises, assertive behavior, conflict resolution and anger and stress management. This organization also organizes awareness raising activities on gender and violence against women through seminars, newspapers, newsletters, research studies and training materials.

Rozan developed a unique program to promote community and police collaboration and cooperation regarding violence against women in which the police force is trained on violence against women, gender sensitization, attitudinal change, as well as communication skills and anger/stress management. Rozan intends to address the abuse of power by members of the police force, as well as the fact that police officers often ignore domestic violence and honor killings because violence in the home is still considered a private issue to be dealt with by families and communities, instead of the police or legal system. This initiative is unique because the police approached Rozan and expressed their need for a programme to promote attitudinal change and interpersonal skills training of police trainees.

Workshops for the police force were organized to focus on sensitization to community issues. The issues included gender-based violence, power relations, tolerance, developing communication, stress and anger management skills, as well as self-awareness- raising activities. Additionally, police and community collaboration sessions were organized in order to improve the police system, develop a partnership and trust between members of the community and the police, and to provide a forum for participants to explore issues and feelings in a safe environment. The workshops were successful in allowing the men to feel safe to express their fears and feelings, analyze their own social conditioning, feel empowered to change, and become allies with women and communities to help eliminate violence against women.

Rozan and the White Ribbon Campaign

Rozan commemorates the White Ribbon Campaign every year through various activities such as awareness- raising initiatives and training on gender and violence against women for men, who then organize awareness-raising activities on violence against women themselves. Rozan strongly promotes partnership with males to end violence against women, and in this regard, Rozan organized events to celebrate the White Ribbon Campaign in 2002. Prior to the campaign events, 30 male volunteers were selected to take part in a sensitization workshop, where the men were educated about violence against women and men's roles in ending it. The male volunteers distributed bumper stickers, white ribbons and flyers to be filled out by men who committed themselves to speak out against this crime and never carry out acts of violence.

The flyers explained the importance of men's involvement in ending violence against women, and gave recommendations on how to create violence free environments and take steps to end violence against women in communities. The flyers the men filled out contained coupons for a lucky draw with prizes and certificates. In addition, men set up stalls at gas stations and distributed flyers and write-ups on men's commitments to end violence against women.

A radio program was also aired to inform the community about the campaign. In addition, a list of men who committed themselves never to condone, commit or ignore violence against women was published in newsletters and also displayed on a public mural. To follow up with the volunteers about their experience with the campaign, the volunteers were asked to share their thoughts and suggestions for improvements. A closing ceremony was also organized, which involved students, journalists, NGO activists and government officials. The ceremony included the distribution of the lucky draw prizes, presentations by staff from ROZAN, as well as a guest speaker presentation on power relations and violence against women.

PROMOTING WOMEN'S RIGHTS THROUGH PARTNERSHIPS

The "Men's Action for Stopping Violence against Women" (MASVAW), a community-based grassroots initiative and member-based network of male activists, focuses on mobilizing men to end violence against women, awareness-raising among youth, the public and local government, as well as advocacy with media, the government authorities, NGOs and universities. SAHAYOG, a non-profit organization promoting sustainable rural development in Uttar Pradesh and Uttarakhand over the years evolved into an organization working on women's empowerment, women's rights, and health issues.

Concerned and active men from SAHAYOG created MASVAW as an initiative with the objective of involving men in the issue of violence against women. The founding male activists wanted to draw attention to the fact that violence against women is not a private issue or a women's issue, but one that society as a whole, including men, must take responsibility for. SAHAYOG holds the secretariat of MASVAW and provides capacity building and resources for MASVAW members.

The objectives of MASVAW are:

i. To increase the visibility of VAW and facilitate the process of challenging the attitudes and beliefs around it;

ii. To develop a rights based approach among NGOs for addressing and mainstreaming VAW and forming a network of organizations in the region;

iii. To increase awareness among men about violence against women as a larger social issue; and

iv. To motivate men to shun violence, protest against violence, support survivors and provide new role models.

The initial activities of MASVAW involved conducting consultation meetings with male heads of NGOs in the region working on women's issues to share ideas and experiences, with a view to create a network of NGOs working on violence against women, and start a campaign on VAW led by men. The NGO participants of this consultation expressed their commitment to organize a campaign to involve men in ending violence against women and became the partner organizations of MASVAW. MASVAW prepared interactive materials such as posters, games, bookmarks, pocket planners and flashcards to be used as sensitization tools for the communities on violence against women.

These materials were distributed to the participants, and later used in meetings with communities. The next phase of MASVAW's work programme involved providing trainings to the partner organizations on violence against women and gender issues, as well as providing capacity building training on organizing activities on women and violence and field level training on networking to end violence against women. The training included discussions on patriarchy and the institutions that uphold it, feminism, violence discrimination, sex, gender and 'self gender analysis'.

An important part of MASVAW's work involves providing technical training support to the partner NGOs that organize meetings with community members in the region on violence against women, and sensitize communities on men's involvement in eliminating violence. The NGOs organize community meetings that involve intellectuals, activists, teachers, local government representatives, media, youth in order to raise awareness and garner support, and motivate individuals to work towards eliminating violence in their communities. Community participants commit themselves to changing their attitudes and behaviors, and have discussions on the role of tradition and religion in society.

These community meetings serve the purpose of bringing the issue of violence against women out into the public, furthering communities' realization that violence is a social issue and that men have the responsibility to eliminate it in partnership with women. Several youth committed themselves to organizing meetings on violence against women themselves, and teachers promised to bring the issue of violence against women up in the classroom. MASVAW and the coordinating NGOs that organize the meetings regularly use training tools such as a games, flash cards, group discussions, role plays and simulation exercises to facilitate learning and active participation and engagement.

The trainings also often include the drafting of individual and organizational work plans to ensure follow-up and the continuation of activism on eliminating violence against women. Networking is one of MASVAW's central objectives. The member's organization has extensive contacts to other regional organizations working on men and violence against women, as well as national and international NGOs with whom regular correspondence and coordination is maintained. MASVAW also coordinated a review meeting to provide a forum for follow-up and sharing experiences and lessons learned, discuss potential problems, and to find a strategy for the future on working against violence and ways to further male participation in the campaigns.

At this review meeting, it was decided to continue with the networking, capacity building, community and media advocacy, trainings, to develop stronger relations with government offices, the media, feminist organizations, and to target policy makers, law-makers, youth, students, reporters, NGOs, as well as doctors in their campaign. MASVAW is a unique grass roots and networking campaign effort in view of the fact that it was initiated by concerned male activists who worked on the issue of violence and noticed the need to focus on men's involvement and increased male activism in campaigns to promote the elimination of violence against women.

Given the pervasive gender discrimination in the South Asian region, it is commendable that despite stigmas attached to men being outspoken and involved in efforts to combat issues such as violence against women, the founders of MASVAW realized the need to engage men and start networking and organizing a male lead campaign. The contacts already established by the organization SAHAYOG are also very useful for MASVAW, and the fact that SAHAYOG can provide assistance in coordination and capacity building, as well as assisting MASVAW with organizing campaigns and trainings is very advantageous. Using SAHAYOG's existing wealth of knowledge and experience helps MASVAW in building alliances with other members in the communities and other organizations at the regional and the national level.

CAMBODIA MEN'S NETWORK

The Cambodia Men's Network (CMN) is a network of men from the NGO Gender and Development for Cambodia (GAD/C), based in Phonm Phen. Gender and Development for Cambodia (GAD/C) is a local NGO that promotes gender equity in social, economic and political processes through advocacy, networking, training and research in partnership with other Cambodian NGOs, international and multilateral organizations, state institutions and other civil society organizations. Similar to MASVAW, the Cambodia Men's Network was formed by concerned men who firmly believe that men must address and commit themselves to gender equity and eliminating violence against women because violence is a societal problem and not a women's problem.

Representatives from grass-roots NGOs were selected to form the corps of the network, and these representatives received training courses in gender theory, men's roles in ending violence, and the root problems of violence against women. The CMN objectives are:

i. To encourage men to be responsible parents and loving partners within the family;
ii. To act as effective role models for children and instill values in them, which contribute to peace and harmony within the society;
iii. To reduce destructive aspects of male behaviour such as gambling, drinking and extra-marital sex;
iv. To raise awareness among men of the benefits of monogamy and fidelity and of the health risks involved in promiscuous sexual behaviour;

v. To be leaders in creating a society in Cambodia which values good behaviour, trust in each other, loyalty, honesty, and giving service to others;

vi. To educate all Cambodian men to reject all forms of violence against women including physical abuse, psychological abuse, discrimination, harassment, and abusive language and, instead to be chivalrous and show respect; and

vii. To be active in lobbying for the elimination of the sex trafficking of women and young girls.

CMN provides a forum for men to discuss the issues of concern, gives capacity building training to NGOs based on the network's objectives, holds conferences, disseminates information, and facilitates advocacy, campaign (including the yearly White Ribbon Campaign) and lobbying efforts to reduce violence against women. The network operates in ten provinces and two municipalities of Cambodia. CMN members, who are only men, can register to become a part of the network at no cost, and thereby commit themselves to never perpetrate acts of violence.

The organizational structure of the network is very organized and efficient, and includes representatives in regional committees, technical committees, central committees, as well as a student committee, who have regular coordination and planning meetings. CMN is supported financially and reports to GAD/C. As with MASVAW and the organization SAHAYOG, this is a very effective strategy, because CMN is able to use the resources and contacts of this successful existing NGO to carry out its mission. The network currently has around 500 members and it actively lobbies for new members through white ribbon campaigns, as well as through its WebPages. CMN is a successful initiative because of the firm and underlying belief in men's responsibility in eliminating violence, supporting women's empowerment and promoting peace in communities.

Women for Women, an NGO in Bangladesh, in a review of the situation of violence against women in 2000, found an increasing trend in violence against women, despite expanded actions to reduce violence against women in all countries. In Thailand, the Ministry for Social Development and Human Security presented statistics from various sources showing that reported cases of physical and psychological violence against women is increasing. These alarming trends need to become high priority issues for national governments in the region. Gender-based violence is a complex multi-faceted issue that needs to be solved with a multitude of responses at the international, national and local level.

It is a severe human rights violation of women, and is not a private domestic issue. Legislation, community-based services for victims, national laws, policies and programmes, as well as police, judiciary, welfare agency and NGO mechanisms must address and work to combat violence against women simultaneously and cooperatively. The United Nations and its entities must build the capacity of governments to implement regional plan of actions to combat gender-based violence. To supplement these efforts, it is clear that men need to be involved at all levels to end violence.

Men's groups mobilizing for change, efforts to re-educate, sensitize and encourage men to be advocates, as well as police training on violence and gender issues, community activism strategies and campaigns targeted at men are all venues to effectively involve men in the struggle to end violence against women. Male socialization practices must change in all societies, and men must be made aware of the benefits to them and societies as a whole of gender equality and the elimination of violence against women. Men must be involved form an early age in efforts to end violence against women in public and private spheres.

For example, programmes for youth can focus on engaging men in discussions of gender inequalities, assuming responsibilities in issues of childcare, HIV/AIDS prevention, sexual and reproductive health, as well as encouraging non-violent means of resolving conflict in all areas of life. Involving men who have influence as roles models is a successful strategy, as the example of an organization in Canada using posters of famous sports stars or local celebrities speaking out against violent shows.

When focusing on the involvement of men in efforts to end violence against women, many issues need to be addressed. In order to involve men in activities to end violence against women instead of alienate them, issues of men's hostility, rejection, defensiveness or denial when confronting or engaging men must be kept in mind by taking care of the use of appropriate language. If men are put in a position of blame, they will not become allies and supporters in the struggle to end violence. Men must be provided spaces where they are made to feel comfortable in sharing their feelings and express their fears; otherwise they will not be engaged.

In any efforts to engage and motivate men, men need to be approached in a respectful, open-minded manner and values of equality, responsibility and honesty should be promoted. Lastly, involving men in actions to end violence against women must take place parallel to efforts and strategies to achieve gender equality and realization of human rights. Movements to involve men should not be viewed as a threat to actions for gender equality on the part of women's organizations; rather, they should operate in conjunction and cooperation.

7

Media
Development and Exploitation of Women

Recently, there was much excitement in the United States over the anti-indecency drive in the media. This move gained more prominence after pop singer Janet Jackson exposed a breast on national television during the Super Bowl XXXVIII (02/01/04) halftime performance. Since then, the Federal Communications Commission has been looking into complaints about TV programmes that may have crossed the "decency line." Interestingly, Peter Bowes (BBC News, 4 February 2004) commented, that there was more naked flesh on advertisements during the entire game (Super Bowl) than in the Jackson-Timberlake stunt itself.

At the same time, however, sex advertising is nothing new but an age-old phenomenon. The voyeuristic portrayals of women as things not only to be looked at but also to be desired have always been used by some magazines in order to maximize sales. Examples include Playboy, Penthouse and Hustler. Recently, due to technological advancements, advertising is all over the place - in newspapers, magazines, billboards, pavements, sides of buses, radio, television, and on the Internet.

The power of advertising lies in persuasion and its ability to influence people's behavior. This ability has been enhanced by globalization. Globalization and the advancement in new media technologies are transforming how sexuality is viewed and treated around the world. The result is the beaming of homogeneous images in the media and the tendency towards increased cultural and social uniformity. This is exemplified by the way films and glitzy advertisements have helped the spread of sales of products.

The result can be seen in discriminatory advertising, and the spread of imposed images of femininity and female roles. A recent survey in the United Kingdom, for example, shows that about two thirds of women thought that advertisers go too far in using sex to sell product. They found explicit billboard advertisements more offensive (Media and Gender Monitor Issue 8). Recent French Reports also highlight the promotion of sexual values in advertisements that increasingly show degrading portrayals of women with overtones of violence, sexual domination and bestiality (Media and Gender Monitor 2002, Issue 10).

A classic example is the Barbette brand cooking cream advertisement in France that shows a headless torso of a woman with the caption "I do what I want with her" (Rosella Melanson 2001). This exploitation of female sexuality in advertising has negative consequences for women. Images of thin models seen, for example, in TV and magazine advertisements, and good-looking muscular men appear daily in magazines, films and television. Thanks to beauty pageants such as "Miss World" and "Miss Universe", as well as locally organized beauty pageants, teenage girls now define beauty by the shape and size of their bodies with the impression that being skinnier is sexier.

More young men are also turning to drugs such as steroids to help build muscle strength. This unrealistic importance given to body image has been blamed for the poor self- esteem and unhappiness among ordinary people, particularly the youth. While doctors do not agree on the extent of this problem, eating disorders such as anorexia have been affecting more young people (Cooper 1997). Great concern has been expressed about the role of the media especially as an agent of socialization.

Critics often blame the policy of pandering to the audience's desires and prurient tastes on the competition between media corporations for the advertisement dollar. Advertising is very important to profit-driven media conglomerates more interested in delivering viewers to advertisers than in serving the needs of the public. In her article titled: "Real Women Elude Ad-driven Magazines" Sheila Gibbons (Women's Enews, 5 July 2003) points out that advertising pays the lion's share of publishing costs, and without it, a magazine just can't make it.

Consequently, dependent on the advertisement dollar and faced with fierce competition, media corporations resort to the policy of pandering to the audience's desires and prurient tastes. Today, the media industry is worth billions of dollars. Examples of such corporations include, General Motors Corporation, the world's largest company that now sells more graphic sex films every year than Larry Flynt, owner of the Hustler empire; DirecTV, a subsidiary of General Motors; EchoStar Communications Corporation; AT&T Corporation, America's biggest communications company; and Cybervision, a film production company based in Cape Town, South Africa.

Armed with new technology, these corporations are increasingly able to spend more money on sophisticated ways to sell their products. This situation has exacerbated media homogenization of women's images, resulting in the link between pornography and advertising becoming increasingly blurred.

The consequences, del Nevo points out, are that: "References to obscenity and indecency cited in many codes of conduct or self-regulatory guidelines are no longer applicable. The general observation is that the depiction of women as objects of desire in advertising effects gender relations and society's attitudes towards women and women's sexuality" (Patrick Stewart (Star Trek actor) cited by Jeremy Lovell, The Independent Online Newspaper [IOL], 5 March 2004)

Realizing the enormous problems women face in this regard, the Fourth World Conference on Women in Beijing, China in 1995 identified the continued projection of negative and degrading images of women as a critical area of concern in the Platform of Action. Yet, five years after Beijing, some of the same concerns still remain (Shivdas 2000).

Since Janet Jackson's stunt with Justin Timberlake, and under pressure to crack down on the growing coarseness of television and radio broadcasts by parents groups and lawmakers, the Federal Communications Commission (FCC) has ramped up its efforts to pursue complaints and issue more penalties against media indecency (Aliza Dichter, World Association for Christian Communication [WACC], and 26 February 2004). On 18th March 2004, the United States communications regulators went directly after profanity on television and radio broadcasts as part of a campaign to crack down on growing coarseness on the air.

Earlier on, Canada had to engender its advertising codes in order to address this problem. With particular reference to the 1994 gender portrayal guidelines of the Canadian code of advertising. Avoiding the inappropriate use or exploitation of female sexuality is one of the key commitments of such clauses (Media Awareness Network, October 2002). Formulating and applying ethical codes for the communications media and for advertising might go a long way in promoting respect and common good.

This is particularly so for television, which beams homogeneous images right into people's homes and around the world. However, confronting the negative effects of the new media on women requires focusing on the entire spectrum of media representations that limit, demean or degrade women. This includes the Internet. Internet advertising is growing bigger by the day and the medium is greatly increasing the influence of media corporations, and the opportunity for pornography considered by many feminists, as degrading to women.

Information from the various regional reports indicate that although some progress has been made in implementing recommendations from section J, a lot of this has to do with the sustained monitoring, networking and lobbying efforts of women's organisations and media watch groups. This is indicated in NGO as well as government reviews and analyses. Official governmental reviews submitted to the UN and NGO reports indicate that there has been an increase in the number of women entering media organisations at the professional level and there is an increase in the percentage of women students graduating from journalism and mass communications courses. The women and media situations in both Asia and Latin America regions conform to this trend.

However, there is a continued negative portrayal and representation of women that may be linked to the lack of implementation of national media codes and, in some cases, even the lack of existence of such codes. Further, women continue to have limited access and participation in decision-making in the media industries and governing authorities and bodies that oversee formulation and implementation of media policies. Women media practitioners continue to face gender-based discrimination including sexual harassment at the work place. Therefore, the power to shape and influence media still eludes women. From the foregoing it can be said that more still needs to be done by GOs, media organisations and NGOs to achieve the two strategic objectives outlined.

Even captured some of the concerns of women activists, researchers and women media practitioners in its analysis of the women and media situation, not all dimensions of the women and media relationship are explored. The economic and political realities within which transnational media corporations perpetuate inequalities and inequities are not addressed and women's vulnerabilities as traditional keepers of indigenous knowledge within this environment are not acknowledged. Women are concerned with the absence of analysis of the globalisation of media, particularly mergers of transnational media corporations and changes in media ownership at national levels that have a bearing on media content and intent.

The Asia report points to the strangleholds of transnational media corporations that are edging out nationally owned media enterprises leaving even less space for women in both the mainstream and alternative media. In addition, globalisation of the media paves the way for increased commercialisation, consumerism and more importantly, homogenisation of cultures resulting in the marginalisation of the voices of minority and indigenous cultures and peoples. In Latin America and the Caribbean, women assert that giant multimedia organisations control different kinds of media resulting in unequal representation of all social actors.

Meanwhile, such crucial issues as freedom of expression and information, and mechanisms for accountability with increased use of ICTs engage women in the UN European region. Women in the Arab world acknowledge that though women are in key decision making positions in media organisations and institutions, more advocacies still needs to be done to counter women's stereotyped images in the media. The monitoring of implementation is not without problems. The structural and procedural policies and processes in place in many of the countries make assessments and evaluations difficult to achieve.

The report from ECE suggests that some governments have restructured their national machineries for the advancement of women without necessarily integrating its mandate for gender issues into other national and regional institutional mechanisms governing media and those governing the development of ICTs. In many cases, the national machineries for women's advancement that have the mandate to monitor implementation of the BPFA have neither the resources nor the power to exercise it. Another important factor to consider in the UN and NGO reviews of the implementation of the BPFA is the absence or minimal acknowledgement given to the media sections in the various Regional Plans of Action that were adopted before the Beijing Conference.

It is felt that the media sections in the Regional Plans of Action are far more reflective of the prevailing media situations and the recommendations were more grounded in contextual realities. For example, the Asia Pacific Plan of Action described the changing media situation and the threat to indigenous forms of communication and cultures by the increased flow of foreign and homogenous images. The document also outlined ownership patterns and drew the connections between corporate intents and media contents. Although the BPFA attempted to elaborate the global media picture based on the different regional situations, the politics of exclusion based on perceived national interests in UN deliberations, limitations of UN procedures and other factors severely limited the scope.

In addition to substantive limitations pertaining to intellectual scope and analyses, the politics of global negotiations, and structural and procedural obstacles to reviewing implementation outlined above, Section J of the BPFA also has problems linked to assessments and evaluations given the political and socio-economic realities of different countries. The Latin American analysis points out that the weak democracies in most of the countries in the region function within inflexible structural adjustment programmes imposed on them leaving their institutions, the media among them, vulnerable to vested economic interests.

This has implications for media's role in mobilising civil society and promoting democratisation and political participation. Information from Africa asserts that Section J has limitations in assessing commitments and actions of governments with regard to new ICTs as the global document does not anticipate the rapid growth and expansion of ICTs and does not fully assess its influence and impact.

All of the above analyses on the review of implementation of Section J of BPFA point to the complex layers and dimensions that need to be deconstructed and understood within relevant frameworks that include the socio-political and economic realities of all countries that make up the global community. This report is calling for a deeper understanding of the connections made between globalisation and women's media portrayal and access to expression and decision making in all media including ICTs.

GAINS

Just as there is a notable increase of women in mass media educational institutions, more women can also be found in television, radio and print. This increase in women's employment in media institutions has resulted in increased coverage of women's issues. While most women media practitioners are still in the reportorial level, there have been a few exceptions where a number of women have risen to higher level positions-e.g. the editorial level and management of advertising agencies-as in the case of Indonesia, Malaysia and the Philippines.

The increase of women media practitioners has also led women to form professional associations where they can address media issues in their countries. For example, there are active women's media associations in countries like China (All China Women's Journalist Association), the Islamic Republic of Iran and in South Korea (South Korea's Women Journalists Club). However, even as more women's issues are being covered, women's portrayal, on a general sense, remains negative. This may be attributed to the absence of a critical mass of women in decision- making positions and more importantly, the media enterprises that they work for are driven by profit and women's issues are not seen as profit-making.

The new information technologies (ICTs) have allowed women to link and network with each other more effectively and share information and resources faster. The women's movement in the region has increasingly used the electronic medium to put forward their advocacy and build solidarity. In Central Asia, e-mail has become a valuable tool in exchanging ideas and information among organisations as well as a way of combating the relative isolation of the countries in this sub-region from the global movement. In most former

Soviet states, mass media is still highly censored and the Internet has become a way to go around censorship and the repression of information.

However, Kazakhstan recently passed a law that threatens the power of information and communication in the region. Its policy "On Establishment of Billing Telecommunication Tariff Center" enables the tracking of all e-mails and Internet for censorship of "unwelcome" information. Another recent development is the use of ICTs in enhancing the social use of traditional media like radio.

At present, there are already innovative models of using ICTs to extend radio's reach and capacity to interact with users, and to improve its cultural relevance and programming quality. Women's radio programmes making use of this convergence of technologies are now being broadcast in countries like Sri Lanka and Nepal.

Radio is the most accessible form of communication in South Asia, the Pacific Islands, Southeast Asia particularly the Mekong region. Women's radio programmes can be found in these countries despite the little support they receive from governments or private sources. The generally low levels of literacy in the non-NIC countries (except for the Philippines) also accounts for radio's popularity. Findings from a 1998 research on radio show that radio reaches between 60 to 88 percent of the population in the region. Print materials targeting women have also seen an increase.

In China, there are 42 types of women's periodicals and three women's newspapers. Japan has three major women's newspapers and during the economic boom of the 1990s, Indonesia, Malaysia and Thailand saw a boom in women's magazines, in particular glamour and fashion magazines. Women's groups in the region are increasingly using the Internet to network and share information. In addition, women are engaging in influencing the technical tools themselves by developing multi-lingual index databases that are accessible via the web and provide information on various issues in Japanese, Filipino, Korean and English.

At this point the database is being used as a model for sharing resources on contemporary issues of concern to women in the region in various languages. While a greater number of women's organisations are discovering the effectiveness of the Internet for communication and information retrieval, many of them have yet to initiate disseminating their own information through the Internet. Some of the National Machineries that have their own Websites and are capable of sharing their expertise with women's groups in other countries are Australia, Japan, Malaysia, New Zealand, Republic of Korea, Singapore, and Thailand.

LATIN AMERICA

Women's right to communicate is an inalienable human right that requires a plurality of information sources and media besides a democratic and transparent administration of communication policies, equity and gender justice. In the last decade, women achieved several goals in their relationship with the media in Latin America and the Caribbean. Probably, the main reason for this is the importance gained by Journalism and Social Communications as a career in universities.

For example in Argentina, women students account for 52 percent of registrations in graduate courses, while 70 percent of students in postgraduate studies in the region are women. The fact that more women were better trained in the communications field enabled them to work in the private and state-owned media, especially in radio and television, not only as presenters, but also as journalists, programme conductors, interviewers, and information analysts. Their participation in radio and TV as producers of journalistic programmes also increased. Main daily newspapers hired women journalists to write on politics, economics and social issues.

Although the participation of women in the decision making level in the media is notoriously low, the fact that there are many women working in the media contributes to the visualisation that they will be playing new roles, expressing their opinions, conducting interviews and programmes. This helps society build a different image of women as they contribute their knowledge and actions in different fields. Within this framework, women in Latin America and the Caribbean consider advances through new information and communications technologies as helpful in throwing open important possibilities to make visible women's contribution to society.

The year 1995 marked the boom in commercial internet connectivity in the region. Since then, there has been a progressive increase in internet access, but mainly for people with higher education and a comfortable economic situation. The proportion of women users is increasing, but is still much lower than that of men. According to UNDP, in 1998 only 0.8 percent of the region's population had internet access. Of these, 90 percent were from upper income groups. In Brasil, only 25 percent of internet users were women. A study carried out in México in 1999 revealed that 33 percent of users were women compared with 18 percent two years earlier.

Aside from the commercial use of Internet, civil society organisations began to use electronic communication in the region as early as the late 1980s, and there was a significant increase in use by women's organisations as of 1994-1995. Women's organisations have continued to use these technologies creatively, particularly to coordinate activities and exchange information via e-mail and lists, and their presence is also increasing on the World Wide Web. Women are of the view that it is important to generate a new audio and visual culture in favour of gender democracy, in order to promote equal opportunities for women and men at all levels, including decision making at the political, economic, social, cultural and communications levels.

Women are challenged to work for strategies and proposals that result in public recognition of the new roles played by women in private and public life and their contribution as actors in civil society. Women are working towards building an integral image of women as communications subjects and citizens with full rights. The Women's Offices in Colombia and Venezuela have taken these principles into account and reflect them in the TV programmes that they regularly produce. The need to put into action the exercise of their rights in the communications field made Chilean women struggle for a place in the National Television Committee.

In community media, women play important roles in both conducting and planning the programming and in its decision making processes, direction and administration. The World Association of Community Radio Broadcasters (AMARC) in the Latin American region developed a Women's Programme with the aim of training radio women and formulating programming with a gender perspective. Its radio campaigns "Women's rights are human rights" and "We have the right to a life without violence" gained international recognition and were broadcast by thousands of community radio stations in the region.

Though, it is true that in most countries community radio and TV stations struggle for a legal status, it is worth noting that in Colombia a new law on broadcasting passed in 1998 has legalised community media. The workshop "WomenAction 2000" that took place in Quito, Ecuador witnessed women's communication networks develop a strategy for participation in the Beijing+5 process. On this occasion, participants produced a document "Nosotras cumplimos" (We have accomplished... and you?) in which they recognise the achievements obtained by the women's movement in the region that have been true to the Beijing agreements and question the lack of response from media companies and governments.

UN EUROPEAN REGION

There are some notable exceptions to a generally negative situation, often as a result of advocacy by women's organisations and media monitoring groups who have played an active role in promoting change. Although a wide variety of women's media initiatives are making a positive impact, the beginnings of change have also come from education and positive role models. In educational publishing, work has been going on since the early 1970s to combat stereotyping in school texts and illustrations. Media practitioners too have initiated changes in media content; for example, in Canada, broadcasters distanced themselves from a popular chat show which used sexist language and violent sexual imagery involving women, after the CBSC (Canadian Broadcasting Standards Council) ruled that the show had a "fundamentally sexist disposition."

There have been a few worthy governmental initiatives, though these are still too scarce. An exception is the 1997 European Commission-supported study on the Images of Women in the Media. While the research offers important recommendations and proposals that can be implemented immediately, few have been put into practice. In its Resolution (A4-0258/97), the European Parliament (on the basis of a report by the Committee on Women's Rights) noted that the national and European legislation to protect women against degrading images in the media was inadequate. Therefore the Committee called for legislation to prohibit all forms of pornography in the media and advertising.

Advertising for sex tourism was another issue denounced in this Resolution. Other areas where gains were made include the spread of ICTs and monitoring of media content by media watch groups. The 'Women In Trades and Technology' (WITT) National Network, with funding from (Human Resource Development Canada) HRDC, launched Women in Information Technology (WinIT) to support girls and women who wish to explore careers in IT. With ICT training being pushed down to the provincial level, most provinces have undertaken various training initiatives during the last five years and three have focussed on women's organisations.

Health Canada, through its five Centres of Excellence for Women's Health, supports web pages and listservs related to women's health. There is a case where ICT has been used by women with the aim of achieving equal representation of women in the new legislature of Nunavut. Short term funding was also given to Pauktuutit, the Inuit Women's Association, to include electronic networking to further this aim. The Status of Women Canada (SWC) funded research in 1996 on the connectedness of women's groups. Unfortunately, the report has recently been withdrawn from the SWC web site.

BEST PRACTICES

The following is a listing of some of the best practices by women's groups, government and intergovernmental bodies in Asia, Latin America and the UN European region.

Asia: Women's media organisations in the regions lead the way with innovative practices:

In Japan the Forum for Citizen's Television and Media (FCT), a voluntary citizens' group, works to change the media environment. FCT holds an open forum three times a year to discuss media issues based on its research. It also publishes a newsletter and conducts nationwide television monitoring to raise awareness on media and thus empower citizens through increasing their media literacy.

The Women's Media Centre of Cambodia carries out media campaigns on various issues concerning women and produces video and radio programmes. It also conducts media monitoring activities and is recognised by the Cambodian government as a partner in improving the status of women in media.

Isis International-Manila, an international women's NGO has taken the lead to bring together women's media groups, individual women media practitioners, media activists, academics and policy makers in the region. It organises regional and international conferences, workshops, fora and other events to discuss issues around women and media. It provides training for women on radio production, electronic networking, and database and resource centre management. It disseminates information to women across the world through its monthly newsletter, a magazine, Website, and electronic mailing lists. Isis is currently taking the lead in establishing an international code of conduct for media practitioners.

The Asian Women's Resource Exchange (AWORC) is an Internet-based women's information service and network made up of women's information, media and communication organisations in Asia. It seeks to develop cooperative approaches and partnerships in exploring applications of and increasing women's access to the new information and communication technologies (ICTs) for social and economic empowerment. This network aims to facilitate regional and national network-building in the women's movement through the promotion of electronic resource sharing and building a regional information service that will support various advocacy programmes.

Kali for Women in India is one of the leading feminist publishing houses in Asia. One of their first books in 1984 was Women and Media in Asia. Since then, their books have continued to highlight various issues affecting women in the region, particularly in South Asia. These books are sold internationally and many of them have been translated into other languages.

Jagori, a women's NGO and resource centre based in India, produces booklets, posters and audio cassettes. Jagori challenged the idea that writing is the only or the best mode of communication and experimented with the use of different media to carry the messages of the women's movement.

Latin America and the Caribbean: In the last five years, women's organisations have raised awareness of the right to communicate as part of the rights of citizenship.

The Women's Programme of the World Association of Community Radio Broadcasters in the Latin American region encourages training with a gender perspective and co-ordinated continent-wide campaigns for women's rights, particularly on raising awareness about violence against women. All this was done applying new communications technologies to broadcasting.

FIRE (Feminist International Radio Endeavour), an all-women radio broadcasters team in Costa Rica, is the first feminist radio station to broadcast on the Internet in Spanish and English. It also develops training for women in broadcasting and the new information and communication technologies.

Fempress in Chile produces feminist articles and radio programmes for the mass media and the Internet. It has published an "ABC of non-sexist journalism" in Spanish.

CLADEM (Latin American Commission on Women's Rights) has launched an e-mail campaign for women's human rights.

Modemmujer in Mexico is an information network on women's issues that reaches hundreds of activists in Mexico and the rest of the region.

ALAI (Agencia Latinoamericana de Informacion) Women's Programme in Ecuador provides advice to women's regional initiatives and networks in planning their communication policies, including the Internet, and facilitates information links with other social movements.

Media monitoring exercises have taken place in several countries and the outcomes have not only contributed data that strengthen the position of women and the women's movement in arguing their case for changes in media practices but also opened channels for possible dialogues on gender and communications issues. Groups in some countries, for example, Red Ada in Bolivia, Grupo Mujer and Chiclayo in Peru, have conducted studies on women's images in TV programmes produced and /or hosted by women.

Geledes, an Institute of Black Women in Brazil, leads the movement against the negative images of black women in soap operas broadcast by TV Globo. They have presented their case to the National Council for Self-regulation.

UNIFEM gives an Award for non-sexist publicity during the Ibero American Festival of Publicity in 1998 and 1999. The Centro de Estudios de la Mujer and World Association for Christian Communication-Latin America were among the local sponsors of the jury.

The UN European Region is leading the way in addressing women and media issues including use of ICTs to change the status quo.

The Toplink office was set up in 1995 in the Netherlands to increase women's involvement in management and government agencies.

The office maintains a database of women who are qualified to participate in advisory councils for the government, social organisations and company boards. This database now includes 900 women and has resulted in an increase in the number of women who have been appointed to executive posts. On average, the office mediates 40 to 50 posts per year.

KILDEN, an information and documentation centre for women's and gender research in Norway shares premises with the Gender Equality Ombudsperson and the Centre for Gender Equality. One task shared with the latter group is the further development of electronic directories published by the Centre for Women's Research.

Croatia: B.a.B.e., in 1998, for the 16 Days of Activism against Gender Violence, made a song and video with young female rappers. The song got great media coverage and publicity, and was a success. It tackled difficult issues in an upbeat and entertaining way. For 1999, they decided on a jazz song. In developing the story line, the organisers asked men what they thought a powerful woman would look like. The men could imagine only an "amazon". Since it was election time, it was decided to make a video with a female president and ministers, showing them making changes in policies that affect women.

Germany: "Media suitcase" developed by the German Association of Female Journalists but only available as a prototype. It is aimed at providing media observation groups with the tools needed for the critical examination and analysis of media content, and ways and means of making complaints and comments better known.

Canada: MediaWatch Canada organised a Global Media Monitoring Project in 1995 to look at issues of portrayal and position of women in media.

Over 15,000 news stories on TV, radio and in newspapers by hundreds of volunteers in 71 countries were analysed. In collaboration with WACC, this will be replicated in the year 2000, and over 85 countries are expected to take part. Consistent monitoring and sharing the results can result in more awareness, and eventually, change.

E.U.: European Women's Lobby, the largest co-ordinating body of national and European non-governmental women's organisations in the European Union, with over 2,700 member associations in the 15 Member States. The EWL systematically monitors European legislative activity and takes action when necessary. As the European Union's sphere of competence continues to grow, the EWL is seeking to ensure equality between women and men as a mandatory criterion for European construction.

USA: Independent Women's Action Project, an organisation committed to limited government and economic opportunity, has joined forces with the E-Freedom Coalition (e-freedom.org) to promote low cost Internet access and continued growth in cyberspace.

France: Les Penelopes has developed an interactive TV programme "Cyberfemmes" with accompanying online discussions and background texts to elaborate on the context.

International: Over the years, the International Women's Tribune Centre, has emphasised the importance of making appropriate and relevant information available–through translation, cut-and-paste newsletters, posters, brochures, story boards, flip charts, role plays, street drama, discussion groups, not to forget the fax!.

International: Women's International News Gathering Service, women's radio news programs on the internet, including programs archived for net casting on the web site, and radio exchange programmes.

ARAB WOMEN STRIVE FOR CHANGE

This is the Women and Media section of the Arab Regional NGO Alternative Report:

On the national level, the Syrian Women's Union is currently overseeing the production of a radio and television programme on the family, in addition to producing the "Arab Women Magazine." The Women's Union is also supervising the work of the Cinema Club and is working at discovering female acting talents. In Yemen, a woman occupies the position of Secretary General of the Ministry of Information. In addition, the percentage of women working in the Ministry of Information is 15.9 percent compared to 10 percent of women working in Yemeni Television.

In Palestine, special TV and radio programmes have been produced which are aimed at eliminating the stereotypical portrayal of women in Palestinian society. The General Union of Palestinian Women, in collaboration with other NGOs, is utilising all media forms to trounce stereotypes of women in films, studies, newspapers, and radio and TV programmes. The Ministry of Information is currently in the process of creating a comprehensive database on all aspects of concern to Palestinian women which will be utilised when formulating strategies, policies and action plans for eliminating stereotyped images of women in the media. The Gender and Development Planning Department, in cooperation with other governmental and non-governmental agencies, conducts training workshops on gender, information and communication.

In Kuwait, the state has guaranteed women equal access to top level positions in the media sector. As a result, Kuwaiti women have occupied the position of directors of various departments in state-run media institutions, in addition to the position of assistant secretary general in the Ministry of Information.

In the United Arab Emirates and Bahrain, women's presence in the mass media is strong in terms of the decision-making positions they occupy, the discussion which they engage in, and in terms of the issues that the various media institutions address in these two countries.

The National Committee for Women in Egypt has adopted several objectives with the aim of improving the manner in which women's issues are dealt with in the media and of eliminating the negative stereotypes that Egyptian women suffer from. This is being done through projecting positive images of women such as those of successful Egyptian women.

In Jordan, the national plan of action for Jordanian women emphasises the importance of developing media programmes to incorporate a gender perspective and encourages the participation of women in formulating media-related studies, plans and policies. For instance a Jordanian woman was recently appointed as head of the official radio institution. One NGO has produced a radio programmed entitled "Women on the Road of Altruism." The Sisterhood is Global Institute implemented an information-sharing project which connects women in the South with other women in the country and in the world by using new information and communication methods.

In Iraq, clear criteria have been set for the production of all information material dealing with women's topics which in turn contribute to the formation of public opinion. Iraqi women's NGOs have also developed various training manuals and programmes on women in media. The Iraqi Women's Federation also supported the development of the technical department of Iraqi radio and TV to better enable it to produce print and audio-visual material on rural and urban women in Iraq.

A network of Arab journalists concerned with development issues has been recently established to facilitate communication and collaboration among journalists. Established in 1999, this network that is based in Damascus and consists of 30 journalists also aims to upgrade its members' journalistic skills. In addition, the network also focuses on follow up work to the International Conference on Population and Development and the Fourth World Conference on Women.

GAPS

The last decades of the 20th century marked the shift to a global information economy characterised by the dominance of giant media and transnational corporations that are able to dictate the production of information worldwide. Information and communication technologies have played a crucial role in this global trend. This same ownership pattern and control has resulted in highly unequal access for majority of the world's population. This inequality contributes to increasing the gap between those who have access to abundant information resources and those who are deprived of this access. Poverty and illiteracy continue to prevent women from having access to not just new information and communication technologies but also to all forms of information and communications.

It is this marginalised sector that has no means to shape information, and therefore unable to project themselves and the issues that relate to them. ESCAP notes that women continue to form the bulk of the poor, with the vast majority living in the rural areas where the preconditions for escaping from abject poverty seldom exist. Globalisation is acting to transform the nature and structure of the media from that of a public trust to a transnational business enterprise. The process of globalisation is also acting to concentrate media ownership and control in the hands of a few, thereby further limiting the ability of many sectors of society, including women, to influence media.

There is a lack of coordinated effort aimed at improving and changing the status of women within the media, information and communications industries. Sexual harassment of women in media organisations is widespread. This is a denial of women's human rights and acts to hinder women's full participation in the media industry. Women continue to experience barriers not only in accessing new information and communication technologies but also hindrances in participating in technology development and policy making. Language continues to serve as a major obstacle to access to the Internet as the English language dominates, the Web.

For many women, lack of training opportunities, the high cost of hardware and software and in some places, the high cost of getting connected as well as the absence or lack of basic infrastructures to support this technology, further marginalise women. The Internet has also been used as another venue to exploit market and traffic women. While a notable increase in women's presence in media institutions is recognised, particularly on television and radio, women continue to have limited participation and access to decision-making in the communications industry and in governing bodies that influence media policy. Because of this lack of critical mass it has been noted that despite the increase of women in media institutions, women are still unable to shape programme content and ensure coverage of women's priority issues and concerns.

Negative and stereotyped representations of women in the media continue while the projection of the cultural diversity and varying realities of women's lives remains absent. Women from marginalised sectors of society are further invisible as their ethnic, racial, and class groups, religion or sexual orientation are minimally or never represented in the larger sectors of media. Media codes of conduct at national levels have not been effective in ensuring positive portrayals of women in the media. On the other hand, gender coding operates as many women media practitioners still tend to be assigned to "soft" issues such as culture, arts and lifestyle while men are assigned to "more important" issues like politics and the economy.

Local and global, geographical and economic differences, structural gaps between the genders, ethnic discrimination and the cross-cutting of all these and other factors contribute to the fact that, at the dawn of the 21st century, women's disadvantaged status is particularly glaring when it comes to strategic technologies, power and decision making. Globalisation of communications has meant, among other things, the arrival in the region of dozens of cable channels that broadcast their programmes from outside Latin America.

Media concentration in many countries has resulted in big multimedia companies owning and having a monopoly of newspapers, radio and TV networks. This trend has been counterproductive to the democratisation of communications and to a more equitable representation and voice of social actors, particularly of women. The limited or weak democracies that govern in most of the countries, within the strait-jacket of structural adjustment programmes imposed by the international financial system, are vulnerable under the pressure of big economic interests, and the media among them. With economic deregulation and free market as an excuse, principles of ethics and equity have been left aside. Information is no longer considered as a right but has been turned into a commodity. The media now have very tenuous links with the concept of public service that was considered a privilege when they were created.

Media monitoring shows that in South America, 23.6 percent of women who make the news are as victims compared with only 9.3 percent of men in the same situation. In Central America and the Caribbean, one out of five women (19.1 percent) who make the news do so in the role of victims. Some experiences of media monitoring that took place after the adoption of the BPFA reveal similar findings. In October 1997, Cotidiano Mujer, an NGO in Uruguay, monitored 9000 newspaper pages, 95.32 hours of TV news in prime hours in the four air channels, and 400 hours of radio broadcasting which covered four journalistic programmes in the three radio stations with the biggest audience in the country.

Only 8 percent of the newspaper news coverage had to do with women, and issues such as women's human rights and sexuality were not even mentioned. In televised news, only one woman was interviewed for every 7 men, and for each hour that a woman journalist spoke on TV, men journalists spoke for four. In radio, out of 7000 minutes of broadcasting analysed, only 301 minutes were dedicated to women's issues. Men were interviewed for 2384 minutes, whilst women were listened to for only 449 minutes.

In Bolivia, la Red de Trabajadoras de la Información y la Comunicación-Red Ada led a similar experience in a week in July 1998 during which the monitoring covered the five most important newspapers in the country which are published in the main cities. In that period, the participation of women in the news was 18.49 percent. Most women who made such news appeared on the pages describing social events (20.3 percent); whilst in issues like education, women or women's issues were mentioned only in 6.25 percent of the news; and in health and legal issues, 2.34 percent.

The data obtained in these surveys clearly demonstrate that to change the status of women in media, it is not sufficient to insist that women undertake training as journalists or social communicators or that news and information be treated with a gender perspective. Changes would also depend on public policies and ethical codes in media that promote affirmative action towards a greater participation of women as information sources and agents, respecting their right to communicate and offering them opportunities to put into practise this right in both private and state-owned media.

Regional/national political shifts, such as those reported in Albania, Austria, Poland, Romania, the Slovak Republic and the United Kingdom., have resulted in interruption and/or re-arrangement of their respective national institutional mechanisms. This has adverse effects on all aspects of women's advocacy efforts, particularly on those that focus on complicated policy issues such as the ones mentioned in Section J of the BPFA.

For example, November 1997 marked a collapse of activities for gender equality in Poland because parliamentary elections resulted in a more conservative government that took power. The Office for Women's Issues was replaced by the Office for Family Issues. From the very beginning, this new mechanism had been strongly influenced by a conservative religious perspective, manifested as a de facto policy in the cessation of most of the women-oriented activities. The present government's focus has been switched to family issues that, according to the ruling politicians, adequately encompass all women's issues.

Most immediately, in Austria, women's organisations and projects are faced with the possibility that they will not receive enough or no state funding at all as a result of the new government's controversial decision to abolish the Ministry for Women's Affairs. Women's Affairs have been demoted to a junior department in a sprawling Ministry of Social Affairs. In addition, its budget for this year will come to only about 40 per cent of last year's level.

During these last few years, the European Commission has also experienced dramatic turmoil, culminating with the forced resignations of all top level Commissioners. Prior to and immediately after these events, what little funding there has been for women's groups was threatened by the requirement that all projects were examined.

Several countries reported that more training of journalists and other media makers is needed. However, while there are a few notable efforts in this area, in many cases governments have not implemented even easily achievable recommendations from the BPFA. In Germany for example, the NGOs note that there is no mention by the government of "Women Oeckl", a comprehensive list of women experts in the media that was repeatedly demanded in discussions long before the Fourth World Conference on Women. This is actually a commitment made in Section J (paragraph 241) that few, if any, ECE governments have implemented or supported.

In Germany too, women's groups have learned that although the legislation and policies are in place and the monitoring machinery is in place, the state lacks the ability to disseminate the tools to the very groups who are likely to take up the voluntary task of conducting observations of media practices. The "media suitcase" developed by the Association of Female Journalists is still only available as a prototype because it has been waiting in vain for two years to be copied and distributed.

The suitcase is aimed at providing the tools needed by media monitoring groups. This includes not only information necessary to undertake the critical examination and analysis of media content but it also provides crucial information regarding ways and means of making complaints and getting comments heard in the public domain.

Very little has changed in the portrayal of women in media since 1995, whether in advertising or news media. Negative, stereotyped, inaccurate and violent images of women are pervasive. Some groups of women are simply invisible, such as those from minority populations. Women are still described in terms of appearance rather than abilities. Moreover, the increased commercialisation of every medium has intensified the visibility of negative images, from billboards to television to newspaper. New media are perpetuating and accentuating much that is negative in the portrayal of women, notably in computer games, on the Internet and in music videos.

Media convergence and the parallel convergence of the Internet with mass media are intensifying all the negative practices to a dizzying degree. A worrying new trend in the U.K. is the increase in sexual violence by boys under the age of 18. Factors that play a role here include declining achievements at school by boys compared with girls, and the proliferation of violence in media, on the Internet and in computer-based games. Czech media have managed to maintain traditional, patriarchal views; expressed explicitly through advertising, these media images very often trespass the bounds of good taste and ethics. In Croatia, where the media do not have gender-sensitive editorial policies or may even have anti-women policies, the portrayal of women is decidedly sexist and there is little awareness of the need for gender equality.

In fact, Croatian state-run television has few, if any, positive educational, political or social programming addressing the problems and status of women. Radio, which is considered independent, is worse; it regularly provides examples of sexist intimidation of women and the use of sexist stereotypes. There is no socially responsible and gender-sensitive journalism to the extent that women's condition in the print media accurately reflects the deplorably prevailing low regard for women's human rights. Drives to quickly develop the market economy have encouraged the production of pornography, and in some highly commercialised private publications, soft pornography has become the foundation of market strategy.

New women's magazines belonging to commercial media groups differ but not in a substantively positive way. They tend to offer a mixture of fashion, glamorous gossip, nationalist and anti-women values, and portray women as fancy escorts to important men or as "self-confident" vamps who participate in the entertainment business. Other more traditional women's magazines focus on motherhood, fashion, the family, entertainment, tourism and provide advice on cooking, health-care and beauty. These magazines are sometimes in favour of women's rights and the pro-choice position but, except for Zaposlena (Working Women), they position women's issues outside of the country's social and political realities and always distance themselves from or denounce feminism as being nothing more than a cheap political trend.

There is obviously great enthusiasm for the possibilities that ICTs offer women in all parts of the region. But it must also be pointed out that ICTs are double-edged swords: so often owned by multi-national corporations and/or outside of our own control, we cannot adequately know what is going on at all times. There continues to be a deeper exclusion for those who do not have access, and the "digital divide" has gone from being a theoretical talking point to a reality since Beijing, while we have seen few programmes aimed at reducing that gap for women. Changes continue apace, too fast for our meagre resources to be up to the immense task of grasping their implications and responding with intelligent and appropriate gender-sensitive policy proposals.

Some of the policies currently on the pipeline in the region, or recently passed, mention nothing directly about women, are not gender-balanced and could in fact represent a further widening of the digital divide in their application (cf., the USA "Digital Privacy" laws, the UK "E-Commerce" and updated domestic security proposals, OECD proposals that have influenced recent European Commission directives). Concern must be expressed about current trends towards ICT and media concentration (cf., AOL/Time Warner merger), which is seen as a potential threat to women's freedom of expression, to their privacy and to their right to pluralistic information sources. One important structural limitation in the context of women-centred ICT initiatives since Beijing is the severe lack of funding in some parts of the region, particularly in countries considered 'developed'. Government funding to women's NGOs accessing, developing and using ICTs continues to be small and intermittent. Ironically it is the 'rich' countries most affected – western-European countries in particular-as there are relatively well developed sources of funding in the USA and, to a lesser extent, Canada and the northern European countries.

However, there is funding available for undertaking projects in the Central and Eastern Europe/Commonwealth Independent Soviet (CEE/CIS) sub-region. This must be seen in the context of a gain for less developed regions of the world and any future gains on this score must not be at the cost of others. The problem is that there are few, if any sustainable methods of income-generation that allow women-centred ICT initiatives to function with minimal external funding input, just as this is the problem in less-developed regions of the world. As a result of this reality, there is a lack of continuity in planning and programming by women's organisations with respect to ICTs.

At the level of awareness and sensitisation, the European Parliament failed to win its request for the proclamation of a "European year against violence". The resources that a genuine "European year against violence" would have provided would certainly have made it possible for this theme to reach more media and citizens. NGOs in the United Kingdom note that there are very few campaigns to promote critical thinking about the content of mass media by younger people and there is perhaps less public awareness of the damaging power of gender stereotyping today than prior to Beijing.

With regard to monitoring media content, many National Plans of Action failed to clearly indicate strategies and actions with respect to Section J. In the Ukraine, Section J of the National Plan of Action was implemented only partly and did not have clear indicators for monitoring the implementation. In many countries in the ECE region, there has been a stated policy by the governments not to directly interfere at a legal level with their media but to rely on some combination of media licensing, voluntary codes of conduct, national complaints commissions, etc. There are several gaps in this approach.

NGOs in Ukraine point out that monitoring the control on prohibitions of violent advertisements in the mass-media is impossible because the press should be regularly monitored and assessed in retrospect yet no national machinery exists with the remittance and funding to undertake this work. Another gap is pointed out by NGOs in the United Kingdom where its Press Complaints Commission's "Code of Practice" contains no specific clause dealing with women/gender stereotyping. It may seem obvious, but clearly, monitoring is worthless if there is nothing stopping the abuses from occurring in the first place.

OBSTACLES

Although there are regional differences in the type of obstacles encountered in implementing Section J, there are many common impediments including those based on gender bias and discrimination. These are outlined here.

Patriarchal societies: One of the biggest obstacles to women's access, participation and control of the media is the patriarchal structure of societies where men continue to see women as subordinate to them. Patriarchal attitudes of governments and media are manifest in their being predominantly male institutions which tend to view women as an undifferentiated mass of low status in society. Gender biases and gender-based discriminations therefore result in stereotyped attitudes, sexual harassment, pay inequities, discriminatory treatment in assignments and promotions, traditional gender hierarchies, including a premium on family responsibilities, lack of support mechanisms for working women and low education that deter women from joining the media or assume decision-making positions.

Ownership of media: The threat to the democratic right of citizens to a plurality of information sources and the means of expressing their viewpoints is endangered by the power exerted by a few transnational media organisations that control the different media. Ownership monopoly, control of media by men, and cross-cutting corporate interests would inevitably influence media content and policy. There is increased concern over the levels of media-industry concentration being attained through the convergence of communication and information technologies with other, more traditional media, bringing up issues of control in many countries. Further, globalisation and monopolisation of media is blurring the lines of accountability as sub-regional, regional and international conglomerates buy and trade national broadcasting frequencies, print, television programmes, cable and films with little or no accountability to government and civil society. The possibility of citizens influencing mainstream media policy and content is complicated when the decision-making centres are ever more distant and unreachable, propelled by profit motives rather than social responsibility considerations.

Lack of gender perspective on issues and gender bias: Few journalism schools have incorporated gender issues in their curriculum. Journalists who attempt to introduce a gender focus in their work often meet resistance or ridicule from their colleagues or bosses. Women communicators point to discrimination and sexual harassment to be among the main obstacles to professional advancement. It is also extremely difficult to open a public debate on issues of communication and democracy, codes of ethics or the social responsibility of the media, when many media directors and even some journalists refuse to recognise this responsibility, and very few are willing to air the issues publicly. The continued projection of negative and degrading images of women, of gender stereotypes and violent and/or pornographic examples in media have an overall negative impact and thus hinder women's full participation in society.

Lack of women's access to and growth in media institutions: As gender issues are not seen as important or profitable, women face difficulties in entering media institutions and organisations. Opportunities for women within the media industry, in employment and decision-making, continue to be limited. Not enough women in media organisations have attained senior programming positions as these opportunities are not yet open to women based on a routine but fair professional upgrading. Even the few women who exercise some control in media organisations operate within patriarchal systems of management and are dictated to follow the interest of profit margins. While it would be naive to state that profit is not important, the current situation of media is one of commodification, commercialisation and consumerism.

Lack of women's access to ICTs and gender biases in the development of ICTs: Women's lack of access to basic infrastructure such as electricity and phone lines makes broad access to new technologies a very distant possibility, further complicated by factors such as illiteracy and economic restrictions. Even in urban centres, the main obstacles to access and use of ICTs, are equipment and service costs, lack of training, and language (dominance of English on the Internet). There has been little commitment from either public or private institutions to address women's situation vis-à-vis ICTs. It is widely acknowledged that the development of new technologies does not take into consideration women's practices and needs. The majority of the computer industry is instead developing for the adolescent boy or adult male game user: bigger, faster machines running bigger, heavier software. This has the effect of pricing computers beyond the reach of many women as well as reinforcing a women-unfriendly view of computer technologies in general.

Lack of women's full participation in media processes: The participation of women in communication processes is largely related to their economic status, geographic locations and ethnic identities. Women who suffer economic, racial or other forms of exclusion are usually also excluded from the means to communicate. National and international regulatory bodies are commonly conceived as technical entities, in many cases with no space for citizens to participate or express their opinion. Even where such spaces exist, women's organisations are often not aware of them. At another level, significant areas of journalism are still male preserves and inherent gender biases and discriminations within the system constrain women media practitioners from participating fully in shaping media content. Another point to note is the relative isolation of women media practitioners. Many of them work within patriarchal structures and do not often have links with the women's movement in their countries. Even if they do, they risk being marginalised within corporate organisations.

Lack of effective media policies: Media policies against sexist and stereotyped coverage, representation and portrayal of women remain as a big gap. Existing media codes and guidelines are mainly concerned with "lewd", "obscene", "indecent" exposure of human bodies, "immoral" sexual relations, sexually "provocative" material, and pornographic content. Current policies are framed around questions of morality, rather than recognising sexual violence against women as a violation of human rights. There have been some efforts to establish or maintain self-regulatory mechanisms on media content. Governments in general take little responsibility for regulation of media industries with regard to gender stereotyping. Action is left to voluntary measures on the part of media enterprises or insufficiently effective national compliance/complaints authorities, who often lack monitoring capabilities and whose legal framework often lack gender-equal policies. To this end, there is no practical monitoring or enforcement of government requirements in many countries and where standards exist, they are often not upheld. Too often, the task is left to private citizens to watch, challenge and litigate.

Lack of effective sanctions against violators: Although calls have been made for codes of conduct with minimum international standards and requirements to be instituted at the international level, the failure to respond to this need bears on the continuing absence of sanctions against violators of women's human rights in the media.

Systemic challenges: In many countries issues agreed to in Section J are not that straightforwardly easy to put into action and often require radical transformations of existing systems. For example, concepts such as increasing women's participation or contribution can often be misinterpreted by the public as women's desire for domination or control. As a consequence, calls by women for greater participation and positive portrayal are trivialised in government consultative and policy making processes.

Threats to media practitioners: In several countries, there had been threats against community radio and TV stations. In some cases, such as Paraguay and Uruguay, people in charge of them were threatened with imprisonment, as if they had committed a serious crime.

MEDIA POLICIES

While there are media policies in many countries covering women's portrayal, there are fewer policies in place that are comprehensive enough to address all aspects of gender discrimination and bias. South Korea and China have enacted legislation that aim to be comprehensive. The South Korea's Women's Development Act of 1995 promotes gender equality and provides the legal basis to rectify gender discriminatory factors in employment and other areas. The Act provides for an increase of women's presence in various oversight broadcasting committees to 30 percent by 2005, the creation of objective standards to evaluate gender-based stereotypes in mass media and the expansion in the production and distribution of public advertisements dealing with women's issues.

However, women's groups involved in the monitoring note that enforcement of the laws and policies remain problematic due to the lack of political will by government machineries and private enterprises. China has laws, policies and guidelines covering women's portrayal in media. It has several anti-pornographic laws which ban, criminalise and punish the production, import, export, sale, and dissemination of material that violate the provisions in the Protection of

Rights and Interests of Women, a policy prohibiting discrimination, ill treatment, and injury to women. It also has the Development Program for Chinese Women (1995-2000) which gives a general guideline for the representation of women in the media. The guidelines are enforced through the Administration for Press and Publication and the State Council oversee the enforcement of various regulations.

Elsewhere in Asia, Malaysia has one provision, Section 5 (Role of Women), of the Advertising Code for Television and Radio. It generally states that men and women must be projected in their participation, contribution and positive image to family life, the economy, society and development of the country. The Ministry of Home Affairs, the Ministry of Trade and Consumer Affairs, and the Health Ministry monitor this code. India, for its part, has the Indecent Representation of Women Prohibition Act whose main thrust is to monitor the depiction of women in print media. First time violators are fined and liable with up to six years of detention; and a further fine for a second conviction is the current sanction.

In many countries in Asia, journalists' associations have their own codes of ethics and/or canons not necessarily guiding them on women's issues but ethics in general. These include journalist associations in Cambodia, Indonesia, the Philippines, and South Korea who have their own codes of ethics enforced through their own ethic committees. Publishers and editors associations have their own canons of journalism in Japan, Indonesia, and the Philippines. There are separate codes of practice for programme standards in radio and television for broadcasters in Japan, the Philippines and other countries. Advertisers are guided by ethics in Indonesia, Japan, and Malaysia.

In some Latin American countries, the Office of the People's Defender (Ombudsman) is the only body that intervenes when citizens pursue a case of media sexism. In Argentina, the Office of the People's Defender in the City of Buenos Aires intervened in three important cases that had to do with infant pornography, the sexist undertone in the apology for violence against women in a popular salsa song and sexist advertising. In all the cases, the Defender applied the Convention on the Elimination of All Forms of Discrimination against Women (CEDAW) principles that in Argentina have the status of a national law. While in most countries in the region, community radio and TV stations continue to struggle for legal status, it is worth noting that in Colombia a new law on broadcasting passed in 1998 legalised community media.

In the ECE region, Canada's gender and media policy consists of enforced self-regulation, operating as a partnership between government, the media industry and NGOs. It requires programming to be of a "high standard." It complements the Canadian Charter of Rights and Freedoms. However, in the United Kingdom, there are a number of regulatory mechanisms in place, set up independently from Government and within the terms of the Broadcasting Acts of 1990 and 1996, some of which have even been recently strengthened.

The Broadcasting Standards Commission is the only organisation to cover all television and radio, and it has a Code of Guidance with a brief reference to stereotyping. Other mechanisms include the Committee of Advertising Practice, which looks at both broadcast and non-broadcast advertising. A key player for newpapers is the Press Complaints Commission (PCC), an independent organisation set up 'to ensure that British newspapers and magazines follow a Code of Practice, drafted by newspaper and magazine editors, and adopted by the industry'. The PCC receives and adjudicates on complaints about possible breaches of the Code and gives general guidance to editors on ethical issues.

EMERGING ISSUES

Privatisation and Mergers of Media Enterprises: The merging of media technologies and owners, especially in the context of globalisation, is changing the nature and structure of the media industry. Media has become a transnationalised business enterprise tied to international trade bodies/

agreements (WTO, GATT) whose main purpose is profit generation rather than to provide public service. As such, it is difficult to regulate the movement of media even by governments. During the last decade the communications industry has been characterised by privatisation of telecommunications, the introduction of new communication tech-based systems (satellites, cable TV, digital and wireless technology, internet, and cellular phones), concentration of media ownership, etc. These changes have been accompanied by modifications in the legal framework where these systems operate, spurred on by recommendations from the World Trade Organization (WTO) and International Telecommunications Union (ITU). The situation points to the urgent need to develop policy proposals from citizens' standpoint, so as to ensure pluralism and democracy in access to information and communication.

Effects of Globalisation of Media: Globalisation of the media has paved the way for widespread promotion of commercialism and consumerism. Of serious concern is the homogenising effect of globalisation on culture and societies resulting in an essentialist, universalistic, diluted reflection of neither reality that does not take into account nor mirror realities that stem from the diversity of races, class, caste, ethnicity and lifestyles. The strangleholds of giant transnational corporations are edging out nationally owned media enterprises. Given this broad scope, there is now even less space for smaller, indigenous media outfits, for women media practitioners and producers to have the production or editorial control that they had, albeit on an already generally limited scale, within the traditional and alternative media. Legislation and jurisdiction have also become problematic given the increasingly transborder character of media.

Violence against Women: The use of the Internet to traffic women and sell pornography has aggravated the exploitation of women. The lack of mechanisms to regulate the use of the internet has worsened this situation. While the issue of pornography and exploitation of women has always been there, it is now more difficult to monitor and curb these activities. The targeting of women and girls through pornography, sex tourism and the sex trade has been exacerbated by electronic communications. The sex trade can now use Websites for their portrayal of women, with the capacity to reach many more people. In the UN European region, the result is an increasing number of women-hating Websites; this, and the use of flaming and stalking, tends to dissuade women in these parts of the globe from using the Net.

Women's Media Initiatives: In community media, women play important roles, both in conducting and planning the programming and in its decision making processes, direction and administration. This is the case in Latin America. There are many groups in Asia making inroads in changing the status of women in media. They have conducted researches and developed models to change the current situation as goal, but these efforts are neither being documented nor explored as models for implementation. Knowledge is a key issue too. In the information age, women face the challenge of not only developing and systematising their own knowledge, but also of ensuring that it is used for their benefit.

Other Issues: Issues of privacy, freedom of speech, freedom of information, etc., as they relate to ICTs, media and women's issues, are increasingly becoming important for women. The scope for women's expression through the alternative media within the current model of communication with its heavy emphasis on ICTs under control by powerful media conglomerates has to be explored further.

In concluding this assessment we would like to highlight the constraints and limitations that necessarily accompany any such endeavour on global implementation. While we recognise the immense diversity of media situations that call for diverse amelioration measures, we would like to place on record two key limitations of the BPFA. The first has to do with limitations of the UN structure and processes that make it difficult to bring in any accountability measures that are binding on members states. We realise too that any negotiations or commitments arrived at are fraught with the politics of inclusion and exclusion. The second limitation has to do with the recommendations outlined in the BPFA which palpably presume that all regions and, indeed all countries, are at the same stage of media development. While we note the need to collapse diverse countries into regions based on geographical locations to facilitate the organisation and administration of the reports, we feel that this approach does not provide for specific and contextual issues to be addressed. As pointed out, the UN process has also left out reviews of the regional process in its 'global' assessment exercise, thus causing assessments in themselves to become, as it is, problematic.

At the level of individual governments, more need to be done. Because governments are accountable to their citizens, women around the globe will be watching their moves, and demand their rights. In recognising women's rights as full and equal partners in development, this report outlines key recommendations to governments, the media industry and the public.

Media Portrayal:

The media need to refrain from presenting women as inferior and exploiting them as sex objects. On the contrary, the media could be a useful tool to promote a positive and realistic image of women. All media presentations should be in line with the demographic context of the community. Gender stereotyping should be eliminated through an exertion of will and foresight on the part of the media industry, who, for starters, should also seek to eliminate violent and degrading portrayals of women.

States need to formulate international ethical standards, based on equality between the sexes, that could be reflected in all communication productions, including programming and media portrayal.

The lack of specific research on media portrayal is one of the most critical barriers to ongoing and effective analysis. Studies should be funded in order to raise the awareness about gender-fair images in relation to policy-making. Regional differences should be identified and the implementation of law should be based on comparative research in this field.

Media Policy:

Governments and NGOs have to ensure that regulatory mechanisms on media are guided by the values of gender justice, human rights, sustainable development and respect for cultural diversity and of cultural expression, sexuality and lifestyle.

There is a need explore the development of an International Convention on Women and Media which addresses problems of diversity, human rights and gender issues using existing international conventions and instruments.

Governments must continue to support community radio, alternative video and access to television, public-calling stations, and community Internet, computer networking and alternative print media.

Governments and relevant bodies should commit resources and implement programmes that will increase women's access to communication resources and knowledge, especially to new communications technologies, in a framework of respect for cultural diversity and for regional and local needs and priorities. It must assign resources to promote gender equality through mainstream and alternative media and the Internet. It must also promote public debate on the social responsibility of the media, and draw up and implement ethical codes of conduct.

Decision-making:

There is a need for gender balance at all decision-making levels within the media industry. This could be achieved through measures such as affirmative action and quota systems. Existing attempts at promoting voluntary equal opportunity policies, training schemes, etc., among media industries have not so far proved successful in breaking through the glass ceiling by women. Further efforts are needed to improve women's employment opportunities and career paths. Guidelines must include sufficient encouragement of women´s participation at all levels of decision-making in media industries and in senior positions in technology industries and on government-convened advisory boards.

Advocacy:

Both audiences and journalists need to be sensitised on how women and men are portrayed, and to what extent and on which issues they are or not given a voice, including how the lack of women in decision-making position affects these portrayals. Further research needs to be done and courses and study groups encouraged. New equality projects in the media must be launched and supported.

Immediate steps should be taken to establish and support centres which are responsible for monitoring national media in all countries. All forms of media should be monitored including ICTs. Support should be given to help women develop their monitoring and analytic skills.

The United Nations should embrace our aspiration to include the right of women to communicate as a priority in its agenda for the 21st century and thus contribute to the present and future goal of building democracies based on pluralism and a culture of peace.

Propose that the United Nations convene a World Conference on Communications as a venue for the community of nations, communication media and systems, and civil society would have the opportunity to discuss an ethical framework for action in the realm of global communication that embraces democratic practices and social responsibility.

Governments should revise their policies on financial support and international cooperation with regard to giving priority to the strengthening of women's communication networks and media, and their gender dimension.

Governments that have failed to state plans for any 'Future Actions' in accordance with the BPFA format must be compelled to do so or else explicitly state that they have no such plans.

Bibliography

Adepoju, A. (2002). Fostering Free Movement of Persons in West Africa: Achievements, Constraints, and Prospects for Intraregional Migration. *International Migration, 40* (2), 3-28.

Alexander, P. and Frederique D. (Eds.). (1987). *Sex Work: Writings by Women in the Sex Industry.* Pittsburgh: Cleis Press.

Annamanthodo, P. (1992). *Red Light Traffic: The Trade in Nepali Girls.* Kathmandu: ABC/Nepal.

Barry, K. (1995). *The Prostitution of Sexuality.* New York: New York University Press.

Bertone, A. M. (2000). Sexual Trafficking in Women: International Political Economy and the Politics of Sex. *Gender Issues, 18* (1), 4-22.

Biddulph, S. and Cook, S. (1999). Kidnapping and Selling women and Children: The State's Construction and Response. *Violence Against Women, 5* (12), 1437-1468.

Brown, H. (1999*). Sex crimes and tourism in Nepal. International Journal of Contemporary Hospitality Management, 11* (23), 107-110.

Chew, L. (1999). Global Trafficking in Women: Some Issues and Strategies. *Women's Studies Quarterly, 27* (1/2), 11-18.

Chutikul, S. (1995, Spring/Summer). Women and Commercial Sex Trade in Thailand. *Canadian Women's Studies, 15 (2).*

Constable, N. (1996). Jealousy, Charity, and Abuse: Chinese Maids and Foreign Helpers in Hong Kong. *Modern China, 22* , 448-479.

D'Cunha, J. (1991). *The legalization of Prostitution: A Sociological Inquiry into the Laws Relating to Prostitution in India and the West.* Bangalore: Wordmakers.

D'Cunha, J. (1998). Feminist Perspectives on Prostitution and Trafficking for Prostittuion. In S. Kudchedkar. and S. Al-Issa. (Eds.). *Violence Against Women, Women Against Violence.* Delhi : Pencraft International.

Eviota, E. U. (1992). *The Political Economy of Gender: Women and the Sexual Division of Labor in the Philippines.* London: Zedbooks.

Farrior, S. (1997, Spring). The International Law on Trafficking in Women and Children for Prostitution: Making it Live Up to its Potential. *Harvard Human Rights Journal, 10* , 213.

Girdler-Brown B. (1998). Eastern and Southern Africa. *International Migration, 36* (4), 513-551.

Hamal, P. (2000). NGOs working Against Trafficking in Girl Children of Nepal. *Population and Development in Nepal, 7,* 219-234.

Hughes, D.M. (2000, Spring). The Internet and Sex Industries: Partners in Globalizing Sexual Exploitation. *IEEE Technology and Society Magazine,* 35-42.

Kempadoo, K. (2001). Women of Color and the Global Sex Trade: Transnational Feminist Perspectives. *Meridians: Feminism, Race, Transnationalism, 1* (2), 28-51.

Kempadoo, K. and Doezema, J. (Eds.). (1998). *Global Sex Workers: Rights, Resistance and Redefinition.* New York: Routledge.

Kyle, D. and Koslowski, R. (Eds.). (2001). *Global Human Smuggling: Comparative Perspectives.* Baltimore: Johns Hopkins University Press.

Lydie, N. and Robinson, N. J. (1998). West and Central Africa. *International Migration, 36* (4), 469-511.

Mensendiek, M. (1996). Women, Migration and Prostitution in Thailand. *International Social Work, 40* (2) 163-176.

Miller, J. and Jayasundara, D. (2001). Prostitution, the Sex Industry, and Sex Tourism. In C. Rezetti, J. Edleson, and R. K. Bergen. (Eds.). *Sourcebook on Violence Against Women*, 459-480. Thousand Oaks, CA: Sage.

Moon, K. (1997). *Sex Among Allies: Military Prostitution in US-Korean Relations.* New York: Columbia University Press.

O'Dea, P. (1993). *Gender Exploitation and Violence: The Market in Women, Girls and Sex in Nepal.* Geneva: UNICEF.

Phizacklea, A. (Eds.). (1983). *One Way Ticket: Migration and Female Labor.* London: Routledge.

Piper, N. (1999). Labor Migration, Trafficking and International Marriage: Female Cross-Border Movements into Japan. *Asian Journal of Women's Studies, 5* (2), 69-99.

Raghu, M. (1997). Sex Trafficking of Thai Women and the United States Asylum Law Response. *Georgetown Immigration Law Journal, 12* (1), 145.

Skrobanek, S. B. S. and Jantateroo, C. (1997). *The Traffic in Women: Human Realities of the International Sex Trade.* New York: Zed Books Ltd.

Sturdevant, S.P. and Stolzfus, B. (1992). *Let the Good Times Roll: Prostitution and the US Military in Asia.* New York: The New Press.

Taylor, I. and Jamieson, R. (1999). Sex trafficking and the mainstream of market culture. *Crime, Law and Social Change, 32* (3), 257-278.

Truong, T.D. (1990). *Sex, Money and Morality: Prostitution and Tourism in Southeast Asia.* London: Zedbooks.

Tzvetkova, M. (2002). NGO Responses to Trafficking in Women. *Gender and Development, 10* (1), 60-68.

Uchida, A. (1998). The Orientalization of Asian Women in America. *Women's Studies International Forum, 21* (2), 161-174.

Williams, P. (Eds.). (1999). *Illegal Immigration and Commercial Sex: The New Slave Trade.* London: Frank Cass Publishers.

Index